DAVE MEUNIER 2019

Dave Urwin lives in Somerset. This is his second book and he also ghostwrites professionally.

WHERE HOPE SPRINGS

Where Hope Springs

Copyright © Dave Urwin 2019 All Rights Reserved

The rights of Dave Urwin to be identified as the author of this work have been asserted in accordance with the Copyright, Designs and Patents Act 1988

Cover image by Wayne Hughes
carrotgraphix@gmail.com
W B Hughes #Art4Fun on Youtube
WHughesart on Instagram
Wayne thanks his late Uncle Stephen and Grandad
Brian Wyatt – two who gave him hope

All rights reserved. No part may be reproduced, adapted, stored in a retrieval system or transmitted by any means, electronic, mechanical, photocopying, or otherwise without the prior written permission of the author or publisher.

Spiderwize
Remus House
Coltsfoot Drive
Woodston
Peterborough
PE2 9BF

www.spiderwize.com

A CIP catalogue record for this book is available from the British Library.

The views expressed in this work are solely those of the author and do not necessarily reflect the views of the publisher, and the publisher hereby disclaims any responsibility for them.

ISBN: 978-1-912694-79-2

ebook ISBN - 978-1-912694-88-4

WHERE HOPE SPRINGS

Dave Urwin

SPIDERWIZE
Peterborough UK
2019

CONTENTS

Foreword by Wojtek Godzisz 1

Introduction 7

'LIFE' 11

Conner's Story Part 2 15

Farewell to Twilight: Wojtek's Story Part 1 22

Possibility 32

Conner's Story Part 3 36

The Continuing Story 40

Hope in Nature – A World Outside the Smart Phone 45
featuring Andy Hamilton

Conner's Story Part 4 51

Origins of Hope 54

Consideration 59
featuring Gary Stringer

Conner's Story Part 5 68

Don't Forget About Grenfell 72
featuring Steve MacKenzie

Drink the Sunshine 82
featuring Ross Cummins

Conner's Story Part 6 94

Beyond Punishment – The UK's forgotten IPP prisoners 100
featuring Joanne Hartley and Rico Costanza

Conner's Story Part 7 114

Two Hours or so to Change Your Life.......................................117
featuring Adharanand Finn

Wojtek's Story Part 2 – The Frontman 124

Conner's Story Part 8..129

Guilty Until Proven Innocent – The Abolition of the
Welfare State? 134

Today is a time of Instant Gratification 144
featuring Declan O'Shea and Christian Montagne

Conner's Story Part 9..151

In One Single Moment..158
featuring Adam Fouracre

Self-Medication in The Face of Rejection 168
featuring Danny McCormack

Conner's Story Part 10..177

'You Don't Get Old if You Keep Moving'....................................184
featuring Justin Gloden, Toni Bernado and Janus Eigaard

If Jesus Came to Weston on a Saturday Night.........................198
featuring James Wotton and Billy Isherwood

Conner's Story Part 11..207

PS4 or PSL? 217

What is Ambition? 232
Featuring Charlie Carroll and Gideon Amos

Wojtek's Story Part 3 – Polish Rider 246

Conner's Story Part 12..253

You Might Get Hit by a Bus 261

Epilogue...271

*"Yesterday was deplorable,
Today was despicable,
But tomorrow may always be delightful."*

Steve MacKenzie

FOREWORD BY WOJTEK GODZISZ

***(Musical maestro of many avenues, including
as part of the popular 90s band Symposium and
his own critically acclaimed solo career)***

Hi, my name is Wojtek, but you can call me the Polish Rider if you like. I'm writing this, and you're reading this right now, because someone called Dave Urwin had an idea for a book, and he did something about it before the idea had a chance to die, just like thousands of ideas before it had. That finished book is now in your metaphorical or literal hands (or in your ears - I'm available for voice work if it comes to it, Dave).

I didn't really know Dave in the 1990s, and he didn't really know me, either. But he thought he knew something about me, because he'd listened to songs that I'd written. Now, after a good few hours spent talking on the phone and messaging each other, we know a bit more about one another. We've moved a bit closer to what might be considered the truth about ourselves. Hopefully.

Our memories are always playing tricks on us, but I recall that Dave contacted me once (maybe a year ago?) during the total blizzard that my life has become since having two daughters over the course of the last three years. That blizzard means I'm a lot more forgetful and tired (obvs), I have trouble remembering what the hell it is I'm supposed to be doing (on a day to day and on a zoomed out larger life scale basis), I neglect friends even more than I used to, and I've really stopped caring about grammar or punctuation in text messages that I send. For anyone who knows me, that last point is the one that really sticks in my craw.

To cut a longer story shorter (Dave only wants me to write one page for this thing), after contacting me, introducing himself and the nature of this book he wanted to write, and a fair few meandering conversations and questions, Dave bowled me over by inviting me to write the foreword which you are presently reading. I considered it a huge honour, and a huge challenge. As someone with huge pretensions to grandeur, and life-long ambitions to be an insufferably pompous polymath, I have always harboured a secret desire to add being a published writer to my quiver of renaissance-man arrows. And I don't care how many mixed metaphors I have to deploy in attempting to do it.

So, ego duly coaxed into action, here we are. And where I am, exactly, right now (writing now), is in a backstage dressing room (are there any FOH dressing rooms in existence anywhere?), 59 minutes away from taking to the stage at a sold out 1,700 capacity music venue in Guildford on a fairly typical, standard rainy Wednesday night in November. Some may view this as success of a sort, or maybe even boastful. I can get behind that. Others may view it as a type of failure. Seriously, believe me, I know people who do. There are people playing with me tonight on stage who wouldn't tell their other musician friends about the tour we're on because they'd be embarrassed. Maybe it's something to do with snobbery, or identity, or shattered dreams. Who knows? It's all a sliding scale, I guess. I won't use the term 'relative', as I don't wish to insult Einstein. I might have not done what once I'd hoped when I was a child. Maybe one day I still will. But I've got new hopes now, too. Hopes die and hopes are born. Just like us.

Anyway, what I'm trying to say is, meeting (not in the flesh - yet!) Dave, in the midst of my maelstrom, talking as we did, and finally having just finished reading the first manuscript draft of his book, has had, I finally realise, something of an effect on me. I completely identify with his sentiments to cherish and nourish the idea of living for the day (in the most non-new-age-self-help-book way imaginable) and truly attempt - at least just some of the time - to really APPRECIATE what we might actually have around us. Family, talents, health, abilities, compassion, empathy, opportunities, nature, intelligence. I could go on. I'm in the middle of a big tour for a big company, playing piano each night as if my life depends on it, and that's because in a sense my family's lives do depend on it. I want my daughters to be fed, sheltered, educated, and loved by a happy dad (that'd be me). Tomorrow I've got a day off, and I'm getting a train into London to meet my wife, who I've missed for a while now. I'm going to hug her and kiss her and tell her how much I love her and appreciate her. And hopefully that will make her a bit more happy, and she can take that back home with her and share it with the kids.

Now read the rest of the book. I've got a show to play.

Wojtek Godzisz was the bass player and principal songwriter in Symposium, and has released two critically acclaimed solo albums. He has his fingers in many musical pies today, and music has been his profession for over twenty years.

For Mum and Dad.... Thank you for never giving up hope in me no matter how many reasons I've given you to xxx

INTRODUCTION

Cold water cascaded into the canal. Having held his breath as the pressure built in his head, one thought kept repeating: "I just want this to end."

It was too late.

Was this what happened when people drowned? An unshakeable realisation that nobody would be coming to the rescue, and that you were powerless to help yourself? A slow realisation that the isolation would remove the chance of salvation? Nothing left to do but accept the situation? His grip tightened on his right knee as the water flooded even faster. It's only water. Yet water is a powerful creation. It gives life and it takes life away. Too little will kill you, too much will kill you. Just the right amount? With life it will instill you. It covers more than half of the earth and makes up more than half of the human body. Deny a person of it for just a few days and they will probably die. Leave a person underneath it for a few minutes they will not survive. Their body needs it to live but is not designed to live within it. What a crazy conundrum. Does water exist to teach us the importance of moderation?

A loud pop, a feeling of a large mass having been dislodged, of a weight lifting. Then the pressure receded as quickly as it had intensified. Henry exhaled in three short bursts as he fell forward, blinking several times and opening his eyes wide. He was alive. Did this canal have a plughole?

"All done"

Henry stayed still for a moment, then craned his neck, turning his head slowly to the right. As he glanced downwards he almost recoiled at the size of the lump of earwax floating in the metal dish. It made ripples like a log in a river. The thought of it being lodged in his ear made him shiver. Several more pops rattled through his ear canal like bubblewrap bursting in a confined space, then everything seemed to be amplified. The smack on the glass table as Doctor Taylor placed the dish down, the swoosh of his coat through the air as he turned back around. Everything made a sound.

"Are you feeling Ok?"

He didn't really have the answer to that question, but he smiled and nodded anyway.

"Yeah. That's much better thanks."

"Excellent," smiled Doctor Taylor, "Well if you have any more problems you come back and see me. Ok?"

Henry smiled again and stood up, turning to leave the room. When he got outside the surgery his hand instinctively shot towards his phone in his pocket so he could call a taxi to take him the half mile back to his house, but today something stopped him. He was seeing the world differently, or should I say hearing the world differently. He could hear everything. The folds of the fabric on his clothing ground together and rustled like leaves. The leaves themselves rustled in the gentle breeze. The breeze was amplified like the flame on a hot air balloon.

He stood still and took in the sensory overload. If he wasn't careful his brain would explode. Just one big block of earwax had gone and it was like he'd been born again. How could this be? A crisp packet rattled across the pavement, guided by the wind, and it sounded like someone typing on a typewriter in one of those old movies his parents used to enjoy. He thought he heard the sound of distant traffic, but then realised it was just a deep breath going in and out of his nostrils. Had Doctor Taylor spiked him? No, why would he? It was just that until now his ears had not been able to do as good a job as they were designed for. Today they were working properly for the first time. It would be something he'd get used to, but for now he'd just continue to be amazed.

He did something he hadn't done in longer than he could remember and just sat on the grass near the surgery as he took in the cacophony of sounds. As it built to a crescendo the one sound that overtook them all was a thought that made him leap to his feet. 'How sick will my new speakers sound now???'

A light came to Henry's eyes that only really came nowadays when he was thinking about technology. The world of people, with their unpredictability, fickleness, disappointments and unkindness, was a harsh place that would grind you down time and time again. A computer would only let you down if you couldn't afford a decent one. He could. And the best connection. His machine. His lovely, submissive machine. It would never let him down.

He broke into a run. Something he never did nowadays unless the situation truly demanded it. So he ran on past the leaves rustling in the breeze, the birds tweeting in the trees, the sun illuminating the surroundings, the park with its freshly cut grass and ornate fountains and to his front door. He turned the key and flung the door open, stepping in and closing it behind him in one fluid motion. He bounded up the stairs two or three at a time and stepped into the room where he spent most of his life. No children, no pets, no housemates, no parents, no wife. Nothing to distract him from what got him where he was today. Everything he needed was right here anyway. He was Henry VIIII, his people hung on his every word and his kingdom was all contained within these four walls. He sat on his throne, which creaked like a wooden rowboat as he made contact, now the barriers of sound had been removed. It was time to address his subjects.....

That story was not true. At least not literally. Bear it in mind though as you read on, because it says a lot about what almost everyone I spoke to for this book said when I asked them what they didn't like about the modern world. Now for a story that is true.....

'LIFE'

That single word emblazoned on a half-full bottle of water on the other side of the room gave Mark something to focus on. He turned to my cousin, Emma, and said that the word was a sign. For what must have seemed like hours they had been waiting for news of their eldest son, Conner, who had been admitted to hospital with a bleed on his brain. Conner had just recently turned seventeen, and here they were just waiting and waiting for further news on how critical his situation was. Mark knew he had to stay calm for the sake of his family, and had to just try and fill the time before the doctors returned. What was already starting to feel like the worst ordeal was only just beginning. He clung tightly to that one word as the chaos unfolded around him.

Around five months later Steve wakes again during yet another restless night and switches on his TV to be greeted with images of an inferno in a London tower block. As one of the UK's leading fire safety experts, he knows exactly where he'll be heading. He's prepared, and his wife fetches one of the 'Grab bags' he's put together for this kind of situation while he gets himself together; think of a scaled down version of a 'Bug-Out bag' someone might have prepared for the collapse of society. The same day I will stand in a queue in the bank and see these same images on the TV screen in the corner, but I won't know the full extent of what they mean until hours later. Steve's mind is flooded with memories of that fateful day when he was sent home from school. When he got home the building where his Uncle lived was on TV, and this young boy's life was about to change forever because a gas explosion had killed four of his family members. The families of many people trapped in that London tower block would be going through the same thing Steve had all those years ago, and everyone would soon be asking why?

Rewind 10 years, and Wojtek is heading through Shoreditch with the video camera he's been taking everywhere lately. He stops when he notices a single word which encapsulates his current frame of mind spray-painted on a wall. Now 30, he already hit peaks a number of years ago that many spend most of their lives trying to reach, but just a year or two later he'd pretty much lost it all, and had spent years now trying to rebuild. He's now heading in the direction he wanted to all along, but little does he know the biggest challenges of his life still lie ahead.

Every day many wake up in prison cells, having made mistakes years previously that still resonate, and characterise their whole existence. They have no idea when, or if, they will be released, and are so institutionalised that the prospect makes them nervous even if it will happen. They are trying to make straight their paths but their environment makes this a constant challenge. Forgotten by all except those few who can see beyond their mistakes, they remain in limbo. Others on the outside stay in metaphorical prisons; the addictions they can't break free from, the past regrets they can't move on from, the demons that torment them, the struggle to find a reason to believe in the future.

Each new day the sun rises, each new season colours change and new scenery appears along with new life. Amid this constant renewal there are some things that never change but offer comfort with their steadfastness. It can seem like the world is full of reasons to languish in despair, so everyone needs just what made Wojtek pause and fire up his video camera that day in Shoreditch. The word on the wall was 'Hope.'

People find hope in different ways, in different places, in different words, in different faces, but it's something we all have in common. We all need hope to save us from despair. I wrote a book already about my own search for hope amid despair, so this one isn't all about me. This is about all of us, but of course it's only literally about some of us. There are a number of stories about what hope means, and has meant, to a whole range of people, including myself at times. My reason for writing it is to remind, or reiterate, that there is always hope. Somebody once said to me that the sun is always there, it's just that sometimes you can't see it for all the clouds. Hope is just the same.

Back to the hospital room. Mark and Emma look up as the doors swing open and the doctors walk in.

"I'm afraid Conner's in grave danger," says the lead doctor, "He has a massive bleed on his brain and we're going to have to get him into surgery immediately."

Emma is understandably hysterical, the stark reality that this isn't just a nightmare she's about to wake up from overloading her senses. Mark tries to listen as the doctor goes through the formalities, but he's heard all he needs to.

"Just get him in there," he says, "Just do what you need to do."

The surgeon turns to him and says something Emma doesn't hear.

"Do you want to say goodbye to him?"

"Wait.....What?"

Everything stops as Mark desperately tries to process what he's hearing. Conner has only just celebrated his seventeenth birthday. He still has his whole life ahead of him. He isn't about to die. He can't be. He just can't be.

Mark drew on every ounce of strength he had left, but he would have to tap into resources he never knew he even possessed. He texted his best friend Gary, who was elsewhere in the hospital getting drinks with Emma's mum, Viv. Gary received the text, which simply said 'You need to get back here now.' None of them had seen this coming. They would all need each other now more than ever.

CONNER'S STORY PART 2

My cousin Emma is just a year younger than me. I didn't see a lot of her when we were growing up because my dad had migrated south from the land of the Geordies in his late teens to do his teacher training in Exmouth. Emma's dad, my Uncle Chris, had stayed in South Shields, which is pretty much the other end of the country if you didn't know. Of course if my dad hadn't migrated south I wouldn't have been born anyway, so Emma would have seen even less of me. I do remember one particular summer though when we had an extended holiday up north and my elder brother Joe and I hung out with her a lot. One of my main memories of this time was that she had a cassette tape (remember them?) called Cricket's Clubhouse.... I think it was called that anyway. Cricket, as far as I remember, was a young girl who was the leader of some kind of youth club. It was like the Famous Five but far less dangerous, and there were only three of them. It wasn't really like the Famous Five at all but I didn't want to go down the 'far less edgy Byker Grove' route, as that seemed lazy. Cricket and her friends lived in the times before the internet, and so actually had to find real things to do and to have imaginations.

Anyway, there were several songs on the tape, and one of them had a bit that went "Let's hear it for the Clubhouse.... Hip, hip, hooray!" Then she would sing it again with a gap so you could do the 'Hip, hip, hooray!' part. Then she would say "Come on, you can do it louder than that!" and you'd have a chance to redeem yourself in Cricket's eyes. It turns out though that she was a little too modest about the impact her cassette would have. She seemed to envision that people would listen to it once, and so the "Come on, you can do it louder than that" would remain a genuine surprise. However, Emma and me got wise to this seeing as the tape played several times a day, and so we'd yell "Hip, hip, hooray!" as loud as we could the first time, thereby making Cricket look foolish, highly sarcastic or just plain mean. Sorry, Cricket. We were young and we meant no harm. I guess you must be at least forty by now anyway, and no doubt have bigger fish to fry. In fact it's entirely possible that Cricket was not even your real name and you were a voice actress who would have been an adult back then already, so by now you would be quite advanced in years and might not even remember that you were the voice of Cricket's Clubhouse. Maybe it was just one of many jobs in your youth, and not even one of the most memorable ones. Times have moved on.

So yes, I also remember that Emma loved chocolate biscuits, wore a leather jacket and always wanted to stay up late. She was way cool! One day, after a particularly brutal argument, she ripped the legs off one of my Masters of the Universe figures. They were attached pretty firmly too, so she must have been very angry. Not long after this she was sobbing uncontrollably, and I forgave her, but as you can tell from what you've just read it was something I never forgot. I told her as much at my grandad's wake last year when we were reminiscing, pretending for comic effect that it was the point at which my life turned sour. Oh how we laughed.

I remember she always had a kind heart. Another thing I'd never forgotten about her was one day when we were in the back of my parents' car going somewhere or other and I was having an episode of youthful self-loathing. I'd written '2p' on a sticker and stuck it on my t-shirt, saying it was all I was worth. She looking genuinely upset that I didn't value myself more highly and told me that she thought I was worth way more. We all are of course, but when someone recognises it? Well, it's priceless.

A few summers later Emma had a colossal collection of Pogs. Remember them? There were rumours at the time that kids were stabbed in the playground for rare ones. Emma wasn't any part of that, but the look she gave her mum, my Auntie Viv, when she thought she'd thrown away her Pogs collection last year? Let's just say Pogs were to the kids of the mid 90s what Minecraft seems to be to most kids now. The difference is that we lived in far less throwaway times then. Life was a little slower paced and nothing was just available at the click of a button, and so Pogs really meant something to the kids of that era. During the midst of her Pog obsession was probably the last time I saw her for years. Around this sort of time she met a polite young man named Mark Weatherburn.

Mark tells me that he was a good boy and Emma was a scallywag. Emma is yet to deny this and so let's go with that for now. They met in 1994, in the first year of Secondary School, but didn't get to know each other well until around 1996 when they were in a few classes together. Mark says he liked Emma for a long time before they started 'seeing each other,' which began on April 17th 1997. This would have been just a little while before Tony Blair became Prime Minister, and around the time the Spice Girls rose to fame and Titanic was in the cinema. They were such optimistic times in retrospect. I don't know what it would have been like to have been in my mid 30s in 1997, but social media was still a long way off and people did real things every day without being able to post their thoughts about it online, or share a photo instantly with all of their friends. Not many people had mobile phones, the internet was slow, expensive and made your phone line unusable while it was on. The world as it was in 1997 must have seemed crazy to someone born in 1937, but if they'd know what it would be like in 2017 they would have been utterly shocked.

So, when Mark and Emma were preparing for their exams in the summer of 1999 they received some news that would shake their lives up beyond belief. I remember my mum telling me one morning that Emma was pregnant. I don't remember how I reacted except that I wondered if it meant I would be an uncle. Apparently it actually meant that I would be a second cousin twice removed or something like that. Hey, I'd take it. Emma and Mark in retrospect knew what the doctor was going to say but Emma wasn't showing at the time and so they'd thought her missed period might be down to exam stress. When she finally went to the doctor she was told that she was twelve weeks pregnant, and actually started showing the next day. Mark had already been accepted into college but he ended up leaving after a little while to find a job, realising that college would have to wait, and getting ready to try and support his young family. Both sets of parents were shocked, but they got used to the idea. Just teenagers themselves, Mark and Emma weren't too sure what to do next but they accepted that they were going to be parents, and Conner was born in January 2000.

Conner's name came from my grandad's side of the family. William Connor Urwin was born just before the Second World War, and was evacuated to the Lake District early on. He became a parent when not much older than Mark and Emma were, to my dad, Bill Urwin, and not long afterwards to Emma's dad, my Uncle Chris. He was a very hard working man, spending a long time away on the oil rigs until he was diagnosed with terminal lung cancer in 1979, just before my older brother Joe was born. His definition of terminal, being a tough as nails Geordie, was remarkably different from that of the doctors. When he woke from his radiation treatment he asked "How long have I got?" and the doctor replied "To be honest I didn't think you'd still be here now."

William Urwin was still alive when I was born a couple of years later, and when Conner was born nearly twenty years after that. He was still alive when Conner's brother Jayden was born in the mid-2000s, and it wasn't until August 4th 2017 that he finally died of a stroke, having had one already the previous year. His fighting spirit has always been a big inspiration to me, and the story has always amazed everyone I've told it to. The last time I saw him before his first stroke he was making plans for his 100th birthday. He might not have made it to 100, but according to medical science he should have died when he was half that age. I wish I was as brave as him, and I still aspire to be.

Conner was a very talented footballer from an early age. He was part of a whole team of very talented footballers, who would comfortably win almost every game they played. They didn't escape the attention of the local talent scouts, and the whole team were on the books of Middlesbrough Football Club when they were about six. They were whittled down over time and Conner was released, but Sunderland also showed some interest. He didn't make the final cut at Sunderland either, but it was all good experience, and he still loved to play football as a teenager, as well as going to the gym and riding his bike. He was an active lad and had plenty of friends who he would have house parties with. Mark believes he probably drank alcohol at these parties but didn't smoke or take drugs, as Mark had always instilled in him how much he hated these things, and he thinks it sunk in. Conner had an apprenticeship as a painter and decorator and was working for a local guy with his own business and training scheme towards the end of 2016.

Just before Christmas of that year the guy who ran the training scheme had left, so the boss had to look for someone new and Conner was in limbo for a while. As his 17th birthday came and went there was still no word on when he might be able to carry on, and one day in late January he had been complaining of a headache all day when at Chris and Viv's. Mark had a virus of some kind at the same time. He and Emma had been to a party the night before and had been drinking, but he didn't have a hangover. It was a genuine illness. They naturally assumed that Conner had the same thing. There was no reason to think otherwise.

The next day Mark didn't feel like going to work, but as a self-confessed tightwad he knew that he wouldn't get paid if he stayed home, so he never liked to miss a day. During the night Emma had got up to go for a wee and found Conner already in the bathroom. She was taken aback to find him fully dressed with a dressing gown over the top of his clothes. He told her he couldn't get warm, and again this was how Mark had been feeling earlier that day, so they still assumed it was nothing serious. The next morning Emma had gone off to work, checking on Conner before she went. He was asleep, and she thought he must have been exhausted having been up in the night, so she left him to rest. Mark dragged himself out of bed and saw the same thing as Emma, also thinking it was best to just leave him to get some sleep. He dropped Jayden off at school and then went to work, feeling a little sorry for himself, but not sorry enough to miss out on the day's wages. Later on that morning Conner woke from whatever amount of sleep he'd finally managed, and realised something wasn't right. Something wasn't right at all.

At around 1.45pm Emma switched on her phone and noticed she had some missed calls from Conner. She dialled his number and he answered almost straight away. She heard the urgency in his voice and may well always be haunted when she thinks of what he said.

"Please help me!"

FAREWELL TO TWILIGHT: WOJTEK'S STORY PART 1

One night in the mid-90s as the clock strikes midnight the caretaker of a London school hears a commotion. Pacing around the corner with a little trepidation, he spots a bunch of lads guzzling champagne. He is duty bound to report them, but these five lads are in a band and are signing a record deal. He lets them have their moment, thinking better of trying to move them on.

Do you know the name Wojtek Godzisz? In the late 90s he was one of the most famous people in the world to me. Every week I would eagerly await the arrival of Kerrang magazine, and hardly a week would go by when Wojtek's band, Symposium, were not within its pages. At the time it seemed like Wojtek, along with his bandmates Ross Cummins, Joe Birch, Will McGonagle and Hagop Tchaparian had pretty much the coolest life I could imagine. They made a living playing music and touring the world with their best friends, and were just a few years older than I was. Will looked about twelve to be brutally honest. I wanted their life back then, but would I have wanted it if I'd known the reality, rather than what I assumed it was like from the way the magazines portrayed it? Was it just the 90s equivalent of seeing an old school friend's life on Facebook or Instagram and getting depressed about your own, not seeing the cracks that hide between the images and bragging status updates?

"I'm not really sure I appreciated what was happening then," begins Wojtek, "To me it had been a choice between continuing my stage acting course and being on the dole or taking off on the road with a band I originally had no intention or desire to succeed with, but which now had a very real potential of doing so. I have vivid memories of staring out of van windows on tour and crying my eyes out."

This definitely wasn't what I was expecting, and as I hear more it's clear that Wojtek had originally wanted to be a singer, rather than the bass player, and despite enjoying the opportunity he had to make a living from music, as he had always wanted to, it was nothing like he'd imagined. One of the most enduring images of Symposium is from a gig they played to a packed Brixton academy supporting No Doubt when singer Ross was giving a typically energetic performance and leapt into the air, landing and crumpling in a heap on the floor during the first song.

"We were laughing at him to begin with," recalls Wojtek, "We thought he was embarrassed because he'd fallen over."

Ross kept singing but during the final chorus he changed the words to 'I've broken my 'eff'ing leg!'

"He just kept repeating that," continues Wojtek, "We were looking at each other and the atmosphere changed, then the house lights came on and the St.John's Ambulance guys came onstage."

Ross was stretchered off, and the rest of the band were told that their upcoming tours would have to be cancelled while he recovered. They were due to be supporting Echo & The Bunnymen and Sleeper around Europe, then Blur around Japan and Australia. Some of the band were in floods of tears but Wojtek was celebrating inwardly. He'd rather have stayed home, as unbelievable as that may sound when he had the chance to go to Australia and Japan to support one of the biggest bands in the world at that time.

The way Symposium came across in the media was the polar opposite of how he wanted to be seen. They had a reputation as 'boneheads', in Wojtek's words, and were even known in NME magazine for some time as the Voldemort-esque 'The Teenage Band Whose Name Will Never be Mentioned,' due to a fracas between a journalist from the magazine and their manager.

"We were imbeciles," admits Wojtek, "We were young, but we were old enough to know better. I'm amazed we were ever allowed to play Reading festival again after what happened in 1998."

Symposium were, Wojtek believes, the only band to play the festival four years running between 1996 and 1999. The year after they were signed they played the Dr Martens Tent, the next year they appeared in a larger tent, then in 1998 they were popular enough to play the Main Stage in the afternoon. In the second enduring image most people have of the band, apart from the music, shall we say they got a little over-excited, being young men performing their music to a crowd of thousands at one of the UK's best known festivals, and as the final song came to an end they started to trash their equipment along with everything else onstage.

"There were people rushing onstage trying to stop us," says Wojtek, "Looking back now I guess they just wanted their microphones back, which is fair enough. If you watch the footage you'll see that I was swinging a cymbal stand around, trying to stop them from getting to us. Then Ross pushed a speaker stack offstage and unfortunately it landed on a security guy's knee. He was fine in the end but obviously he was hurt at the time. We'd never do anything like that now; Ross is the mellowest guy you could ever meet and wouldn't hurt a fly."

I put it to Wojtek that the audience for the more folk-based music he largely plays nowadays would not appreciate such antics anyway. He laughs at my joke. Reading 1998 was no laughing matter though – shortly after the set the festival organisers came to their dressing room and basically said they'd have to leave the site immediately for their own safety as there were people who wanted to harm them.

"It was pretty scary, and they were extremely angry with us. Mind you, Green Day made a bonfire onstage later on and I don't think they got in trouble. It wasn't a controlled fire – they just put all their equipment in a pile and burnt the lot. What we did was pretty tame in comparison."

On later tours Wojtek would make a point of putting his bass guitar very carefully back in its stand at the end of the set, partly as a nod to their previous destructive ways and partly because he just didn't want to be known as a vandal.

"Sometimes we'd be doing an interview and I'd inwardly be thinking 'Who are these people?' when looking at my bandmates," he reflects, "I was a little older than the rest of them, and we'd only become good friends when we formed the band. I was basically filling in on bass for some younger kids but then it became more permanent. I get on well with all of them now; age difference means less as you get older, and we did share something pretty special now I look back on it."

On one American tour he had spent over £1,000 on a fender jazz bass but ended up smashing it to pieces when a gig at New York's Bowery Ballroom went badly. After this he realised that their destructive behaviour was not sustainable. It was costing them a lot of money, and sometimes they'd even switch to cheaper guitars for the last song because they knew what might happen. Having heard the stories so far you might think it was relentlessly awful being in Symposium, but this just isn't true. Sometimes it was wonderful.

Symposium had started out playing small gigs – when they first got signed their average show was in a tiny, sweaty venue where they would be constantly colliding with each other because they were in such a small space. They would play some huge shows as well though.

"We went from playing to a few dozen people at the Dublin Castle in Camden on a Tuesday to opening for the Red Hot Chilli Peppers at Wembley Arena on the Thursday," he remembers, "It was a symbolic gesture from our agent to show us how powerful he was. I was standing in the blinding lights of Wembley Arena, hardly knowing which direction the audience were in, then I turned round to look for Joe on the drums and saw a tiny speck on a drum riser way off in the distance – a distance you could fit several of the tiny venues we were used to playing into."

He admits that he didn't appreciate what was happening back then, but if he looks back now he wishes he'd made more of it and taken Symposium as far as they could go. He certainly worked hard, along with the others, to get them to where they were.

"In 1995 I got serious," he says, "I stuffed hundreds of demo tapes in jiffy bags and got us loads of gigs all around London. We were playing in pubs to a tiny audience almost every weekend. A year later we felt burnt out and frustrated, at which point most bands would probably give up and go and live a 'normal' life."

So few who set out to make a living from music every get beyond this stage, and when they do it's often through being in the right place at the right time. So it proved for Symposium, when Hagop got chatting to a neighbour who happened to be a manager and publisher in the music industry. He came to a gig and saw plenty to work with, so he became their manager and started a 'bidding war' with various record labels. In the end they signed to Infectious Records, for the reason that they offered the band complete creative control, which Wojtek reflects now they probably didn't need.

In a way it was everything he'd dreamed of: -

"Before getting signed we played at the Bull & Gate in Kentish Town one rainy and cold night to the proverbial two men and a dog. It was dispiriting to say the least, but after the gig I was outside with Will and we were looking at the Kentish Town Forum next door, which was the 2,000 capacity venue for 'proper' bands. I said we'd play there one day, then three years later Will and I were beaming from ear to ear onstage there as we were playing a headline gig and I reminded him of the conversation we'd had. That was perhaps as big as we ever got, and that moment might have been the zenith of it all."

Symposium gave plenty of hope to young people growing up in the 90s with their optimistic sound, and the success they achieved allowing people to believe maybe they could have it too. After fleeing Reading Festival in 1998 they regrouped to work on material for their second album, which would never be released. Things started to unravel even quicker than they'd built up. At the height of their popularity they appeared on Top of the Pops, TFI Friday and a host of other TV shows, their songs were played on mainstream radio and MTV, they played all of the big UK festivals… basically everything most up and coming bands at the time dreamed of. Perhaps there were always cracks though, and the picture painted in the magazines hid a far darker side.

"We walked away from our deal with Infectious in the end," he recalls, "We had £1.2 million worth of debt from promotions, recordings, video budgets etc. and we wouldn't really have made any money until we paid it all back. Besides, Rupert Murdoch had just taken over Mushroom Records, who owned Infectious, and that put us off working with them."

Prior to this Wojtek had signed a publishing deal with EMI under his own name and made enough money to buy a house for his parents to live in. Their manager had made it happen, and he promised publishing deals to the rest of the band too, but they never materialised. It became one of several sources of tension. Their manager was a volatile character who most record labels weren't too keen to work with, and Hagop became disillusioned, leaving the band and going to university. All of the band members were young and still finding their feet in life as well as in music, and with five of them there was always a strong chance that some would start pulling in different directions. If you watch video footage online of the band playing Reading Festival in 1999 it really looks like they're having the time of their lives and are excited about people hearing their new material. There was even an unreleased song called 'Try Not to Give up Hope,' which seems a very apt title when you think about how it was all over just months after that Reading performance.

"'Try Not to Give up Hope' was in the process of being recorded and demoed when Symposium split up," Wojtek reveals, "I remember one of our best producers, Bryan New, was doing it – he saw some potential in the song. We did it with a drum machine, and I think Ross sang it. It was totally inspired by Idlewild, because I thought they were cooler than us and I wanted to do something less pop and with more 'integrity', whatever that was."

These new songs were being worked on against an increasingly fractious backdrop. The band would frequently argue at rehearsals and some members would stay at home smoking weed a lot of the time because it offered escapism from their growing problems. Maybe none of them wanted to admit quite how bad things were getting, and were desperate to hold on to the dreams they'd had. The image of five young lads leaping around in the artificially created rain in Spain (which may or may not have been on the plain) in the video for their 'Fairweather Friend' single, seems so at odds with the same five lads living in fear and resentment as they grow further and further apart just a couple of years later. Wojtek and Will beaming onstage at the Kentish Town Forum upon the realisation of their dreams seems so bittersweet when they were barely looking at each other as they scowled through rehearsals when the turn of the millennium was approaching.

At the end of a winter rehearsal that year their manager gathered them together and told them they needed to sort things out, that they should just go to the pub and talk things through. There were huge debts, personal differences, changing ideals and all kinds of tension that someone perceiving their lives from the outside would struggle to see. As a teenager reading about them in magazines I always just assumed they were five best friends doing something they loved for a living, making heaps of money, having a wonderful time.

"The debt was definitely a source of fear," admits Wojtek, talking about something that happened almost half his life ago now, "At the time I didn't really think about how bad it was, but now I think of it yeah, it was really bad. It's something I don't think any 21-year-old would find easy to deal with."

After their manager had spoken to them the lads went outside, but instead of going to talk through their differences they just said "See ya then!" and went their separate ways. On 1st January 2000 Symposium officially split up, which was really quite a surprise to me at the time. I remember one magazine reporting that Ross, Will and Joe were on one side whilst Hagop and Wojtek were on the other, and I'm ashamed to admit that my teenage self joked about the guys with the English-sounding names being xenophobic towards the guys with the Eastern European ancestry. I am less ashamed to admit that my mid 30-something self immediately thought of Symposium taking the full force of the millennium bug to save the rest of us and sacrificing their band. I told Wojtek about this. I think he saw the funny side, but he also told me about a documentary he'd seen which explained that the millennium bug was real, and that it never came to anything because of the tireless work of some IT geniuses leading up to the event. I'm yet to watch the documentary but I'm intrigued, having always thought it was false.

"I had to sell my house to pay off the debt," states Wojtek, "I could have declared bankruptcy at any time, which would have made it all go away, so I was never too scared. It wasn't nice to deal with though."

So Wojtek's dreams kind of came true, but he was always going in a different direction to where he wanted to be. Now everything he'd worked towards was no more, and he would have to figure out what to do next. Barely out of his teens really, he'd amassed enough money to buy a house and then had to sell it very soon afterwards, finding himself pretty much back at square one but having lost some friends, lost a lot of money and lost the source of his success. Maybe they were too young to handle the level of fame that was thrust upon them, but is anyone ever old enough to handle fame? It's a strange culture we live in, but Symposium had their success in a time when many people who were famous were still famous for their talents rather than just simple notoriety. Reality TV, social media and all that has gone along with them were either in their infancy or still some way off.

Wojtek had something to work with, having been in a band people connected with, and was still just as determined to earn a living from music as he ever had been. He couldn't imagine himself doing anything else, but there are so many stories of musicians who have some success and then spend many years trying to make ends meet in any way they can. This isn't exclusive to musicians; most people in life aren't making their living in the way they would love to be, but Wojtek was so certain it was what he was meant to be doing, so was there another way to make it happen?

POSSIBILITY

I saw a quote on the internet once saying that nothing is impossible because the word itself says "I'm possible." I disagree. Not because I'm pessimistic, but because by the same logic you could say that there's no such thing as being impolite because the word itself says "I'm polite." Or there's no such thing as immaterial, because the word itself says "I'm material." You could use the former to justify being rude, the latter to scramble fragile minds with questions on the nature of reality. It's a dangerous, lazy and ill-conceived way of looking at things. Like I said though, I'm not a pessimist. I describe myself as being 'optipesstic.' I'm swamped in self-doubt, yet I'm still able to maintain hope. How is this possible? Well, nothing is impossible because the very word says.....

Ok then, let me explain. You may have been spending most of your life gathering more and more reasons to think you'll always be proving the school bullies were right about you. Incidentally, most of those bullies are only the way they are because of their environment at the time. It's nothing personal. However, as anyone who has been bullied will know, those things they said and did can cut deep, and can shape the way you are, no matter how hard you fight to not let them. Anyway, you may have had glimmer after glimmer of possibilities glow brightly before disappearing like sparks from a roaring fire on a long winter's night. You may have blinked and opened your eyes to find yourself hurtling towards a certain age at terminal velocity with the feeling that your life has passed you by. But maybe there's a bearded man in Utah who's about to give you the break you've been trying to catch all these years. You can't see the future, so you really never know what it might hold.

That's not true though is it? The most successful 100 mile runner of all time wouldn't ask an unknown, underachieving fool from across a vast ocean to collaborate with him on his autobiography. That just wouldn't ever happen in these derelict times. It would be like Trevor the just qualified electrician from Delabole being flown over to be the lighting technician for Rio Carnival. This is real life, in which dreams are dashed like waves that crash against cliffs in October storms. Right?

Well actually, no. That's precisely what happened to me in December 2016. Simply because I was in the right place at the right time, I jumped into a virtual haystack and instantly found a virtual needle of hope. What do I mean? Well I'll tell you. Grab a beverage first if you wish. Ok, so this all came about because of something I basically loathe but can't seem to keep away from in the modern world. Social Media. I posted on an American ultra-running group on Facebook. I can't remember what I said, but it was something to do with running books. I got a few notifications, then one of them caught my eye. It said 'Karl Meltzer has commented on your post.' This was particularly intriguing to me, because I happened to know that Karl Meltzer was one of the greatest endurance athletes in the world, and had recently broken the record for the fastest known time thru-hiking the Appalachian Trail.

"Hmmm..." I thought, "I wonder what his favourite book is. Let's have a look at his comment..."

"Just you wait until my book '100 Miles is Not That Far' comes out..." it said, "..now all I have to do is find somebody to help me write it"

It was the moment in the film where the main character's eyes bulge, his mouth falls open, he exchanges a look of urgency with his sidekick and then explodes into action. Is this the real Karl Meltzer? Well the picture looks like him, and he seems to know his own catchphrase ('100 mile is not that far'.) Would he want someone to help him write his autobiography or would he write it himself? He's probably too busy running and recovering from running to have much time for writing. It must be him. Ok, time to reply. Play it cool, Dave....

"Meeeeeeeeeeeeeeeeeee!!!!! I'm a writer!"

Oh. Oops. Has he seen it? Can I delete it in time? Maybe he'll be impressed with my enthusiasm. No he won't. Must delete

'Karl Meltzer likes your comment'

He does??? Well maybe, but a 'comment like' on Facebook can just as easily be a token gesture of politeness. In this instance it probably means "Hahaha. Yeah. Good one, buddy." I imagine seeing my name on the cover of Karl Metlzer's autobiography next to his. Yeah, Ok. Sure. I switch Facebook off and decide it's time to procrastinate no longer over the dishes.

When the last droplet of water has dried from the last roasting tin and it's been placed back in the cupboard I pick up my phone. Oh how life has changed since the '90s. Back then the internet was something that meant you couldn't phone anyone when it was on. Now it's unusual for someone to have a phone on which you can't access it. Anyway, I saw that I had a new message. Who was it from? Oh... Karl Meltzer. What could he possibly want? Well the message is a little cryptic. It says "Yeah, I've been looking for someone to work with for a long time." Ok, so what does this mean? Am I meant to say "Oh man, that sucks. I would have thought writers would be literally falling over each other for the chance to work with you?" Am I a sounding board for this poor guy who has an amazing story but can't find anyone to help him tell it, or is he actually considering the possibility that it could be me who helps him? One way to find out.

To cut a long story short, messages were exchanged and then he said "This is my number, give me a call at 9am." This was 9am his time, meaning 4pm my time, because he lives in Utah and I live in Somerset, England. It would have been better if he'd asked me to call him there and then, because there were a lot of hours between now and 4pm tomorrow. Plenty of time for the negative thoughts that wait around every corner to catch up, swarm around my brain like seagulls around a discarded chip wrapper and to envelop my mind in blackness. I would hear every voice of every person who's ever doubted me, including my own, in a mass chorus of mocking laughter at the idea of me writing a book with Karl Meltzer. I'd convince myself that it could never work and that the fact I even considered the possibility was ridiculous. That's if I listened to the voice of reason. Not this time. When would I ever have an opportunity like this again? I had to try. I guess I should have prepared for it like I would a job interview, but what could I possibly say? "Hey, Karl. I've self-published one book and had a small amount of success with it. Why wouldn't you want me to help you with yours?" I'd just have to talk to him and see what he said.

I can't remember how well I slept that night, but I don't think I was too nervous. I hadn't really had time to get nervous, or to think about how phenomenal an opportunity this could be for a writer trying to catch his break. Of course I was well aware of these things, but they hadn't really had time to sink in. I bought an international calling card and dialled the number on the dot of 4pm.....

Answerphone. Ok, I'll try again in 10 minutes.....

Answerphone again. Well, it was a nice dream while it lasted.

CONNER'S STORY PART 3

"Please help me!"

It has to be any parent's worst nightmare. Emma had returned Conner's calls and heard him say these three words hysterically as soon as he answered.

"What's wrong?" she asked.

"Please help me," he reiterated, "I feel like I'm going to collapse. Please help me!"

"Stay still, son. I'll call an ambulance."

At this point the line went dead. At the same time Mark was checking his phone and saw that Conner had tried to call him too. He rung back but there was no answer. This wasn't unusual, as he didn't always answer his phone, but Mark sent a text as well. A few minutes later Emma called. He barely had time to say hello.

"It's Conner," she stammered, "There's something wrong. I've called an ambulance, you have to get home now!"

Mark's workplace is very close to their home and so after a frantic explanation to his boss he was able to get there in no time. Rushing through the door, he felt a chill as he spotted Conner's phone at the bottom of the stairs. Bounding up the steps two at a time, he stopped momentarily as he saw his teenage son sprawled naked on the floor, a pool of blood-coloured vomit around him. Mark fell to his knees and tried to rouse Conner. At this point he was still awake but was fairly incomprehensible. At this point Emma burst through the door and joined him at the top of the stairs. They both tried to ask Conner what was wrong. Until now their son had never really sworn in front of them but he kept repeating "My 'eff'ing head." They weren't sure how aware he was of his surroundings, but they kept trying to get him to explain what had happened. They managed to get some boxer shorts on him just before the paramedics arrived, protecting his modesty.

The paramedics weren't able to get any more out of him, but they asked Mark to go and check Conner's room for empty pill packets. He couldn't find any, and all Conner would say still was "Ah 'f...', my head." They carried out a number of tests but all they revealed was that his temperature was a little low, and that there was a slight imbalance in his blood. Conner has no memory of this day, and we may never know what was going through his head at the time apart from horrific pain. We don't know if he was distressed, or even very aware. All we do know is that he was in agony.

It was 3pm when the ambulance arrived. A while before this the paramedic had been speaking on his radio, perhaps explaining the urgency of the situation, or asking for opinions when the tests had revealed so little. As they took Conner into the ambulance Mark and Emma were left to try and process what was happening. Their eldest son was very unwell, and they didn't know why. For now the good news was that he was alive, and that he was conscious, but he had severe head pain and seemed to have lost consciousness at some point. He had vomited blood, and wasn't able to articulate what he was going through. They didn't need the paramedics to tell them that this was serious. Their younger son Jayden would be going to his grandparents' house for a while; he shouldn't see this. What exactly was this though? What was wrong with Conner? This was only a matter of months after his Great Grandad had his first stroke. What more could life throw at them?

After quite some time the paramedics returned and said they were taking Conner to the hospital, asking if Emma wanted to go with them. She did. Mark would follow in the car. When they arrived they waited in the same room while the doctors and nurses carried out more tests. At this point they were concerned but not too afraid. Conner's language was still a lot more colourful than they'd usually hear from him. He was doing his bit to reinforce Geordie stereotypes with what he was saying.

"This is unusual," said one of the nurses, "Normally I can call an illness by now, but it's not obvious what's wrong with Conner yet."

Mark and Emma looked at each other and then back at the nurse.

"I'm sorry, would you mind waiting through there for a while? We'll come and let you know what's happening. We have to fit a catheter."

There wasn't really any urgency in what the nurse said and so they went to the waiting room. They may not have been panicking but they were becoming more concerned by the minute. After around fifteen minutes the nurse came back out.

"We've moved Conner to a bed right in front of the nurses' desk in A&E so we can keep a closer eye on him," she explained, "if you follow me I'll take you to him."

This time the atmosphere was a little different. They arrived to find cannulas being fitted into Conner's hands, shins and feet. One of the nurses was talking to the doctor. Mark and Emma couldn't hear what they were saying but there was tension in the air. The doctor came over and started to use medical terminology to try and explain what was going on. Everything became a blur, but one sentence leapt out.

CONNER'S STORY PART 3

"I believe Conner may have taken an overdose," stated the doctor, "That's my hypothesis, but we need to test him also for meningitis. We will need to carry out a CT scan."

"Conner wouldn't take drugs," said Mark immediately, "Get the other tests done now."

Conner had been with his grandparents all of the previous day and at home all of that day. Mark knew that he couldn't have been spiked, because it would have to have happened a couple of days ago. This was nothing to do with drugs. Meningitis can be gravely serious, so why weren't they testing for that straight away? All Mark and Emma could do now was wait, and it was unbearable, but it was the only choice they had. They knew the doctor was wrong about Conner taking drugs, but they were no closer to discovering what had really happened. All those years ago when they'd first discovered they were going to be parents they had no idea of the nightmare they would one day face. It was hours ago now that he had picked up the phone to Emma and begged her to help him. It was all she wanted to do now, but it felt like so much time had passed and she'd never felt so helpless. She and Mark were told to wait outside the room while their first born child was taken in for his CT scan. They didn't know what they would be told when they next saw him. There would be so much more waiting for them to do, and if they felt helpless now it was nothing compared to what was coming.

THE CONTINUING STORY

Maybe Karl hasn't come to his senses. Maybe he just couldn't get to the phone right then. Maybe he was out on a run and just decided to keep going for a bunch of extra miles, high on endorphins and lost in the moment. Maybe there was a plumbing issue, his kitchen was filled with water and he was too busy to talk to me right then. Maybe I'd calculated the time difference wrong between Somerset and Utah and I was actually meant to call him at 6pm. Maybe he was watching a really gripping episode of something on Netflix and he just had to find out what happened there and then. Maybe someone else had called him and he couldn't get off the phone. Maybe he was polishing his trophy collection and lost track of the time. Maybe he was nervous to talk to me for some reason. Maybe his breakfast had taken longer to prepare than anticipated and he couldn't answer the phone on an empty stomach because he might get hangry and snap at me, which would make him look unprofessional. Maybe he'd got a letter from a long lost relative with some revelatory news that he was trying to process. Maybe he was learning Russian on the DuoLingo app and he didn't feel he could stop until he'd mastered lesson 3. Maybe he'd overslept.

There could have been thousands of reasons why he hadn't answered the phone, but not one of them, even the more sensible ones of those above, seemed more likely to me than the possibility that he'd just changed his mind. I figured I may as well send him a Facebook message anyway....

"Hey, Karl. Are you still free to talk this morning? I tried to ring."

Within minutes I got a reply. It turned out he'd been for a run and forgotten to charge his phone while he was out. He asked if I could speak in a couple of hours' time instead.

"Nah, mate. You had your chance – good luck finding another writer."

So, a couple of hours later I called. Of course I hadn't really said that. I'd actually said "Ok, cool. Will speak to you then," but if I'd replied with my actual thoughts it would have been more like "Yes please, Mr Meltzer. Please, thank you, are you sure? Ok, thank you!"

Those extra couple of hours gave me plenty of time to wonder why he was going to spend some valuable minutes of his day talking to a pretty much unknown author from England. Did he think I was a more successful writer than I was? Was there a famous author with a similar name to mine he could have confused me with? Was this the real Karl Meltzer? Were there other Karl Meltzers who were just imitating, and was this one of them?

So, Karl answered the phone. To be fair he did sound a lot like the Karl Meltzer I'd listened to on the Talk Ultra podcast a few years previously. This was a good start. Forty minutes went by, and the conversation ended with me being reasonably convinced that I would soon be helping the winningest 100 mile runner of all time to write his autobiography. We'd seemed to get on quite well. He laughed when I said "You never know" after he'd told me his best years of competitive running were probably behind him, and seemed to warm to me as soon as I'd said it. I told him what I could offer, and after listening to it all he said that the conversation had ticked a lot of boxes for him.

He didn't say yes, but he definitely didn't say no. I liked him; he seemed humble, he had a sense of humour, he seemed like someone I could comfortably talk to in real life if I was thrown into a potentially awkward social situation with him. Definitely somebody I'd like to write a book with. I didn't have to wait long before this became a reality. I think probably if I hadn't been a little bit irritating by messaging him every so often to subtly try and move things along then it would have taken longer for things to get going, but over time it began to make sense why he wanted to work with me.

I don't want to give any spoilers for the book, but basically Karl wanted to tell his story in his own way. He didn't want it to be boastful, even though for a man who's had as much success as he has it could be hard not to be boastful just by stating facts about his running career. He wanted it to be authentic. So why did he need my help at all? Well it turns out that Karl is a very busy man. To be as good at running as he is takes a fair bit of training. On top of that he has clients to coach, races to run, interviews with a whole bunch of people who want to hear what he has to say, and of course all the unexpected things that crop up in adult life that need his time and attention. Plus he's married. Plus he likes to keep his lawn tidy. I mean really tidy. To the extent that it could be described as a little bit obsessive. Plus he likes to do active pursuits in his spare time and doesn't really like sitting down to write books. He admitted to me that if he didn't have someone to work with then his book would never get written, but he did want to tell his story. That's where I came in.

Karl isn't someone who likes to do things the 'right' way. By that I mean he's the kind of guy who might forget to charge his phone in preparation for talking to a guy about writing a book, because he was focused on his run. This isn't because he doesn't care about the guy he's going to be speaking to, just that he loves what he does and sometimes that distracts him from the odd thing here and there, but everything will get done in time. How many of us can relate to that? I think in me he recognised a guy who would get that, and wouldn't mind if the book wasn't done in a particularly structured way. He was right. I won't say I wasn't desperate to get it done so I could tell every potential future ghost writing client, publisher, agent and person I met who I needed to break the ice with that I'd worked with one of the greatest endurance athletes of all time on his autobiography. For absolutely ages after work began I couldn't quite believe my luck. I still don't. There is literally no logical reason why I should have been the one Karl chose to work with. It's completely bonkers! I started this book probably about a year after I'd first spoken to Karl, and it's entirely possible that this one will have come out first. You may not believe me that the other one is coming, but Karl said he didn't mind me including this. You should read his story when it does surface; it's pretty amazing.

So why did this chance ever come about? Well essentially it's because I was in the right place at the right time. Why was I even in that right place? Several times I've deleted, or should I say deactivated, my Facebook account. If I'd not been on Facebook I would never have been able to set this opportunity up. The Facebook group I asked the question on I'd nearly been banned from almost as soon as I joined several years previously. I'd been trying to sell my first book on there when it was against the group rules and I hadn't realised. As it happens I've now left the group for different reasons, but if I'd been banned from it originally I doubt Karl would ever have seen any of my posts. If I'd not written my first book I would have had no leverage to try and convince Karl I could help him with his, and so I'd never have replied to his comment in the way I did. If I hadn't made that post on the Facebook group at that time then this opportunity would never have happened. So what's the lesson here? There isn't one. I got that opportunity through a completely random chance. There's no way you can plan for that. The message though is just don't give up. You might have been feeling for years like you're getting nowhere in your field, but there might just be a bearded man in Utah who can change your life by offering you an opportunity you'd never bargained for. You just never know.

I could tell the rest of the story of how we wrote the book, the process of it and everything but that feels kinda self-indulgent and unnecessary. If you have specific questions and are interested then you will find out how to get in touch later on and you are welcome to do so. The point of me including this in the book though is that it's a personal story of hope, about how opportunities can come from nowhere. At the time of writing I've just been lucky enough to get an allotment plot with fruit trees and bushes, heaps of space, a shed and all manner of things I couldn't believe I'd be so fortunate to have. Again this was just by being in the right place at the right time. Sometimes, or maybe a lot of the time, your efforts aren't rewarded with what they might deserve. Sometimes things can just work out for you because you happened to be somewhere when that thing was available. That's basically how I got to work with Karl Meltzer.

HOPE IN NATURE – A WORLD OUTSIDE THE SMART PHONE

Author Andy Hamilton has a walk he does almost every day. He's got to know every inch of it, but he still sees something new each time purely because he's looking.

"The walk takes me from my house just into the suburbs of Bristol to my office, which is moments from the main train station," explains Andy, "It takes me through a wooded area of a park, through a knocked down fence into a 44 acre graveyard. Even in the midst of winter, when everything seems dead, there is a new growth. The trees lose their leaves and thus there is a light and warmth hitting the bare earth. Opportunistic plants then start to shoot up and you get this slow winter growth."

Throughout the seasons there are familiar sights and sounds that I find rejuvenating. A carpet of bluebells in the woods in spring along with clumps of wild garlic and three-cornered leek in between the armies of daffodils and primroses. Throughout the spring and summer the palette of colours increases as migratory birds return to these shores and butterflies, moths and dragonflies emerge. Perhaps my favourite sight in all of creation is the leaves ablaze with the warmth of their autumn colouration. Reds, yellows and oranges provide a four course dinner with after eight mints for the eyes. Even winter can have a striking atmosphere when Fieldfares and Redwings return. They spend the summer further north, but in the winter months they can be seen gathering in UK trees and fields, and if you're out on a November night you may hear the softly piercing call of the Redwing as it migrates. A winter sunset can be charming, with the charcoal outline of the branches against the twilight, and of course there's atmosphere in a frozen river or a glistening frosty branch.

"I really don't like the winter months – the lack of light really effects me," admits Andy, "However, by focusing on nature I am filled with hope. You have to focus on the small things, look for them and focus on the kindness. I can't say it without sounding like The Lion King but it brings me close to the circle of life."

Like me, Andy seems to have preferred the world as it was in the 1990s to now in a number of ways, and feels we are less connected rather than more so since the digital revolution began.

"What I don't like about the modern world I try to exclude myself from," he says, "I don't have a smart phone and I only check my e-mails and social media three times a week during office hours. I don't like that my mum asks for my wi-fi password as soon as she walks into my house or that when I walk past a bus stop everyone is on their phone and nobody chats."

Don't get a smart phone, Andy. I've owned one for a couple of years now and having the internet in my pocket has overshadowed all the knowledge I have about the level of screen time that's healthy for me. I can't resist the urge to look at it every so often, just like I could once not resist the urge to light up a cigarette. The internet has revolutionised self-employment for sure, and has opened up a whole new world of possibilities for people like me, but I rarely just stop when I've sent that e-mail I was planning to or made that post I just thought of. An honest intention to spend five minutes online can so easily become forty extra minutes of wasted time before I even know what's happening. I am one of many who has let this happen and just writing this makes me determined to change my ways. I don't see anything wrong with a little internet time each day but there's so much more to life and I know it.

"I used to get a bus across town one winter at the same time all the kids came out of school," Andy recalls, "All of a sudden I noticed the bus had gone quiet. All of the kids were on their phones. Christmas had passed and they'd all got devices. When they did talk it was all about how they looked in images, or what they thought someone meant by something they'd said on snapchat. You could see the birth of their anxiety and the loss of communication. That I didn't like."

The hope of every generation is that their children will have a better life and do a better job of things than they did, but to me it's pretty frightening when children are obsessed with technology and with the superficial. It was much the same for my generation in a sense – all the kids were obsessed with football and the latest bands or TV shows in the 90s, and I remember three kids walking along Dawlish Beach one day ignoring their surroundings and discussing Nintendo 64s and Sega Megadrives. I can't help feeling though that back then kids actually did more and had more varied interests on the whole. There weren't quite so many distractions, or at least they weren't quite so intense and all-encompassing. When I reminisce with people of my age about our youth there's so much to discuss, and it's a genuine fear that when the kids of today reminisce in twenty years' time they'll not be able to remember much but a blur of meaningless screen time. Maybe I'm being a little dramatic, but when I think of how much the world has changed in the last fifteen to twenty years I can't help but feel deeply unsettled at the thought of what it might be like in another ten. Thinking about it really makes me want to smash every phone and computer I can find, but of course I won't. If I do then typing up this chapter was utterly pointless for a start.

Andy was on my Creative Writing course back in the early 2000s and it's certainly quite a different world nowadays. Even more so than when Andy and Adharanand Finn, who you will hear from later, knew each other as kids. However, what was beautiful about the world then largely still remains in nature. Andy wrote the book 'The Self-Sufficient-ish Bible' with his brother Dave (most people are called Dave really), and has written a couple connected with his passion for foraging, which he often combines with his liking for a drink or two. 'The Perfect Pint' has recently been released.

"I'm trying to get to those who still would find a foraging walk a little bit 'fringe' and giving people a touch of plant knowledge in the form of a drink is very enjoyable."

Andy is able to make a living from his passion for nature but admits it has been tough some years.

"I somehow muddle through," he says, "I think as most self-employed people would admit, you don't make a living from doing just one thing or doing the same thing all the time. I constantly evolve what I do."

Aside from his books and newspaper columns, Andy leads foraging walks but is moving away from the straightforward ones and is hosting wild cocktail and gin nights. Having said that, some of his most rewarding experiences have come from the foraging walks.

"I've met people from Shanghai and taught them foraging; it was amazing to see their reactions. They said it was one of the best experiences of their lives, and it was in the driving rain in the north of Scotland. We only spent an hour or so on the walk, but even these real urbanites knew a lot about nature.

After all, we use 'nature' like we are separate from it, but even in the city there's the wind and the rain. What are we if we are not nature?"

Indeed, with all the movement towards the digital nowadays it can feel like we've never been so far removed from nature. When you go to a library and find a machine doing the job a librarian once did, or like recently when I went to a petrol station and a robotic voice reminded me to fuel safely, as if I would otherwise forget. When everyone is sat looking at their phones in the evening rather than talking to each other, and when very few people write letters any more. However, Andy argues that if you take a step back and open your eyes to what's happening away from the mainstream there's actually quite a move back towards traditional ways going on, and that foraging and fermentation are becoming more popular than he has ever seen.

These traditional ways, and the appreciation of nature, can fill you with tranquillity. On the other hand though, Andy has experienced the threat of opposition from the government to living a natural life.

"There was an attempt to criminalise foraging that came from Westminster," he states, "Their lawyers created some bylaws and then forced councils to adopt these chapter and verse. Their hands were tied when it came to changing them, thus the local government have to take the flak for a national government policy."

The law stated that you couldn't remove or damage any part of a plant, which of course could be interpreted to make foraging illegal.

"I went to the press and it hit the national news," recounts Andy, "I had a meeting with the local council, who insisted they wouldn't ban foraging and in the end they didn't adopt the bylaw. It felt good to highlight it, though in the end how can it be enforced?"

How indeed? Wild garlic grows everywhere in the spring, blackberries grow everywhere in the Autumn, elderflowers are widespread in the summer. Are the local councils really going to take steps to prosecute everyone who picks them? All the same, this possibility led to Andy creating the Association of Foragers.

"Having slagged off social media," he laughs, "I have to make a concession. The Association of Foragers was founded by starting a Facebook group. I do have to say that it became something more than just a group when we actually met up, and I can't take credit for the hard work that others have done to grow it."

Social media does have its uses, but what exists outside of it and always has is so much more nourishing and enriching. Andy is someone who seems to have the balance just right – he harnesses the internet for the great mass communication tool and resource it can be, but has enough distance from it to realise how much of a problem it is becoming. There is an illusion that the internet opens our eyes. Well, perhaps it's not an illusion if it's only used sparingly, but in reality the internet threatens to dull the senses and rob people of so many real life experiences that are taken for granted. The internet is one of many things in my life that I've lost control of, but like all of those other things it's within my power to take control back. Today is day one, and there is always much hope to be found when you reconnect with nature.

CONNER'S STORY PART 4

Something was gravely wrong, and they were beginning to realise it. I'm lucky enough to have rarely found myself in situations where the lives of people close to me have been in immediate danger. I can only imagine that up until this point Mark and Emma had been deeply concerned, but still believed everything would be Ok. Now there were doctors and nurses rushing past them and a screen was being placed in front of the door where Conner was having his CT scan. What the heck?

"It was one of those Oriental screens like you would get changed behind," recalls Mark now, "I don't know how long we were outside that room. It could have been minutes, it could have been hours, but as soon as that screen was put outside the room we knew something was really wrong."

Emma was crying, and one of the nurses was rushing past but caught sight of her and stopped immediately.

"We've found a bleed on Conner's brain," she said as she hugged Emma, "We're trying to get in touch with the RVI."

She was referring to the Royal Victoria Infirmary; a specialist hospital in Newcastle. Mark remembers the next short while as being a bit of a blur. Emma tried to call her mum, Viv, but she couldn't get the words out and so Mark did his best to explain what was happening. He then rang his friend Gary to ask if he could give them a lift to the RVI, knowing he was far too anxious to drive them there safely himself. A little while later they were getting some air outside the A&E department, still not being allowed to go into the room with Conner, and some nurses came out to tell them the ambulance had arrived to take him to the RVI.

"Can we call you a taxi?" asked one of the nurses.

"We're sorted, thank you" murmured Mark.

"Can I go in the ambulance?" asked Emma.

"We'd advise against it," replied the nurse, "Everyone who's in there already could potentially save Conner's life, and one of them would have to stay behind if you were to go."

She asked them to wait for a second and got the lead paramedic from the ambulance. As he stepped out Mark was taken back to a poker game he'd been involved in at a work colleague's house. He'd played cards before with this guy who now had his eldest son's life in his hands. Such a different atmosphere. There would be no attempts at bluffing this time.

"I'll get him there as soon as I can," said the paramedic.

"Please take care of him."

"He's in the best hands."

'Best hands' – if this was a movie that would have been put in the script intentionally as a poker reference. Mark was just desperate to know that in these circumstances the paramedic would have a Royal Flush. Did he really have the best hand?

There was not another second to waste. Mark and Emma rushed to the car; it wasn't far to their home, where Gary and Viv would be meeting them. Mark was relieved to let Gary take over the driving, having found it difficult even to drive the short distance to meet the others, but on the way to the RVI the ambulance pulled in front of them at a roundabout. This was purely coincidental, but seeing the vehicle her son was in, where she'd been unable to join him, made the flow of tears unstoppable. Just that morning they'd thought he'd been sleeping off the same virus Mark had come down with.

Now they were trying to make sense of this living nightmare. Would it have made a difference if they'd known how ill he was that morning? How could they have known? Why did he not collapse when one of them was still there? Why was this happening at all? How could it be?

When they arrived at the RVI they quickly found the A&E reception, explaining who they were.

"There's no information at this time but we'll find out for you as soon as we can. If you just take a seat for now we'll be with you when we know more."

Not more waiting. They kept stepping outside just trying to make the time pass until they could see Conner again. Of everything that was going on it was the waiting that was driving them to distraction. If they could find out what was happening at the very least that would be something.

After some time they were taken through to the side room where Mark would see 'LIFE' on the label of the bottle. Just how much longer would it be? Somebody had to know something. They had to have some idea.

ORIGINS OF HOPE

For hope to exist, living beings who can experience hope have to exist. There are a number of theories about how we came into being, but there are two main ones – evolutionary theory and creation. The big bang/evolutionary theory, which is taught as fact now in most schools, goes a little something like this as far as my Google-based research goes. I'm not an expert, this is just what I gather....

From basically nothing came a giant explosion. Immediately after this the temperature in the atmosphere was around 5.5 billion degrees Celsius. For an idea of how hot this is, last week at the time of writing there was a 'heatwave' in Australia during which temperatures of 50 degrees Celsius were recorded, and the tarmac on highways literally melted from the heat. Meanwhile, the boiling point of water is 100 degrees Celsius. Therefore, the temperature at the point of the Big Bang was 5,499,999,900 degrees Celsius hotter than the temperature at which water will boil in a pan, and 5,499,999,950 degrees Celsius hotter than the temperature at which even Australians will say "Crikey, mate – bit hot out here isn't it?!" as the tarmac melts on their highways. The explosion, as the theory goes, also sent crazy numbers of neutrons, electrons and protons into the atmosphere, some of which combined as the universe got cooler over millions of years, eventually forming planets, stars and ultimately life. Visible light wasn't thought to be around for about 380,000 years after the Big Bang, but something known as the Cosmic Microwave Background (CMB) appeared when free electrons combined with nuclei to create neutral atoms. Like I say, I've done limited research on this, and so if you're reading this and thinking "No, no, no! That's not it at all!" I apologise for my rudimentary scientific understanding. Anyway, I shall continue.

Ok, so if we fast forward over 13 billion years, a couple of scientists in New Jersey - Arno Penzias and the less exotically named Robert Wilson - were building a radio receiver and picked up temperatures that were higher than expected. They thought they had struck gold at this point and found something they could blame on the pesky pigeons that tried to roost inside the antenna, emptying the contents of their pigeon guts everywhere. This would be justification, in their eyes, for mass pigeon murder, and so that's exactly what they did. However, their scientific findings did not back up their theory when the temperature remained the same despite what they had done. However, a team from Princeton University were trying to find evidence of the CMB at exactly the same time, and told the New Jersey scientists that since they had eliminated the pigeons, both literally and metaphorically speaking, as the cause of the raised temperature around their radio receiver, the only other possibility must be that the CMB was causing it. I don't really know how this works to be honest. Someone with a more scientific mind must have a fairly convincing-sounding explanation, because it is now accepted as fact by many. However, by using this observation, and by gazing far into the night sky with jolly big telescopes, scientists believe they have been able to map out the history of our universe.

Now, there is a lot more to this theory of course, but in a nutshell it's that a big explosion set into motion expansion and a lot of reactions. Over time the universe cooled, life began with single-celled organisms and over billions of years these adapted to their environment, the fittest survived, some species thrived, and multiplied, changes took place through time and space, eventually leading to the human race. Scientists will admit that they don't know how or why a lot of this occurred, but from fossilised remains discovered, rocks uncovered and observations made they are confident that they can map out how and when life began, and what changes have happened over time to lead to what we see today. They believe they can plot an exact course from bacteria deep in the ocean 3.8 million years ago to The Only Way is Essex. How could these primitive marine organisms at the beginning of life on earth ever have known that the answers would one day be discovered in the salons and nightclubs of a county in the southern reaches of East Anglia? Does the Cosmic Microwave Background's warm ambient glow radiate today in the fake tans that adorn the flesh of these modern day celebrities? Do the first stars that twinkled in the darkness now twinkle…. Actually no, never mind.

Now, I don't actually believe in this theory, for I am one of them Christians. I believe that the universe and all of the species that live within came from intelligent design. I find it harder to believe that this all happened basically by accident than I do to believe that we were created for a purpose. The one similarity between our views is that the universe came from basically nothing. That's something it seems we can all agree on. However, instead of a huge explosion starting everything, I believe that God created the universe and that creatures didn't evolve over billions of years but were created; some of them have survived, others haven't. A lot of people would consider me to be delusional and unintelligent for having this belief. I wonder if those same people imagine creation as a bloke with a beard plonking planets in the sky? To me it would have been more like a deity beyond our comprehension using methods far beyond the capabilities or imagination of humankind to create life not all that far removed from that which we find today. Some species from then still remain, others died out. Humans were given free will, and with that free will they constantly went against the wishes of their creator, which is why we live in such an imperfect world today, and why so many people feel at odds with themselves.

I have done the same with my free will as so many others have before me. I'd be the first to admit that, and so I'm not going to say you should be like me if you want to be at peace with yourself, to be a shining example to others and to successfully live with hope at the forefront of everything you do, but that's what I'm aiming for. I'm a work in progress. We all are. Literally nobody alive today is perfect. I've made some very regrettable decisions. Every day I do or say something I regret at some point, and I've never met anyone in my life who's been perfect with every word and action. If you spend enough time with anyone you'll start to see their flaws, no matter how perfect they may seem on first impression. If this wasn't true there would have been no need for God to send his son to earth to die on the cross to pay the price for all of our sins, giving hope to anyone who would trust in him that there is something better beyond this life. Yeah, I believe that too. Even though I believe this to be true I still make a lot of mistakes, and I still wake up feeling very negative some days. When I read the Old Testament I read constant examples of people who have struggled with hope even though God had given them reasons why they should never doubt Him. That's why Jesus came to earth. If you believe in the gospel then that's a reason in itself to have hope beyond hope, even if some days you struggle to keep it at the forefront of your mind. So what if you don't believe in the gospel? Where does your hope come from?

I guess there's not a single answer to that question, but to get through any adversity hope is vital. Hope is everywhere. Hopefully you will find plenty of it within these pages.

CONSIDERATION

"When you say hello to someone at a bus stop and they scowl at you it's so easy to just think 'What an idiot' and to judge them, but the fact is you don't know what's been going on in their life. They might have lost somebody, they might be in pain. It would be easy to scowl back but being kind and compassionate goes a long way."

Wise words in one of the broadest Somerset accents I've heard in some time, from a man in his early forties who I first became aware of when he was barely out of his teens. Reef were a bunch of Somerset lads who formed a band, moved to the big city and caught their break when they were featured on a minidisc advert. Gary Stringer was their vocalist, his voice an explosion of power. Most people discovered Reef through the advert at the time, but they have fared a lot better than the product they were helping to sell.

"A minidisc was like a recordable CD," laughs Gary now, "We got a lot of flak for doing that advert, which was the way at the time. You were called a sell-out and were really looked down on, but we'd been on income support six months before that. We were young lads and suddenly we were being flown to New York, taken to the airport in a limousine. We didn't care what people thought."

I'd forgotten all about it until Gary mentioned it, but back in the 90s there was a real conviction among alternative music fans that bands who had music on TV adverts were somehow breaking an unwritten code and letting us down. I probably thought so too, or at least I said I did without really thinking about it. Like most, I didn't see these bands as being made up of real people with financial concerns and futures to think about; they were just there for my entertainment. Looking back now I can see things differently. For bands people like to keep making music they normally have to make enough money from it so they can afford to live in the meantime (no pun intended; 'In the Meantime' by Spacehog was another famous advert tune from the 90s.) If not they either have to get another job to supplement their income or just choose to be extremely poor and deal with it. I wonder how many of the people who called Reef sell-outs would have refused a huge bonus from their work if offered it. Gary and his bandmates - Kenwyn House, Jack Bessant and Dom Greensmith - saw an opportunity to come off income support and so they took it.

"We did make a deal with our record company though," explains Gary, "The song from the advert wouldn't be our first single, because we thought if it was then people might lose interest in us quickly afterwards. We probably could have had a number one single, but we wanted to be in it for the long haul."

What Gary describes is basically what happened to several other bands from the same era who had a very successful single on an advert but were never anywhere near as popular again. The minidisc never really caught on, because MP3s were on the horizon and the way most people discovered and listened to music would soon be changing.

"I reckon just about any band nowadays would bite your arm off to have their song on an advert," says Gary, "Most people don't listen to the radio nowadays and there's far less music on TV. A new band today would take any opportunity to get themselves heard."

CONSIDERATION

So much has changed since Reef started out. The evening of the day I speak to Gary they are due to head off on tour along with several other bands who were contemporaries, including Danny McCormack's The Wildhearts. Along with Terrorvision and Dodgy, also on the bill, and a bunch of others, they were part of the 'Britrock' scene during the 90s. Symposium were part of it too, and Wojtek explained when I spoke to him how helpful the guys from Reef were to him. The Britrock scene wasn't something they chose to be in, it was more a way for journalists at the time to categorise a bunch of bands, but for me they encapsulated the optimism of the 90s. I may look back on it with rose tinted spectacles, but I see it as the last age of realism before everything went digital. Gary tells me how almost no studios record music onto tape anymore; it's all on huge computer files.

"I was trying to explain to my kids the other day about the time before mobile phones," recalls Gary, "I talked about how you would call someone from a payphone and if you went to their house there wouldn't be a running script of where you were and what you were doing. They'd just have to wait for you to get there."

He was given his first mobile phone in the Sony offices a year after Reef got signed. Sony were trying to push the minidisc at the time and they thought Reef were the band to help them sell it. The minidisc might not have gone anywhere but Reef gained quite a huge level of popularity. Their second album, 'Glow', was one of the best known rock records of the era, had several hit singles and was absolutely bursting at the seams with Westcountry optimism. Real instruments, real accents and lyrics about swimming, coming back brighter, everything being alright... nowadays if I heard an album like that I'd wonder if the band who made it had their eyes open. I had the album on cassette tape (it was the actual bought version, Gary – not a copy!) and would frequently play it in my Renault 5. There was a song called 'Consideration' that really typifies hope for me.

"I still love singing that one now," enthuses Gary, "What it means is that you don't have to take from someone else to be strong yourself. When I moved to London as a teenager I felt physically strong and mentally strong, and like I could take on the world, but I never looked at life as a competition and just wanted to do the best I could for myself."

This is where the observation at the beginning of the chapter came from. Gary really believes in showing compassion, and sees many of the world's problems stemming from a lack of it.

"If someone is shown kindness and compassion they're far more likely to show it to others," he argues, "It's easy to see where peoples' bad moods come from. It's so hard to make ends meet nowadays because everything's so expensive and people are moving so fast just trying to get by. It's like they're running around in a hamster wheel. They don't have time to show compassion."

This brings to mind some words from the author Charlie Carroll, who I also spoke to for this book, about how it can be hard for homeless people to have ambition when they're so focused on survival. Is it just homeless people though? Are more people than not just desperately struggling to get by, and do they have almost no room for anything else in their lives? It reminds me of a tap that erupted once in a friend's flat. We didn't know where the stop tap was, so I was desperately bailing water out of the window using the washing up bowl in between my frantic attempts to locate it. The gush of the water was relentless, and I was beginning to wonder if that was going to be my life now. Could I keep bailing water forever? Eventually we found the tap and shut it off – it wasn't in an obvious place

– but persistence was rewarded despite all seeming hopeless for a while.

Life is kind of like that nowadays for many. It seems like all a lot of us are doing is stemming the tide of problem after disappointment after stress, clinging on to the odd moment of joy in between. This is what Gary describes, but hope is to be found in a story he mentioned as soon as our conversation began, and there's a spoiler alert here for anyone not familiar with it. The story of Touching the Void; a book and documentary film about true events that took place when climber Joe Simpson broke his leg near the top of a huge Peruvian mountain, then his climbing partner Simon Yates tried to lower him down in stages on a rope. Things were going along relatively well until Joe was lowered over a ridge and his weight was nearly pulling them both off the mountain. Simon faced a life or death decision – he could either cut the rope and potentially save himself, or they would almost certainly both fall to their deaths. Simon cut the rope, which he has faced a lot of criticism for, but ultimately by doing this both of them survived. Joe's survival was nothing short of a miracle; he fell into a crevasse, which he lowered himself to the bottom of on a rope having landed part of the way down the side, and then found his way out through a tunnel. He was still pretty certain he would die but over several days he found his way down to the foot of the mountain, literally hours before Simon was due to leave. He was taken to civilisation on the back of a mule, taken to hospital, and he recovered over time, climbing many more mountains. Not sure I would ever have wanted to climb another mountain again if it had been me, but he's still alive. Gary found a huge amount of hope in this story, just as I did when I first heard it, and the lesson I take from it is that you might as well keep trying to move forward when things seem hopeless, because nothing's going to change if you stay still. I have come close to forgetting this, but when I write now I am reminded how important it is to keep it in mind.

Joes' accident didn't stop him from climbing, but he would have been aware of the possible consequences before he set off, and it seems the risk is part of what makes people want to climb in the first place. Again, this isn't something that makes a huge amount of sense to me, but it is true. Generally in life, experiences shape our choices.

"I've become more cautious as I've got older," admits Gary, "Young kids don't realise the consequences of their actions and so you have to teach them not to run into the road, or that if they fall off a high climbing frame they'll injure themselves."

Most people become less carefree as they get older too, because life experiences can make you realise how fragile you are, and this extends to your approach to situations. At the same time though, getting through adversity can make someone appreciate life so much more.

"I was diagnosed with an illness in my early thirties," reflects Gary, "I won't go into it too much but there were times when I couldn't get out of bed, couldn't walk, and nowadays I really appreciate just being able to swing my legs out of bed in the morning. We take so much for granted, but to come through something challenging and still be alive can really give you hope."

Gary is medicated for his illness and has it pretty much under control nowadays, but it really rammed home to him how much he had been taking for granted. I've always found that when something has given me a new lease of life I've promised myself I'll make the most of every moment, and for a short time I have done, but then whatever made me feel that way fades into the background and I start to take things for granted again. Gary feels grateful just to be up and about nowadays, and sees plenty of hope in life, despite being as bemused as many of us by some things. This includes how mean people can be on the internet.

"I must admit I often get lost down the Twitter hole in the morning," he says, "I'll see an article being shared and then I'll read it, and check out what everyone has to say about it. The before I know it half an hour's gone. It's weird isn't it?!"

He seems as confused as I am by how the world got so digitised so quickly, and says that people are 'weirded out by facts' nowadays, meaning that everyone has a theory when they're on social media and nobody shows much in the way of common sense.

Just after this he identifies the way that Joe Simpson broke the horrific situation he found himself in on the mountain into manageable chunks and concentrated on getting to the next boulder, or whatever landmark was in front of him. If he could make it to the next one it would represent progress and from there he could set himself a new target. If this kind of thinking could be applied to every situation then everything would surely seem less fraught.

Reef's music has always represented optimism, an appreciation of the simple things, and basically everything I appreciated about life in the 90s. This was exactly what came across during the forty or so minutes I spoke to Gary. He spoke of compassion, taking nothing for granted and making the most of opportunities. Following on from his talk of being fearless when he was younger, he spoke of how his dad would never let him buy a motorbike until he left home but now he understands why, as he doesn't think he's ever known anyone who's owned a motorbike and not had a crash of some kind. Of course, as a father himself nowadays he feels he has to minimise risky behaviour.

"My eldest son's just got his first car," he says, "He's been asking all of us to look in our attics in case we've got an old cassette player he can have."

In a sense there's hope in that alone; how a young lad would choose something that isn't the most computerised, hassle-free version of itself money can buy. 90s living can still be done in a world that's trying to convince us to do the opposite. Every time I step away from the internet and try to do something real, all the tension of the modern world slowly seeps away. This was what I took away from my conversation with Gary, as well as several reminders of hope to be found. He spoke of the image of an oak tree growing from a tiny acorn. I also think of the image of the sun always being there, just sometimes being hidden behind clouds. There are plenty of images that illustrate hope. I get the feeling Gary could reel off a whole host of them.

Not long after completing this chapter, it was announced that Gary would play a solo acoustic set at The Plough in Taunton. I knew I had to go along, and from the back of the room he didn't look a day older than he would have been when I was listening to his albums on cassette back in the day. His long hair was swept back in a ponytail and kept under a hat, but it was unmistakably the same guy I remembered from the same magazines I'd read about Wojtek, Ross and the rest in. What's more, he seemed extremely nervous, and even said so a couple of times. He would have played in front of audiences a hundred times as big, but perhaps that's the point. When you're in front of that many people with the rest of your band there are plenty of places to hide. When you're in a small room with just you and your acoustic guitar it's a completely different situation. Frequent spontaneous bursts of applause broke out when he demonstrated the power of his voice, and each time that happened he chuckled to himself, almost seeming embarrassed. Like he still considers himself to be a lad from Somerset who managed to have some success with his music. There was no ego on display. He was there because he loved playing his songs.

I spoke to him very briefly afterwards and he thanked me for coming. A couple of months later Reef would play Watchet festival, just down the road. People I knew were there and said it was just like seeing them in the 90s would have been, except they were a little older. Bass player Jack Bessant now has a huge grey beard and matching hair, and resembles the characters you see wandering around Glastonbury Town Centre on any given day. They are in their 40s nowadays, but their passion for music has not waned, just as Karl Meltzer's passion for running hasn't. When you love what you do it's easier for hope to remain, and when you are able to do what you have a passion for on a daily basis. Having meaning and focus in life seems to delay the ageing process in a strange kind of way. A couple of days ago I saw a copy of Metal Hammer magazine in a shop and was amused to see that pretty much the same people were in it as when I used to read it twenty years ago. Sometimes, frequently in fact, I look at my life and feel like the world has moved on without me. It's nice to know that some things never change, and when I saw Gary playing his songs in a tiny Taunton venue with the same enthusiasm he did when I saw him on TV playing them at a huge festival back in the day I feel a warming dose of comfort.

CONNER'S STORY PART 5

So now we pick up where the introduction left off. Viv and Gary have returned and they were all taken through to see Conner, who was now hooked up to numerous drips and machines. There were nurses and doctors everywhere, along with the paramedics from South Shields. Mark went out for air at one point and Gary followed him while Emma and Viv stayed in the room.

"I'm not saying goodbye to him, Gary. This isn't goodbye."

"I know, mate."

The paramedic Mark knew came out to wish him good luck before heading back to South Shields. Mark and Gary went back in, and Conner was taken up to surgery at around 9 or 10pm. It was going to be a long night, and that morning Mark hadn't been feeling well but tiredness was the last thing on his mind. Nobody had much to say, they were all just trying to let it sink in.

"I wanna go up to the chapel and say a prayer," said Emma.

They stayed in the chapel for quite some time. I didn't find out what had happened to Conner until the next day, otherwise I would have been praying too. The most amazing answer to prayer I have seen to date was when my close friend's dad was in hospital and twice was said to be on death's door but made a remarkable recovery both times after people had been praying for him all over the world following requests. An admission of one of social media's good points needed here; when you need to call on people all over the world it is by far the quickest way.

Eventually they ended up back in the room and at around 1am they were taken up to the Intensive Care Unit. At reception they were told once again there was no news but someone would be with them soon. It was a sombre and silent atmosphere. What was there to say that hadn't been already? Mark could think of one thing: -

"It has to be good news that they've moved us up here," he said, "At least that must mean he's alive."

No-one could believe they were even having to speculate about this. He'd only turned 17 recently. He was a young lad. At last a nurse came through.

"Could you follow me please?" she said.

No. What is it? What's happened? Why had she only said those words? What was wrong with telling them here? They were taken through to a small room and asked to take a seat.

"He's still in the Intensive Care Unit," she said softly, "The doctor in charge will be with you in a few minutes."

He was alive. He was still on the unit. What was the doctor going to tell them though? A little while later he walked into the room flanked by two nurses; Emma and Sarah. All introduced themselves and asked who everyone was.

"Mum, Dad, Nana and Uncle."

They said Gary was Conner's uncle in case he was asked to leave due to not being a family member.

"Can you explain to me everything that's happened today?"

They gave a patchy version of the story you've read until now. Everyone was too upset to be particularly eloquent, but between them they muddled through.

"Ok," he said, "Well the good news is that Conner's out of surgery. However, he has suffered a massive bleed."

"So what does that mean?"

"Well, there isn't a lot of room in the skull and because of all the bleeding Conner has quite extensive bruising to his brain."

Everyone was silent as the doctor continued.

"I'm so sorry to have to tell you this, but I would advise you to prepare for the possibility that he might never be the same again."

Emma stood up and started pacing around the room.

"You must be wrong," she screamed, "I don't believe it. How could this happen?"

"He is alive," sighed the doctor, "But he has suffered massive bruising and swelling. This could mean permanent brain damage."

"No. you're wrong. Why Conner?" yelled Emma as the others were speechless.

"Because of where the bleed was I'm afraid he's paralysed down his right-hand side. If he does recover he's more than likely going to be wheelchair-bound and unable to communicate."

Knowing there was no positive spin he could put on this apart from the fact that Conner was alive, the doctor explained everything as honestly but as gently as he could.

"You have a long road ahead of you," he concluded.

Mark had listened intently throughout and was desperately seeking for a crumb of hope to cling on to.

"So what happens now?" he asked.

"Well, Conner is very heavily sedated at the moment," the doctor replied, "We'll try and wake him up tomorrow so we can assess the damage. As his brain's still swollen we'll need to carry out further scans and monitor him very closely. He's still very ill and he's not out of danger."

Emma, Mark, Viv and Gary were all devastated. They were all just wishing this wasn't true and that they would wake up at any moment, all of this having been a dream. Sometimes things are just too hard to process, and this was pretty close to being the worst news any parent could hear. How would life go on? What would they tell Jayden? It was one of those times where you wish life had a rewind button, or failing that just a pause. This was too much.

"Can we see him?" asked Mark.

"Soon. I should warn you that the ward Conner's on has a lot of seriously ill patients. We'll just give you a little time to digest the news, then we'll take you to see him. I should also explain that he's hooked up to several machines and has a number of drips going into him. He has a large bolt in his brain to monitor the pressure and the last of the excess blood is being drained. We'll be back soon."

As they left the room nobody could do anything but cry.

DON'T FORGET ABOUT GRENFELL

As a teenager I studied A-level Philosophy, and one of the concepts which always stuck with me was that millions of people were killed during the holocaust, and because of the sheer number of people who died, history mostly forgot the individuals. If you think about that for a moment it's true; the human brain would not have the capacity to remember the names of six million people who died, or any details about the lives of more than a handful of them. The same is true of so many instances throughout history in which a lot of people lost their lives at the same time. The Jonestown Massacre, the sinking of the titanic, the plague…. Events could be listed all day and we would still have barely scratched the surface. The fact is that when somebody dies it impacts upon the lives of everyone close to them. Sometimes it profoundly affects others; some of them might never be the same again. It's hard to come to terms with the fact that someone who meant something to you is no longer in this world, and that you will have to carry on living your life without them. Bereavements are tough, and when so many of them happen in the same place at once it can be too much to comprehend.

The Grenfell Tower Fire in the summer of 2017 was one of these events, and many who survived are still so badly affected that it's as if it all happened yesterday. I was hoping to speak to some of the survivors directly in order to paint the most honest and accurate picture of what happened that day, and to get a true perspective of the impact it has had. I haven't been able to contact anyone who lived in Grenfell Tower as they were rehoused and the community rallied to shield them from any toxic elements. I hope that those who read this will understand that I am writing the chapter because I don't want people to forget, and I hope in some small way it might help people to remember. I don't know anyone who was directly involved. The nephew of a couple I know was one of the firefighters who was sent to help tackle the blaze. Also, I have spoken to Steve MacKenzie on the phone. Steve is one of the UK's leading fire, health, safety, security and resilience experts, and has been heavily involved in trying to ensure that the survivors of the Grenfell Fire are taken care of, and that their voices are heard.

Steve was touched on a deeply personal level by what happened, because when he was fifteen he was sent home from school to find out that his uncle and three other family members had been killed in the 1985 King Park, Glasgow gas explosion. This is why he established the Grenfell Fire Forum as a response and left it as a community legacy. He then moved on to sponsor @globalfireforum, but when he first saw the tower fire breaking on the news he time-stamped, as incident reporters do; 2.05am 14th June 2017. He wouldn't have known then how huge a part of his life it would become, even with his wealth of expertise.

"I don't sleep very well most nights," explains Steve, "I was awake on the night the Grenfell Fire started and I saw the images on the news feeds, which I always check upon waking. I knew I'd be going there, and my wife grabbed me one of the 'emergency grab bags' I have prepared for such situations. Unfortunately it was the wrong one, and I ended up having mild heat stroke as a result of what was missing, but that's a different story. Meanwhile I hit the news desks and my fire service contacts whilst simultaneously gearing up to go in around 2 minutes."

The grab bags of which he speaks have items in such as a prepaid credit card, money and 72 hours' independent life support: food and water, spare seasonal clothes, kit and the like. Basically a bag you might take with you if you were going for a weekend camping trip but customised for each major incident type and seasonal response. Due to the nature of his work, Steve frequently has to go away for a few days to months at short notice, and he's ready. His family are also always ready. He made his way to Grenfell from his home in South-East London, and was there by early morning whilst responding to an avalanche of news desk requests.

"I'd never spoken live on camera before, and only once pre-recorded," he recalls, "And I was put in front of all of the journalists at the incident press conference live point from about 7am until 10pm from Wednesday 14th until Sunday 19th June. When I first got there I'd spoken to a guy I knew from Fire Investigation Private Practice, and from our short conversation we knew it was going to be a bad; a really grave situation with a lot of fatalities."

Steve didn't know all of the facts when he first arrived, but they did know by then that the fire engulfed almost the whole building, and the fire service were unable to control it as they would a conventional fire incident, with many being trapped in their flats and a lot of them losing their lives. The official statistics later confirmed that 72 people died. Many believe it could have been quite a few more. It's known that the fire spread so quickly because of the highly flammable cladding system on the outside of the building, which I must say looks remarkably similar to the cladding on many other tower blocks we know to exist. Grenfell can't be the only one, which of course begs the question 'Could it happen again elsewhere? Could there be Grenfell 2.0?'

"The government have technically defective advisors," argues Steve, "There were 474+ confirmed similar style buildings in the UK to Grenfell and a further 1650+ suspected vulnerable tower blocks with other fire hazards or defective systems, along with other concerns from a fire safety perspective. I was frustrated with the way Theresa May, ministers, government and responding agencies handled the situation. After this happened, government Civil Contingency Act responders should have got implemented major incident emergency arrangements to support the residents and give them the reassurance they needed, along with the local authorities CAT 1 responses, as she did after the terror attacks. This included the single fatality at Finsbury Park on June 19th, which commanded a Cabinet Office Briefing Room A (or B) response."

According to Steve, these are two high tech briefing rooms located in the Whitehall Cabinet Office which are used for a range of incidents. When pressed on this Steve mutters "Official Secrets Act" and quickly redirects the conversation.

This echoes a poem I wrote not long after the event, off the top of my head, which included the line 'Grenfell was a tragedy on the magnitude and scale or the terror over which they say we must prevail.' Recently, during a performance at the Brit awards, rapper Stormzy asked Theresa May to do more to help the residents of Grenfell, insisting that we hadn't forgotten. I have read a number of articles suggesting that survivors have received nowhere near enough support, and as vice chair of the London branch of the Emergency Planning Society, Steve agrees. To my mind, every one of the survivors should have been treated as a high priority by the government, because this was a tragedy that happened in the country they are meant to look after. The whole country; not just those they deem worthy. So many lives were changed forever that day, and it should be remembered as a national tragedy.

"Buildings are essentially your life support," says Steve, "If this is taken away then your health, both mental and physical, will deteriorate rapidly when exposed to the elements. That's why a lot of rough sleepers you see look older or more ill or frail than they should be."

Hundreds of people became homeless because of the Grenfell Fire. The place they could call their own, which is essentially what a home is, was burnt beyond recognition by the flames that couldn't be fully extinguished for SIXTY hours from when the fire services arrived. Many instances of Post-Traumatic Stress Disorder have been reported, along with other mental health issues. Is this at all surprising? Everyone who lived in that tower block would probably have been thinking it was just a normal night before the fire started. When it began they might have been concerned, but none of them knew at that point they were going to die, and those who would survive had no idea of the scale of tragedy they were about to be a part of. As the fire spread, terror is probably the best word to describe what people would have been feeling.

"Human behaviour in fire research and case analysis has proved that people don't panic until death is perceived as being inevitable," explains Steve, "People either act adaptively or non-adaptively. They will experience escalating anxiety until it overwhelms, and will then display irrational behaviour until ultimately acceptance or panic takes hold."

Steve changes the subject again, saying that he will only discuss the forensic depths when absolutely necessary.

"You really don't want to have forensic detail of fire or

fatality incidents or see the world the way expert responders do," he says, and I can tell he really means it.

Despite all of this, the response from the government was not the same as it was after what they would describe as a terror attack. I can't help wondering why. It seems to me like yet another instance of society's most vulnerable people coming last when it comes to proper help and support. Steve, surprisingly, wholeheartedly agrees that this may likely be the case.

The following week, during the Chalcots Camden Towers evacuation due to similar fire safety concerns, Steve started to be recognised by some people in the community as he spent more and more time there. He describes how one elderly gentleman said "You're the Scottish chap on TV?"

"Yes," Steve replied, "How can I help, sir?"

The gentleman responded with a cry for help Steve says he will never forget.

"You're the only one who's speaking out," he said, "The only one making sense. Keep helping us, please."

"Sir, that's the oath I've sworn to and intend to keep," Steve replied without a second thought, "To protect and assist those impacted by fire and other emergencies."

Steve spent time in between news slots talking quietly but listening loudly to many of the evacuated residents' stories, which touched him so deeply. This is exactly what he wanted to be doing, having known personal tragedy and seen it become national news. He has been on Sky News a number of times to talk about the fire, and has set up the Grenfell Fire Forum before meeting with other experts in September 2017, first as a panel of six and then 12+ fire experts, and from January 22nd 2018 other experts and local residents were approached to join. This was Steve's idea, and was to ensure that the community voice was heard, and this wasn't just the formation of an expert forum. The forum was launched during the Terms of Reference hearing of the public inquiry, and they have held a number of meetings since which were aimed at ensuring there is justice.

So how did the 14-year-old Steve who faced that personal tragedy eventually become one of the UK's leading fire safety experts?

"My dad was an alcoholic who drank himself to death," he states, "He wasn't a bad man but one who liked to drink. He was a plumber by trade and so that's what I wanted to be. I got into a lot of fights with bullies at school. I was always ready to take down the pack leader but wasn't always successful. I won a national award at plumbing college, then self-funded study in construction with fire dynamics and building engineering. More medals, awards and scholarships followed despite the fact I was dyslexic. I've worked all over the world on a lot of different projects or research programmes since, including a Successor submarine programme, which was cited as being more complex than a NASA space shuttle."

Steve has determined a successful career for himself, and studied extensively despite his dyslexia, which he says he wouldn't want a cure for if one existed, and is proud of what he has achieved. His 97-year-old gran is also very proud of him. She once told him "Steve, you will never be a rich man but you give so very much." Incidentally, her husband lived to be 103, dying two years ago, and both of Steve's grandparents on his dad's side lived to be 94!

"My dyslexia doesn't affect the way I work," he says, "It makes the way I work better – I have super charged processing speed, problem solving at the 99/98.5th percentile and all other indicators exceptionally high or gifted even. I wouldn't take a pill to get rid of it; I say 'Made by dyselxia.' It doesn't have to be a barrier."

My mum worked with dyslexic kids for many years as a teacher, and when she first started, probably in the early 1990s, dyslexia was only just beginning to be properly understood as far as I can recall. When Steve was growing up it must have been less so, and yet it hasn't got in the way of him pursuing a career that requires studies that would scramble the brains of most, and most can't match the pace of Steve's million zillion ideas. He has received what he describes as some lovely messages via twitter from dyslexic people's families, and says it's great to help that impacted community.

Due to his extensive training, qualifications and professional practices, Steve is a powerful ally for the local and wider impacted residents who need justice. He is the perfect combination; a guy from a humble working class background who has direct experience of the kind of tragedy they are dealing with, coupled with the titles, letters and influence that focus MPs and journalists to listen. On 17th January 2019, which happened to be Steve's 49th birthday, Steve was invited as a fire expert to the Scottish Parliament: Culture, Tourism, European and External Affairs Committee hearings on the devastating Charles Rennie Mackintosh, Glasgow School of Art fires of May 2014 and June 2018. This was one of Steve's proudest moments, and one which showcased his resounding expertise and infallible exertions. Even when he was challenged Steve quickly took all arguments aground.

What's more, it's obvious that Steve really cares. I was on the phone to him for nearly an hour, and felt it would have been more if I hadn't had to wind up the call at that point. During that hour he spoke passionately and with real conviction about the state not just of Grenfell, but of many fire, health, safety, security and resilience issues around London and elsewhere in which local residents are really not getting the support they should be entitled to as a basic human right. He has been with residents to several local councils in order to ask for immediate action to improve their conditions or to demand statutory compliance above the bare minimum level. Why did the government not care as much as he does? Why did they not want to do everything in their power to help the residents rebuild their lives? Unless I see anything that tells me otherwise I'd say it was because the residents of Grenfell Tower were not wealthy high-flyers. In short they were not the people the government set their policies to try and look after the interests of. Did the government feel that they didn't have to give the people of Grenfell much because they would just appreciate whatever they were given?

Of course this is just a point of view, and the only people who truly know why they didn't do more are the government themselves. It's not too late though. They can do more now. Let's not stop talking about Grenfell. Let's not forget. Let's not let the government forget either.

Theresa May recently said she regrets not going to meet with the residents of Grenfell on the day after the fire. She went to commend the firefighters and to thank them for their efforts in trying to put out the blaze, which of course is also important for her to have done, but why didn't she meet with the people who were affected? If she regrets her actions then she could meet with the residents now, apologise for not having done so before, and give some indication that she was committed to helping them move forward. She spoke of there being no magic money tree in the time leading up to the elections, but a magic money tree is not needed to show compassion. I hope she will, but where she doesn't, ordinary people and experts like Steve demonstrate not by strength of words but by strength of actions that they really do care deeply despite frustrations, barriers and hardships they all have to bear.

Steve has now sponsored the formation of @globalfireforum and is interim CEO to the global, national and regional forums. He has also set up #bigfiredebate2019 and launched the site @firesafety2019, continuing to give expert comment and pro bono support on fire issues and responses to major incidents around the globe. I leave you with a short poem of his, which is also in the front of this book: -

> *"Yesterday was deplorable,*
> *Today was despicable,*
> *But tomorrow may always be delightful."*

DRINK THE SUNSHINE

"I'd not been looking after myself for a while," recalls Ross, "I'd been drinking too much and not eating properly, that kinda thing, then Dave saw me and called me over."

I remember it well. Except I don't, because he's actually referring to one of the other Daves of this world, and one far more famous than I. You may have heard of him. He played the drums in a band that myself, Ross and millions of others around the world just couldn't stop listening to in the 90s. Nirvana anyone? Dave Grohl is more famous to the current generation as frontman of the Foo Fighters, and this is how Ross Cummins got to meet him. Symposium were the support band for this leg of their Colour and the Shape tour. Back at the time of the incident Ross is recounting, Foo Fighters were only on their second album. Although still very popular then, Dave's new band hadn't quite pushed the legacy of his old one into peoples' memories. He was still very much known as the drummer from Nirvana. Ross, like his good friend Wojtek, was very famous to me at the time. He was Symposium's livewire vocalist. Anyway, back to the story.

"Dave was like 'You're looking too skinny there, Ross. You need some meat, boy!' and slammed a huge plate of meatballs down in front of me."

Dave was half-joking, but Ross explains that the former Nirvana drummer did look out for him on that tour, and I can only imagine how this must have felt for someone who was still so young at the time and was meeting a guy whose music meant so much to him growing up.

"He was a lovely guy," enthuses Ross, "Touring with them was truly amazing. I remember him joking about getting old and turning into Ozzy Osbourne, as we discussed our rock wounds and achy limbs."

He made his excuses and left before the plate of meatballs was done though, as he confesses the whole thing was freaking him out a little bit. In contrast to Wojtek's image of crying on the tourbus late at night though, I don't get the impression that this was something Ross experienced at the time. Pretty much everything about touring with Symposium was actually everything he had ever dreamt of and more. I will let him set the scene.

"I'd written myself off at an early age as being someone who wouldn't achieve anything in the real world. I was from a working class Irish family, my dad was an alcoholic, we lived in a council flat and I wasn't very academic. The only way out I saw was to form a band, which helped build my self-confidence and ultimately defined my character. So when I was 11 I would just hang out at a local youth club where I had access to some instruments and made some connections with a few local kids. We started a band, and it was literally the only thing I cared or thought about."

Music really was everything to a lot of kids in the 90s. I'm not sure if it's the same now, but I remember when I was a teenager it was all we would talk about at times. For so many, being in a band, getting signed, releasing albums and touring the world represents hope for the future. It's a dream thousands chase, and for a select few it becomes a reality, which perhaps gives false hope to many. Why was Ross one of the ones who made it happen rather than one of the thousands who didn't?

"I don't think I've ever told any of the guys this," he admits, "But when I moved to secondary school my sole intention from day one was to find a bunch of like-minded individuals who I could make music with."

He knew what he wanted to do from an early age, and fairly soon he found Will McGonagle, Joe Birch and Hagop Tchaparian, who shared his enthusiasm. Later on Wojtek would join. In 1993 the three of them with British-sounding names went to see The Smashing Pumpkins at Brixton Academy. Afterwards they were talking about how they would play the venue themselves one day.

"It was 25th September 1993," remembers Ross, "This guy who was off his face overheard us talking and told us we'd definitely play there on this day in a few years' time. We all laughed about it, but then on September 25th 1997 we actually played there!"

Remember Wojtek's similar story about Kentish Town Forum? If I was to speak to each of the five members of Symposium then perhaps there would be five different stories of accidental future prediction.

"Will reminded us what the guy had said and we couldn't believe it was the same date, just as we were told it would be."

So did they encounter a shadowy puppet master who orchestrated every opportunity of the next four years, culminating in their dream gig, or was it mere coincidence? You decide. As it happened though, it wasn't quite the joyful celebration they'd imagined. In fact you may recognise this gig from Wojtek's story.

"Brixton Academy to us was like playing Wembley; it was where all our favourite bands had played, so to us this gig was MASSIVE," he says, "We were super excited, and then literally in the first song I slipped and popped out my knee. I couldn't believe it. There I was at the gig of my dreams, on my arse."

It does read like one of the deeply unfortunate scenarios from Alanis Morisette's 'Ironic', which was from the same era. I remember reading about the incident soon after it happened, and seeing a picture of Ross, with a plaster cast on, in a magazine. He was making a goofy face for the camera, but surely having his dreams dashed in that way must have hit him hard?

"It ended on a good note," he laughs, "Because in true Spinal Tap style we came back the next night and finished the show with me in my motorised scooter."

This was the height of Symposium's popularity, and wasn't long before I'd first discovered Ross when I turned to the inside back page of Kerrang magazine and my brother Joe was staring back at me. I did a double take and then my brother's features materialised into those of a singer from a band who bore a passing resemblance to him. I read the interview and thought this Ross Cummins seemed pretty cool. The only answer I remember though is that he was a little embarrassed to have recently cried at a gig by the band Travis, who would become really rather popular a year or two later. I think it was because a particular song tugged at his heartstrings, but I'm not sure which one, or if he even said. This would only have been a few years after he'd formed the band in school, as so many do, but he made it to where he was aiming for, as nearly all don't.

"By the time I'd reached A-levels we were filling out shows, and it felt like the years of work were paying off. It was an exciting time."

Isn't it ironic, don't you think, that he's talking about years of work paying off at the time of his A-levels but he doesn't mean academically. Everything he'd been working towards during his school years was actually outside of his lessons.

"Getting signed was great," he continues, "It was like a seal of approval for me to know that what I believed in was being taken seriously and we could bring our chaos to the masses."

Ross had worked hard all the way through school, and had seen it come to fruition. Not everyone is academic, but he put his all into something he saw a future in, and unlike so many who end up with egg on their faces and rolling of eyes from those who had doubted them all along, he was exactly where he said he would be.

"I'd never been anywhere other than West London, so to be able to play in America and Europe was like a dream come true for me. I met so many bands and people I admired, and had some amazing experiences. I also did a lot of stupid things."

Sometimes it can feel like you're the only one who does stupid things, but it seems that most of us do. We often don't hear about other peoples', because it's not exactly something you want to broadcast. This point has been made before, but perhaps Ross was lucky to have done these stupid things in the age before social media. Of course there were still magazines, but it was nothing like the modern day, when in any given place most people would have camera phones with direct Facebook and Instagram access. Something tells me he preferred the world the way it was then in a number of ways.

"We live in an age where communication is so easy now, but I feel like it's all at arm's length a lot of the time, which I think is sad," he reflects, "People need to stop looking at their phones all the time and communicate in the real world more. Phone people and have a conversation rather than a lame 'like' or Facebook comment."

With perfect comic, or should I say tragic timing, I was reading Ross' replies to my questions on my phone as I walked into Axminster Town Centre to find a cashpoint, pretty much oblivious to my surroundings. Just after I read what he said about phones I looked up and there was a teenage girl sat glued to her phone screen in the passenger seat of a car. When clearing some metal poles and wooden pallets from the allotment this morning I paused to answer a message from Ross on my phone. I could have waited, but to be fair those metal poles were buried deep in the earth among thick roots and a myriad of stones, and we had a heatwave this summer so the earth was rock solid and needed time for the water I'd poured over it to seep in. Besides, I was messaging him to confirm that Symposium had meant a lot to people in the 90s; it's not like I was sending him a string of hugely forgettable memes.

It can't be denied though, just as was discussed in the chapter with Andy Hamilton, that smartphones are as much a part of life now as the humble Walkman was in the 90s. Remember, an early Symposium song was entitled 'Eddie Vedder Ate my Walkman,' and a song like that just wouldn't make as much sense now. 'Ed Sheeran Ate my I-Phone' just doesn't have the same ring to it.... See what I did there? Also, despite social media allowing opportunities for self-promotion Ross and the lads could have only dreamed of, he doesn't believe it's any easier now to make a living from being in a band. In fact maybe the opposite.

"It's an odd one really," he muses, "On the one hand kids today have the power to control everything they do, but it seems to me with Spotify/downloads etc. that the only way bands can make money is by touring. It's really hard work."

Ross doesn't make his main living from music nowadays, but he still writes songs and plays the occasional gig with his band Paper Cuts, who weren't named after the Nirvana song of the same name but from the cuts he would get from cheques he had to process in an old clerical job. He does say the 'can do' attitude of Nirvana was very inspiring to him. I've heard some Paper Cuts music and enjoyed it a lot, especially the song 'Jai douze ans'; a phrase I actually said to some French girls on a school trip there in the early nineties. Most of what they said I didn't remotely understand, but when one of them said "Quel age as tu" very slowly I managed to reply that I was twelve in French (see previous song title.) I recently had a slightly more successful conversation with a French schoolboy in his native tongue half way up Glastonbury Tor, but before you give me too credit it was basically me telling him I speak a little bit of French but only a little bit and him seeming disappointed and saying 'thank you.' Anyway, sorry for the interjection, Ross.

"The one thing I hope Symposium achieved through our live shows was to inspire people to believe in themselves and be themselves," he says, "Also I hope we made some memories for people and were able to give them some kind of euphoric experience for a short space of time."

This definitely happened. Symposium's live shows were famously energetic and were infectious for many, hundreds of whom still talk about the band on a Facebook page to this day, hoping that one day they will reform. Reunited bands from the 90s have been sought after in recent years. Reef and The Wildhearts, members of whom also feature in the book of course, have been touring again, and Symposium have had offers. Apart from the music I think the appeal of 90s bands reforming is for people to feel like they're back in simpler times. I'm sure everyone takes their smart phones to the gigs. I mean you can't literally step back in time, but when Ross was entering Secondary School and feeling determined but uncertain about his future he found so much hope in music, and that was the same for so many people. His hope was that music would be his way out of difficult circumstances, and so it proved for a time. With that in mind, what became of him when the band fell apart?

"My hope nowadays comes from my family," he explains, "I have three children and an amazing wife. They're the most important thing to me now. Music comes second."

Ross has a regular job and works hard. His work isn't what he imagined it being all those years ago, but in a way he has been proved wrong in that he has found his place in the real world after all. Perhaps succeeding in the field he chose as an alternative gave him the confidence he may have been lacking in other areas. Ross and Wojtek, when in the early days of Paper Cuts, may never have imagined that they'd be family men in their early forties. When I used to read about Symposium every week in magazines back in the day I never imagined that one day their singer would be 'liking' a picture of me having dug up a Rosemary bush on Facebook. I couldn't have imagined it, because I didn't know Facebook would exist, but life has probably turned out differently than Ross, me or Wojtek would have imagined back then. I'm slightly younger than them, but in the 90s I was another lad who didn't see himself cutting it in the real world. I was never in a successful band, and I still haven't cut it in the real world or the 'imaginary' one in which bands, poets, writers, painters, troubadours thrive. I do see some parallels in my story and theirs, and nowadays we're three men in their late thirties or early forties who occasionally 'like' each others' photos on Facebook. Ross and Wojtek still communicate in the old skool way, and thinking of the days when it felt to me like Symposium were one of the best known bands in the world is yet another thing that makes me want to go back to the old skool way of doing things. At the time of writing this chapter, someone I'm very close to has deleted their Facebook account and doesn't miss it. If I didn't have this book and other things to promote I would almost certainly do the same tomorrow, but then Ross might not get a chance to enjoy any more of my allotment photos, and I know this would sadden him greatly.

Something I feel Ross does have a degree of regret about is how differently he would have done things had he known when he was 19 what he knows now. Wouldn't most of us, right? He is well placed though to offer advice to anyone who is trying to get into the ferocious beast that is the music industry so that they don't get burnt, and when he saw a TV show about a young man with a difficult past who got a record deal he got in touch with the guy to pass on some wisdom. He is kind enough to share this advice for the book, lest any prospective professional musicians be reading. I think it makes fascinating reading regardless of whether or not you're pursuing a musical ambition. Over to you, Ross....

"Contracts – Don't sign anything unless a legal rep has checked it. There might be a time when you will have something thrusted at you to sign; don't sign it! Check and check again.

Publishing Deal – Don't blow it. A lot of people do this and end up having to pay it back when they haven't recouped the money spent on album costs. The first thing you should do is get a mortgage or property. That's number 1. For sure I guess that's an obvious statement, but when I was 19 I didn't care about that sort of thing.

Advance Record Deals – Make sure your management spend it responsibly. Ensure you have a trusted accountant who can track where the money is going. Some managers will take you and your label mates out for a meal, or drinks, but you'll be paying for this if you do not have control of your advance money. Just make sure any outgoings are accounted for.

Live gigs – Try to keep costs to a bare minimum for gigs. You don't need 300 roadies. Also, make sure you are aware of touring costs etc. For example, do it in a car rather than a massive tour bus. Make sure you know exactly how much money you've made for doing the show and how much you've made on merchandise.

Trust - Don't trust anyone. Ultimately, all music industry businessmen just want to make money. Very few actually care about creativity unless you get lucky.

Back-up Plan – This is important. Hopefully you will have a successful career, but if it all goes belly up in a year or two's time you need to have an idea of what you will do. It can be a scary thing to think about, but it's definitely worth doing.

Contacts in the Music Industry – Use all contacts to help you for possible future opportunities. When I was in a band I met so many people who could possibly have helped me after the band split, but I lost touch and it was before social media! Here's an example; you know several DJs on BBC6, or have met several TV producers. Think about the other qualities you possess, such as DJing or acting or presenting. Think about your back-up plan if things go wrong or even right actually. There are other interesting avenues you can take, like getting your own BBC6 programme or presenting a show.

Drugs: - Don't do drugs, and watch your alcohol intake. Remember why you are a musician and a creative person. These things ruin creativity from my perspective. You might meet some people who request that you partake in snorting drugs. Just don't do it; these people suck.

Support: - Support loads of bands when you're starting. If you get a good agent you can play massive venues, which can be a lot of fun. Remember their audience could be yours one day!

Burn-out: - Always do 3 days on and 1 day off on tour. Some agents will insist you do 6 days on, 1 day off – this will burn you out. It's not like a 9-5 job. This is 24 hours; travelling, interviews, load-ins, gigs, more interviews, load-outs, into the next town. This stuff is physical! Having said that, you will have long periods of time with nothing to do between soundcheck and the gig. Ensure you keep yourself busy during these times, no matter how hungover or tired you are. Go and check out the town you're in; museums, book stores... anything to fill the time. Otherwise the devil will make work for your idle hands!"

Reading back through Ross' advice, it could largely be taken as good advice for life on the whole – be careful with your money, work out who to trust, look for opportunities through any contacts you may have, don't take drugs, keep busy in order to prevent yourself from falling into mischief. Doing the opposite of these things could basically be said to explain most of what's gone wrong in my life. If only I had the Ross of the future to talk to me when I was 19. My parents told me many of the same things, but being the idiotic youth I was I didn't listen to them. This is one of my biggest regrets. If Ross had been able to come back and tell me where the path I was on would lead I would have turned back to the junction I passed and gone the other way.

Ross also linked me a Henry Rollins video entitled 'Letter to a Young American,' which he says he can massively relate to. Rollins was the singer of punk band Black Flag, and has a solo career nowadays but is perhaps better known for his speaking. In the video he extols the virtues of hard work, explaining that many who have done very well in life have come from very humble backgrounds, and you just have to give your all to what you want to do. This is what Ross did, and he reaped the rewards. If he'd known then what he does now he could have made a lot more of it. Things worked out well for him after all, but there were certainly times when it didn't seem that way. In the video Rollins also speaks of not becoming somebody you don't like and to retain your moral compass. Oh man, I could write another book about times I've not done that.

I think I do have a number of similarities with Ross. Perhaps most of them are down to being a fairly similar age, growing up in the 90s and both being huge music fans then with similar tastes, but both of us could really have done with each other from the future to go back and explain how to do things. Of course this is impossible; people live their lives, they make their choices and they have to live by them. Is there still potential for change though? Well as Mr Rollins says, you have to make the best of what you've got. I don't have a lot of money behind me, I have made a lot of mistakes that still impact upon my life, but I do have a perhaps misguided sense of optimism, and through that I have made some things happen that I will reap rewards from. It's up to me to do this more. You have to work hard. That's rule number one.

Is it possible to live like it's the 90s whilst having one foot in the modern day and taking anything good from it? I'm not sure. Will Symposium make music together again? I'm not sure. None of us are sure, but what we need to do is figure out what's most important to us and give it our all. For Ross it used to be music, and he had many of the successes he dreamed of. Now it's his family, and they gave him a new direction when his reality stopped keeping pace with his musical ambitions. The future is yet to be revealed, but look after yourself or you might just get a plate of meatballs slapped down in front of you.

CONNER'S STORY PART 6

"He's alive; that's what we have to focus on for now," said Mark as he hugged Emma, "Anything else we'll deal with later on but he's alive."

He was alive, but everyone was distraught. Whatever this was, it was only the beginning. Soon everyone would be asking questions. Soon poor Jayden would have to be told what was really going on. Soon they would have to try and make all kinds of arrangements for how life would proceed, because it would proceed. There would be money to be made, special occasions to plan for, another son who needed them, and all manner of things that seemed impossible right now. In the meantime they just wanted to see Conner. If they could be in the room with him they'd be able to see what was happening and wouldn't have to rely on hearing all of the facts from others. They wouldn't just have to wait to find out. It would be a while before they'd known the full extent of the damage that had been caused, but if they could just be there with him the wait would somehow be more bearable. They'd feel like they were doing something.

Soon Mark would put a post on Facebook asking for all messages of support to be directed to him rather than Emma for now, because Emma was feeling far too upset to reply to anyone but was guilty that she couldn't. I was so impressed at the time with his strength, and told him so. Surely anyone in the situation he was in would just feel like everything was falling apart, and would struggle not to fall apart with it. Nobody would have blamed him for crumbling, but he knew he had to look after his family and so he drew on every ounce of his Geordie toughness. I also said that with a dad like him, and a great grandad like William, who had survived for so many years after his terminal cancer diagnosis, Conner would have a lot of fight in him, and that I'd been praying for him. I remember thinking that I hoped I would never find myself in a situation like this but if I did I would show as much strength as Mark had, even if I wasn't feeling like it. That I would be able to resist the urge to collapse in despair and instead would be the glue that held everyone else together. There would be time to cry in private later on. Right now Mark had to fight for his son.

Back in the room, Emma was desperate to see Conner and so they went looking for the nurses. They walked through silent corridors, their footsteps echoing but not a single voice to be heard, or any evidence that there was another person in the building. This feeling of nothingness amplified the detachment from their son. The most unreal day, in the worst imaginable way, was getting even worse. When would they be able to see Conner again? Where was everyone? Anyone? Somebody who could take them to him? The doors were locked, and so they would just have to wait until somebody came back to get them. They weren't about to go hammering on the doors, even though they may have felt like it.

Just as frustration was about to boil over the nurses came back and took them through, finally, to the room where Conner was. Mark recalls: -

"As soon as we stepped through the doors, Conner was in the bed in front of us. It was a horrendous sight; I wish now we had pictures of him so he could see, but the amount of machines and tubes was incredible. He had a breathing tube in, and this was secured by plasters around his face. Thinking about it, he looked a bit like Homer Simpson!"

I'm sure they would have given anything to make what was happening just a cartoon, and not their harrowing reality. I can't imagine how they must have felt to see their son like this. The best way I can picture it is perhaps to remember a documentary I once saw in which a man experienced cluster headaches; chronic, frequent headaches where the pain is horrifically intense. There's nothing that can be done to reduce the pain, but nobody knows what causes them. They are never fatal but can make life truly miserable for the sufferer. The pain they must have felt could be like a cluster headache but with sadness and desperation instead of the physical pain. I imagine a searing emotional agony that just won't relent. Viv was so upset she had to leave the room. Gary went with her, while Emma and Mark fell on each side of Conner's bed, holding his hands and talking to him.

"We love you, Conner. You need to come back to us, son. Jayden needs his big brother."

They weren't sure if he could hear them, but it was something of a relief to be able to talk to him. He was still alive, and as long as that was true there was hope. They spoke to him for a while before Viv and Gary returned, having two separate one-sided conversations. Would this be how it was from now on? Would he ever talk back? What if he didn't? No, none of that was relevant now. They just needed to keep talking to him. They needed to keep believing the doctors could be wrong.

When Viv and Gary returned the nurse was talking to Mark and Emma.

"You two should go home and try and get some rest. Tomorrow will be a long and exhausting day, because we'll be trying to take Conner off the sedation."

"We can't leave," pleaded Emma, "We need to be here."

"I'll be taking really good care of him," promised the nurse, hugging Emma, "I'll take your number and I'll ring you if anything happens but you need to try and sleep for a while."

It was around 3am. They didn't want to leave Conner's side for a second, but their other son needed them too. Viv said that Jayden had been asking for them. He hadn't been able to sleep because he knew that Conner wasn't well, and because his brother hadn't come home he knew it must be serious.

"We need to go and see him," they agreed.

As they were about to leave Emma stopped.

"Wait," she said, "I need to give you this."

She handed the nurse the bottle they'd seen in the room previously. The one that said 'LIFE' on the label.

"You need to keep this by his bedside," she told them, "Nobody can throw it away."

"I promise we won't" smiled the nurse.

They headed back to Viv's, where Jayden was awake, barely having slept. Mark sat him on his knee and tried his best to explain what was happening.

"Conner's very poorly, son," he murmured, "But he's alive. That's the main thing. We'll be going to see him again a bit later."

"Can I see him?"

"Not yet," Mark replied, "He's not ready just yet, but you can see him soon."

What was going through Jayden's young mind at that moment can only be guessed, but at the end of a long and uncertain day it seemed to be an answer for the time being. He hugged his parents and then everyone tried to get some sleep.

Mark has said how everyone tells him about the amazing strength he showed through all of this, but the way he sees it he didn't have a choice and any man would have done the same in his position. His family needed him and so he had to find a way to keep it together. Right now he knew he needed sleep; he was in no fit state to drive, and that's exactly what he'd have to do later in the morning at some stage.

"I can't sleep, I want to go back to the hospital" groaned Emma.

"I can't drive right now. Just let us sleep for a bit" replied Mark.

Ten minutes passed. Emma didn't feel like she could sleep for a second, but she had to try. It was no good.

"I still can't sleep. We have to go back."

"Not just yet. I need to rest."

It was around 4.30am. As Mark dozed off Emma realised she wouldn't be going anywhere for at least a little while, but she knew she wouldn't be sleeping. Remembering when she had gone to the chapel at the hospital earlier that night, she wrapped up warm and headed out of the door to the church around the corner from the house. Unable to escape the frantic worry she felt about Conner back at the hospital, she said some prayers. Prayer can be a way of staying in the calm at the eye of the storm when everything seems overwhelming. It's written in the book of Philippians "Don't worry about a thing; pray about everything." Emma had never been so worried in her life, but while she prayed she was able to do something for Conner even if she wasn't right next to him. Many would pray for Conner over the following days as they started to hear what he was going through, myself included. Imagining how cold it would have been in South Shields at 4.45 on a January morning, I'm impressed that Emma could focus enough to pray for more than just a few seconds, but at that moment I can imagine the cold was the least of her worries. Besides, she's grown up with the harsh Geordie winters. She's accustomed to them.

Just 24 hours previously, Emma would have been asleep in

her bed. When she woke she would no doubt have thought it was going to be a normal day. It scrambles my brain just to think about how much their lives changed from one day to the next. Yet another reminder that we should take nothing for granted, but I know I will take many things for granted every day because life moves on and we forget to appreciate everything.

Now it was time to go and wake Mark.

"It's 6 now, can we go back to the hospital?"

Mark felt like no time had passed but realised he must have dozed off. The digital clock by his bedside read 5.15, but he did feel a little refreshed and so it was time. If yesterday had been a long day this one would seem like a whole week in comparison.

BEYOND PUNISHMENT – THE UK'S FORGOTTEN IPP PRISONERS

"Lock him in jail and throw away the key."

It's just something people say. Maybe it goes on in Third World countries, but not in the UK. It just wouldn't be allowed…..

If this is what you believe then it seems you're just as naïve as I was on the subject until a couple of months back. It's believed that somewhere between 3,000 and 5,000 prisoners in the UK are still languishing in jail with no release date a number of years after their original sentences have been served. IPP (Imprisonment for Public Protection) sentences were the idea of David Blunkett, and were first passed in April 2005. The idea was that prisoners who were considered to be a danger to the public but whose crimes weren't considered to be severe enough to warrant a life sentence were given a minimum sentence, which they would serve, and after this their release would be at the discretion of the parole board. IPPs were abolished in 2012 but there are still several thousand who received them years ago and are yet to be released, having long since served their original sentence. What's more, these people seem to have been forgotten about by all except their families and a select few who are trying to speak up for them. IPPs were brought in around the time a 'chav' culture was being popularised by the UK media and ASBOs (Anti-Social Behaviour Orders) were all the rage. 'David Cameron's Broken Britain' was the tagline.

There are far more reasons for people behaving anti-socially than most will understand. As discussed in another chapter, former Prison Officer Ronnie Thompson wrote the novel 'Knifer,' based on the stories of young men he'd met in prison who had made poor choices, and through the novel he explains what a number of them might have been, and how it's possible for people to change. This is a good starting point for trying to understand the majority of people who are on IPP sentences. Not long after these sentences first started being handed out, David Cameron came out with the 'hug a hoodie' rhetoric, but this is a very complex situation and is beyond token gestures and slogans. It is a genuine ongoing nightmare for many family members of people who have made mistakes and aren't allowed the opportunity to change.

One such family member and activist is Joanne Hartley, whose partner Ian was given an IPP shortly after they were brought in for robbing a client at a prostitute's house and then trying to extort further money from him. His original sentence was three years. He had to be brought back to court three days later so it could be explained to him what his sentence actually meant, because the judge didn't really know. Ian is still in prison at the time of writing and it hasn't been the best environment for him to try and kick the drug habit he is desperate to move on from. He was even moved to a 'drug-free' wing at one stage but, as Joanne explains, "Drugs are rife in prison. There's no such thing as a drug-free wing, and Ian just can't get the one-to-one support he needs in a drug-free environment. All it takes is one bad day and he can get his hands on drugs almost straight away."

Addiction is a cycle. To break it requires strong willpower on the part of the individual, just as it does to break any cycle of damaging behaviour, but it also requires support. You need people around you who also want you to break the cycle, and time away from those who will encourage it to continue. Once you've spent some time clean it becomes more of a habit not to take drugs, and so it becomes something that's more manageable with continued dedication. Something that strikes me about the 'drug-free' wing though is that for such a wing to exist the prison are basically admitting that they are unable to control the flow of drugs into the building, and if they are not able to keep drugs out of the prison altogether then how can they keep them out of a specific wing?

"They know the wing's not drug free," continues Joanne, "Every prison has a 'drug-free' wing, but basically it's just somewhere they can dispense Methadone."

Joanne contributes to the 'Smash IPP' website: a place where the stories of the prisoners who still have no idea when their sentences might end can be told, awareness can be raised and resources can be shared. The campaign is on social media too, and Joanne has done plenty in the way of activism with peaceful protests, information evenings and the like. She has met David Blunkett several times and describes him as a 'lovely guy.'

"He's full of remorse about what's happened, and he admits it was all a big mistake," she says, "But it's the current Justice Secretary who can actually do something about it, and I don't have much faith in him."

The question is why? Why do so many IPP prisoners still have no release date? Why did I not know this was even happening until a couple of months ago? Why is it allowed to continue even though IPP sentences were abolished six years ago? The way things change is often if enough people make a noise about them that the government have no choice but to act. Ian admits he should have been punished for his crimes, as does Joanne. I believe that for violent crime there must be punishment, but I don't believe in prisoners being basically left to rot. I believe that people have the capacity to change, and that the majority of violent criminals are a product of their circumstances, or of a struggle that is hard for people to understand. Yes, we all have choices, but it's a lot easier to make the right ones if you have the right people around you, feel loved and supported and have relatively low stress levels.

A letter from Ian can be found on the Smash IPP website. In it he outlines, "I've spent a lot of time in prison since 1989 due to my own selfish ways. The sentences I never really gave a thought to – they were like water off a duck's back to put it bluntly (sad really.) I was in boarding schools from the age of five."

He was given his IPP sentence in 2006 – remember at the time he was told it would be a three year sentence, but he is still in prison now. The terms of the IPP sentence are vague; the prisoner will serve their original tariff, then it is basically up to the parole board when they will be released. There are usually a number of terms and conditions attached. IPP prisoners often have to complete a number of courses before they can be considered for release, some of which have long waiting lists and some are not available in all prisons. If someone on an IPP sentence moves prisons, which they frequently have to due to overcrowding and other issues, they basically have to start again from square one. This seems to be a common theme, as Joanne has told me how David Blunkett has tried several times to arrange meetings between the families of IPP prisoners and the Justice Secretary. Every time it has been impossible because by the time the meeting is approved a new Justice Secretary is appointed and so they have to reapply. When a Prime Minister is appointed they will ordinarily be in office for five years, but the Justice Secretary seems to change far more frequently, meaning there is no consistency.

Ian has been trying to get a place in residential rehab for years. His first attempt was hampered by a previous attempt at smuggling drugs into prison, which he admits responsibility for, but the probation officers both inside and outside the prison have been dead against his recent attempts, despite financial backing from Preston Adult Social Services. They instead wanted him placed in a Category D prison. When he honestly explained that drugs would be rife there and it would be a matter of when, not if, he lapsed, the probation officer wrote in her report that he was threatening to use drugs if they didn't give him what he wanted and that he was trying to manipulate his release to rehab. To me this seems like the actions of power-hungry individuals twisting words to fit their own agenda. It seems they have taken a dislike to Ian and are blocking his attempts to rehabilitate. It can't be denied that Ian has made mistakes, but his original sentence would have ended ten years ago. A full decade. Doesn't he at least deserve the chance to try and rebuild his life and stay on the right path?

"If I wasn't so headstrong I would have taken my life long ago," Ian says in his letter, "Drugs have been my coping mechanism since a very early age. Thinking about how my family and Joanne would feel and deal with it have kept me alive because I wouldn't want to put them through that sort of thing. This sentence is killing many people within themselves."

A prison sentence is meant to be a punishment, but it is also meant to inspire people to want to change, and why would anyone want to if they felt like they were never going to get out no matter what they did? Even once released IPP prisoners are subject to extremely strict conditions. They are on a 99 year license. NINETY-NINE years. If they slip up in any way during that time, or even if anyone claims they have, they will almost certainly be going straight back to prison. Joanne believes that there are more corrupt prison officers than those who genuinely want to help. I don't know the facts, but just the fact that drugs are so easy to get hold of suggests a high level of corruption.

"IPP prisoners are treated differently to normal prisoners," sighs Joanne, "Also, nobody who has money or influence is on an IPP. They targeted the lower classes."

Joanne Hartley is not making excuses for Ian at all costs and blaming anyone but him for his imprisonment. She is simply fighting for justice. He has long since served his time, and he needs help to move on from the life he is so desperate to leave behind for the sake of his family as much as himself. He is one of many. James Ward, released last year but recently recalled, I believe after the police were called when he was heard to be having an argument with his girlfriend, was given a ten month sentence for stealing a mobile phone but was known to have mental health issues and couldn't get the help he needed in the ordinary prison in which he remained for ten years. During his sentence he set fire to the mattress in his cell as a cry for help, but instead of being moved to a Psychiatric Unit his sentence was increased. A lot of IPP prisoners become so institutionalised that they feel anxious about being released. Many were given their IPP sentences at a young age and so have not really known life outside prison as adults. Believing that they have little prospect of employment, or of making friends who will have their best interests at heart, many will reoffend soon after release if they don't have support networks in place. This is why generally held attitudes towards prisoners need to change.

"It's no wonder people are killing themselves, cutting

themselves or drugging themselves up," concludes Ian in his letter, "I might be Headstrong Heledd, but I honestly don't know how long I can keep going like this. I need emotion, love, compassion. I get that every week on a visit but that's it. The rest is dark and scary."

Many believe that dark and scary is no more than prisoners deserve. This is why a friend of mine (who cannot be named for the purposes of confidentiality) visited Shepton Mallet Prison when it was still open, on behalf of a mental health charity. She was expecting all of the prisoners she met to be monsters, and was afraid to speak to them, but was fascinated at the same time. The reality couldn't have been more different to her expectations.

"The prisoners were all very friendly and just wanted to chat," she explains, "I expect it was partly the novelty, because they wouldn't have got to talk to new people often, but chatting to those people it was easy to forget that some of them had committed awful crimes."

Do we all have it within us to commit awful crimes? Could those who do commit awful crimes have been different people if their circumstances had been different? My friend thinks this is a definite possibility.

"One common theme was that everyone I spoke to seemed to have had a terrible upbringing," she says, "It struck me how many of them had experienced horrific abuse and how readily they would share about it in great detail despite me being a complete stranger."

This experience seems common to a number of IPP prisoners too. It is logical that the less stability you have in your formative years the more likely you are to fall in with people who are a bad influence and to have anger at the world. Having a difficult upbringing isn't a license to commit crime, but that fact is that so many prisoners seem to have lacked the emotion, love and compassion of which Ian spoke. This suggests that the picture is far more complicated than many like to admit. I have shared a number of posts on social media about IPP recently and they have received little or no reaction. Are most people afraid of being seen to side with prisoners? Do most see prisoners as being bad people through and through? My friend certainly had her opinion changed by her visit to HMP Shepton Mallet.

"I was expecting the atmosphere to be really tense like on a TV show but it was almost underwhelming when it was just a room full of blokes chatting and having tea and biscuits," she laughs, "The prisoners were laughing and joking with the guards, and there was someone serving tea and biscuits who I thought must have been a staff member but after I left it struck me that he was a prisoner. That was a real lightbulb moment."

Of course the atmosphere can be, and is, very tense in prisons a lot of the time. Ian Hartley, along with other cleaners on his wing, dealt with some bullies and were praised by the staff for doing so. The bullies were moved to another wing but Ian was later moved there himself, and of course he didn't receive a warm welcome. Prisons are full of rivalries, and there is a constant threat of violence spilling over. This is why the prison guards should be highly commended. Would you want to do the job they do? Those who do the job because they genuinely want to keep the peace and to help prisoners to change their lives just cannot be thanked enough, and in my opinion should be honoured for bravery.

So can criminals really change? Once you've become immersed in the dark side of life, and have spent time in prison after prison, is there any way back? Well let me tell you a story. Back in around 2010 one summer's day I went to my mate's girlfriend's birthday party on the beach at Lyme Regis. I'd heard her dad was coming, and all I knew about him was that he had been addicted to crack and heroin in the past but was now clean. I found him easy to get on with, hilarious and a little mischievous but definitely with no hint of malice. He told my friend Max he was going to 'get it' for repeatedly saying he had hair like Peter Andre, but turned to me and grinned straight afterwards and didn't lay a finger on Max all afternoon. I would never have guessed the full extent of his criminal past, and his daughter seemed to adore him. Rico Costanza went through more as a child than some will in a lifetime.

"When I was very young I was in a car accident with my family and my dad was killed," he recounts, "I became a father very young. I was only 15, and I wasn't able to cope with that I guess."

What followed was a long and turbulent youth. Rico always felt like something was missing – not surprising when you hear about his early tragic loss – and used alcohol and drugs to fill the void. He started with drinking and smoking weed, and at this stage it was all about escapism, but he later got into chemical drugs like LSD, speed and ecstasy and in line with this he lost interest in working. He bought a van and started living peacefully on travellers' sites, but then things got a lot darker when he started taking heroin and crack-cocaine. At this point it became about more than escapism and was a full-blown insatiable addiction. As so often happens in these circumstances, life became all about the next score, and he wouldn't always have the funds to get it, so he would steal or deal drugs in order to raise the money to feed his habit. It got him into a lot of trouble, but the cycle continued because he distanced himself from those who would have been his support network.

"I went to prison about ten times. The effect on my family

was huge. I couldn't be a dad. I had another daughter by then, but my children could no longer trust me. Neither could my mum or my siblings. I couldn't face seeing the people who cared for me and I disappeared from my childrens' lives altogether."

Rico was still a child when he first had a child of his own, and he was still trying to come to terms with losing his own father. He didn't know any other way to cope and the drugs took more and more of a hold on him.

"The last two years of my time in Somerset I lived on the streets of Bristol, begging for change and stealing whatever I could get my hands on. I lost all hope and hated the person I had become. I just couldn't face what I'd turned into and at this point I got arrested doing a robbery with a knife."

This story, or similar, is common to a number of people who end up in prison, but Rico's criminal past took place before the introduction of IPPs and what has happened since shows just what could happen for Ian Hartley and a number of others should they be released.

"The officer didn't recognise me until I gave him my name," he remembers, "He'd known me for a long time but he couldn't believe it was me because I'd changed so much and I looked so ill."

This officer saw that Rico needed treatment and one-to-one support, so he helped him access some drug support services. Somerset Drug Service, as it was at the time, helped him get into a rehab centre near Bristol and then on to a secondary unit in Bournemouth. He was introduced to the Fellowship of Alcoholics and Cocaine Anonymous, completing nine months of treatment and getting a flat in Bournemouth. He thought his problems were over, but without the daily routine of the treatment centre and the constant support he had been used to he felt completely lost. It was only a matter of time before he relapsed, and this lasted four-and-a-half years.

"I went back to my old ways," he admits, "Then I met some guys at a CA meeting I'd been in treatment with who were still clean. They inspired me that it was possible to change my ways. They taught me about my addiction, and that I'd have to admit defeat and realise I couldn't beat it on my own."

He stopped blaming others for his problems and learnt to rely on himself. Once he felt strong in his own recovery he was determined to help others start theirs, and says that helping others has been his main source of strength, making him accountable. Running, walking and yoga have also given him a way of harnessing the energy and focus he used to put into getting his next fix into something more positive, which boosts his physical and mental well-being.

"I have plenty of hope nowadays," he smiles, "I'm trying to better myself as a person, and I'm always trying to be a good father and grandad. I see my kids now and have a good, honest relationship with them. They're now young adults and are moving into the big wide world. I exercise, I pray, I meditate. I appreciate nature. I don't forget where I came from, and I have a wife now. I have plenty of purpose in life. It's important to laugh, and not to take myself too seriously."

Does he worry about his kids following the same path he did?

"I think the main things are education and keeping lines of communication open. Telling them 'just don't do it' isn't going to work, but if they do get in trouble the right person is on hand to offer help instead of judging them. If everyone had that we could do much more good."

If you disagree with what Rico says, just cast your mind back a little. The path to his own recovery began when a police officer didn't judge him but helped him to get support. A person can only be truly helped when they want to recover, but someone wanting to help them who doesn't judge can really inspire this yearning for change. Recently he visited some guys on life sentences in Ford Prison for Cocaine Anonymous and shared his story.

"As I have been to prison a lot I know what these guys are going through. Many times I left prison intending not to use again but I always did because I didn't have a real solution to my problems. One guy in there I'd tried to sponsor years before and it blew my mind when he walked into the meeting. We talked and he said he really wished he'd listened to me before, but you're not done until you're done. Some guys in there had been in for fourteen years but had found a higher power and seemed to have real peace even in those conditions, so would no doubt thrive on the outside. It was a great privilege and a very powerful experience."

Rico is always looking for ways to help others who are in the position he has been in before. He has been clean for 13 years now and believes he never has to use drugs or alcohol again but refuses to get complacent about it because he says he has seen 'better men than him' relapse after being clean for longer, and some have died. Last year he completed the 100 kilometre Trail Walker event with three other addicts. After a guy he sponsored tagged him in a post on Facebook he said 'yes' straight away, but hadn't read it properly and didn't know they'd have just 30 hours to walk the 100k.

"Once I'd found out it was too late to back out, and I'm glad I didn't," he enthuses, "We started a training camp together and the four of us got to know each other a lot better. It was one of the greatest experiences of my life. There were times in the middle of the night with the rain hammering down where it got tough, but we helped each other along. At no point did I think to give up, even though the organiser said it was some of the worst conditions they'd ever seen at the event!"

Rico says he'd definitely do something like Trailwalker again, and describes the Ghurkas he met as 'incredible people who were awesome to meet.' Activity is a big part of his life, and he tries to parent in this way too, taking his kids out in nature rather than putting them in front of a screen, and taking an active role. He hates money and greed, which he sees a lot of in the modern world, and talks about how we want to help someone in another country but are too afraid to talk to or help our neighbours. Is this part of the paranoid culture that has been created by the digital age?

Rico concludes, "As long as I keep doing what I've done these last 13 years and continue to try to be a better person and, most importantly, help others then I'll be fine."

Rico has started his own company, Vapestar, with one of the other Daves of this world, who is also an addict. They began with a market stall and over six years have built it up so they have an online store with two brick and mortar shops. What's more, they have created their own brand of e-liquid, which they sell themselves, and have also started to sell wholesale to other companies.

This is a success story that shows what Ian Hartley and many, many others have the potential to be if they are shown support and understanding and given a reason to hope. Will they be allowed this chance? Do you think they deserve to be allowed to try? If so please tell others about what's happening, because not everyone has someone in a position of influence to help give them the tools to change. Rico did. Just imagine what might have been lost to everyone he has helped, and to his family, if he hadn't.

Well shortly after this chapter was written, Ian was released into rehab. He found it challenging and was soon recalled, so his battle continues. He has a parole hearing coming up. Rico's story tells us that he still has a long road ahead of him, but shows us just what is possible if he can manage to stay clean. Let's pray that Ian and many others like him are offered a similar opportunity for a second chance at life when so many years have already been lost.

CONNER'S STORY PART 7

When it was actually 6am Mark and Emma arrived back at the hospital. They hadn't received any phone calls in the meantime, which had to be a good sign, but was it the best case scenario from a still critical situation or were they about to witness a miracle? At some point during the morning the doctor in charge told them what the plan was for the day.

"We're going to try and bring Conner round today," he explained, "This could take a long time and we don't know yet how he'll respond. He is still very poorly."

They nodded, being reminded, as if they needed to be, of just how ill Conner was. They'd been pleased that he hadn't taken a turn for the worse while they'd been at home, but whatever sleep either of them had managed hadn't made their nightmare go away. When I think of endurance I might often think of it in terms of a workout or something similar but true endurance is what I'm describing right now. I'd rather run all day any day than go through something like this.

During the morning the doctors had to ask them to leave several times while they removed some of Conner's tubes. They described it as 'working' on him, almost as if he was a car or a computer, but they knew what was likely to help fix him the best they could, just as a mechanic or technician would know how to fix a machine. It's phenomenal the amount of trust we put in doctors in situations like these when you think about it. Mark felt his phone vibrate as a message came through. It was his eldest brother, Paul, who had been working up in Scotland. Paul asked if they wanted him to come back.

"It's Ok," replied Mark, knowing that it was unlikely his brother would be able to get the time off, even if it would be great to have the support, "We'll keep you updated."

The doctor came back to speak to them again. He appeared serious.

"Ok, I've got some news," he stated, "Conner's paralysed on his right-hand side. He's not responding to any tests we're doing on his right."

Emma began to sob.

"The good news is that he's responding to tests on his left side."

"What does this mean?" asked Mark, holding Emma's hand.

"Well it's likely to be a long road ahead," replied the doctor, "He could be in hospital for anything up to two years."

He indicated that he would give them some more time to process the news. When he left Emma let her full emotion out.

"He's still here," insisted Mark, "That's the main thing. We'll be here for him every step of the way. Anything else we'll deal with as and when we need to, but he's still here."

Even as he said those words Mark wondered what was truly left of Conner. He was still here in body, but would he recognise them, and would they recognise anything of the boy they knew before all of this? What would they have said to him if they'd known this was coming? They could never have known.

After a while they headed back into the unit, taking their places either side of Conner. A few minutes later the doctors were doing their rounds. The one who had asked if they'd wanted to say goodbye the previous night was among them. When they saw Mark and Emma they stopped and talked amongst themselves. Mark and Emma couldn't make out what they were saying, but they heard that Conner was going to come out of his sedation. Before they moved on the doctor they recognised came over and put his hand on Mark's shoulder.

"He's doing well. He's fighting," he assured.

"Thank you for everything" said Mark. At the time he thought this was the surgeon who'd performed the operation. Later he was to find out it was somebody else who did the main procedure, but this guy had been involved in some way.

They sat with Conner for what seemed like an eternity. Every time they stopped to consider the whole situation it was hard not to feel despair, but they tried to hold on to any positive they could. Sometimes it's hard to see anything good in a situation, and when something so unthinkable happens it takes a huge level of resolve to even try. What choice did they have though?

Suddenly from nowhere, Conner lifted his left hand and squashed his nose with the flat of his palm, the way he always would when itching himself there. Mark and Emma looked at each other to confirm they'd both actually seen what just happened. They were astounded. Was he still in there somewhere?

TWO HOURS OR SO TO CHANGE YOUR LIFE

As we know, many in the UK dream of becoming professional footballers or musicians. Nowadays perhaps you can add Youtube celebrities to that list, but the point of it all is to get paid a lot of money for doing something they enjoy. In Kenya, for a lot of youngsters, it's all about being a professional runner. Kenyans are especially dominant over the marathon distance; apart from Ethiopia's Haile Gebrselassie every male world record holder for the marathon in recent years has been Kenyan, and from any other nation only a couple of other Ethiopians have come close. Apart from the still unparalleled achievements of Paula Radcliffe it's been pretty much the same for women. Running one brilliant race can pretty much set them up financially for life, but the years of training to enable them to run that one race basically have to be done relying on the good will of others to fund their living costs in the meantime. For those who reach the very top the rewards are phenomenal, but more than half of those who attempt to reach those heights never win any prize money, even though if they were from just about any other country in the world their talent would make them a national record holder.

Everyone who has an interest in these things has a theory on why Kenya produces the best marathon runners, but perhaps Adharanand Finn, who spent a long time in close proximity to these athletes for his book 'Running With the Kenyans', is better qualified than a lot of us to answer.

"This is such a big question," says Adharanand, "But roughly it boils down to a few things. Firstly you have to look at the numbers – there are thousands of full-time athletes in Kenya. Nowhere else in the world can you find so many athletes training seriously in the hope of success. This increases the chances of athletes reaching their full potential, but also creates a brilliant environment in which to train, with hundreds of training groups who support and inspire each other."

Indeed, a culture exists in Kenya where those who show natural talent for running can have the best environment to try and make it their career. There are plenty of talented runners in the UK but there isn't a training community in the Cotswolds where heaps of them wake up at dawn and run in the hills then come back and tuck into a plate of locally grown and reared food before resting in the afternoon. That's the life of an athlete in the Rift Valley. It's basically all about becoming the best runner they can be, and nothing else gets in the way. This might seem like an empty, and perhaps selfish, existence but for those who make it to the very top it can set their families up financially for life. As Adharanand explains, it's the whole Kenyan culture as well as this total dedication to athletic pursuits that allows them to be the best they can be.

"There's the tough, rural upbringing that most of these athletes have experienced – running to school, working the land, looking after animals, never travelling by car and never wearing shoes. Growing up barefoot helps them to develop foot strength and beautiful, light running form."

As I consider Adharanand's words I think of an American lad who at one time became the best 100 mile mountain runner in the world. Karl Meltzer was taken skiing by his dad, also named Karl Meltzer, as an 8-year-old and developed a love of the outdoors, which led to an extremely active lifestyle from a very young age. Throughout his childhood he would always be out running or playing sports whenever he could, and would never just lounge around. Through this he grew up with an impressive level of natural fitness, and it's almost certainly what set him up to develop an astonishing level of endurance as an adult. At the time of writing he has won at least one 100 mile race in every one of the last eighteen years, and is still going strong aged 50. Karl Meltzer senior is 75 and is still running, albeit not quite as fast as he used to. There are also the Tarahumara from Mexico; a tribe who live in the Copper Canyons and live very active, simple lives with natural diets and on their feet wear just sandals made from old tyres, so have the same beautiful running form as the Kenyans. They are famed for their ability to run long distances without getting exhausted. The Tarahumara don't have the same culture of athletic aspiration the Kenyans do – their running ability is borne more out of necessity – but when life has been geared towards the outdoors from an early age and a solid fitness base has been built up you will be well placed to become a great athlete who can compete with the very best.

"You also have the huge incentive that running offers," Adharanand continues, "For no cost you can train and win enough money to change your life. This hope inspires so many to take up running."

In the areas of Kenya where all of these athletes train there is almost no junk food, there is clean air from the virtual absence of traffic and a high altitude. This helps runners to be stronger and have a higher aerobic threshold, thereby being more likely to be able to run faster for longer without gasping for air. I've not seen any of the very best Kenyan runners in action face to face, although I did see some evidence of what's talked about in this chapter when I ran Torbay Half Marathon in 2011. Due to the course being two laps I got to see the leaders in action. In first and second place were Isaac Kimutai and Collins Tanui; two UK-based Kenyan runners who looked like they were just out for a jog in the park. They were running gracefully and effortlessly with broad smiles on their faces. In third place, several minutes behind, was Paul Martelleti from the UK, who looked like he was running at the absolute threshold of his ability and frankly appeared to be having a horrible time. At the finish line it was the opposite. Paul looked like he was having a lovely time whilst Isaac and Collins looked somewhat uncomfortable with the attention. Those two Kenyan runners were obviously fantastic athletes but in their own country they would probably not have been in the top 100.

So Adharanand, just how good a living can the most successful of these runners make?

"The very best make great money. Winning a major marathon in a fast time can easily mean a half-million dollar payday. That goes a long way in Kenya. Even winning a third-tier marathon like Edinburgh can get someone enough to buy a plot of land or a house."

Not bad for a couple of hours' work! Of course it's a long and hard road to even get to the start line with a chance of victory, and only the very best can make that kind of money, but it's no wonder so many Kenyans gravitate towards running.

"With virtually every major city in the world hosting a marathon or half-marathon, this adds up to a lot of opportunities to earn decent money and so almost everyone in Kenya's running regions, which are mostly around Eldoret and the Rift Valley, knows a friend or neighbour who has gone abroad and come back either a little richer or incredibly rich."

With so many incredible runners in Kenya it does mean that

there are plenty who sacrifice almost everything to try and get their big payday through running but don't ever make it, which no doubt leads to a whole lot of disappointment and disillusion at best, total despair at worst. If someone from the UK is running the times that the 100th best marathon runner in Kenya is then everyone who follows such things knows their name. Someone from Kenya who was that talented but no better would not be known outside of their family, and the running scene of the Rift Valley. Of course many have dreams that are unfulfilled, and this raises questions about the world we live in. People chase these big paydays because life can be incredibly tough without money in a capitalist society, so what of those who never reach the top? It's unimaginable to have that much talent and not be able to make money from it. A by-product of the lifestyle they have is good health, a phenomenal level of fitness and valuable experience, which would hopefully be enough to give them the necessary drive to get by in life another way. Wealth does bring security; that cannot be denied, even if there is much it cannot bring.

Kenyan athletes are not totally unbeatable. The UK's Mo Farah has beaten them over 5,000 metres, 10,000 metres and half-marathon distance, and is training towards trying to beat them in a marathon at the time of writing. He recently won his first marathon in Chicago in a time that's getting close to that he will need to beat the very best. You could say he has the best of both worlds in that he does a lot of his training in Kenya but can also take advantage of the superb facilities of the west. The marathon seems to be the distance at which Kenyan athletes truly dominate, and just recently there has been talk of when the 2 hour marathon barrier might be broken. You could say this is the modern equivalent of the four minute mile, first broken by the late Sir Roger Bannister in 1954. It has since been broken by many athletes, but at the time it was not known if it was possible. Adharanand didn't hear any talk of it though when he was in Kenya.

"When I was there it wasn't even a thought," he admits, "It's a recent thing that people are getting so excited about it and in my opinion it won't happen in a real race for many, many years. Certainly nobody running today has the ability to do it."

Recently Nike organised an event they called The Moonshoot, in which three elite marathoners – Eliud Kipchoge and Lelisa Desisa of Kenya and Eritrea's Zersenay Tadese (the half-marathon world record holder) would attempt to run a sub 2 hour marathon on a track in Monza, Italy, with a team of elite pacemakers who would take shifts to prevent them getting exhausted and having to drop out. Kipchoge got close, running a time of two hours and twenty-five seconds, which remains the fastest known time over marathon distance but doesn't count as a world record because it wasn't done during an official race on a course that fits in with the criteria. Don't ask me what that is; I don't make the rules. The closest anyone has got officially is Dennis Kimetto, who ran two hours, two minutes and fifty-seven seconds at Berlin Marathon a few years back.... or at least it was when I first wrote this chapter. By the time I came to editing it none other than Eliud Kipchoge had set a new record of 2 hours, one minute and thirty-eight seconds, once again in Berlin.

"It was a remarkable performance," enthuses Adharanand, "And even better than I thought he was capable of. The fact he looked so fresh at the end was remarkable and suggests he can go faster, but he is getting older and has to slow down at some point, so I don't think he'll break two hours. The question is whether he's a one-off or whether someone else is coming through who can pick up the baton. That I don't know. He is a rare combination of Kenyan upbringing, running culture and talent but also an incredibly focused and intelligent mindset. Among all those other runners in Kenya perhaps there's one who will be as good. Geoffrey Kamworor and Rhonex Kipruto are my tips."

You can guarantee the first athlete who achieves the sub 2 hour marathon will be financially set up for life, and it is something that will continue to give hope to young East Africans for years to come. The reason they all dream of success and work hard towards it is the same reason anyone does; to make life more comfortable for themselves and their familes.

WOJTEK'S STORY PART 2 – THE FRONTMAN

So now we resume the story of young Wojtek. Eight years have passed since he bravely sacrificed his band to save us all from the fury of the millennium bug.... Well anyway, the intervening years have not seen him fulfil his original musical ambitions of being the frontman. He played bass in Ross Cummins' new band 'Paper Cuts' for a while, then he was in a number of bands that were very much of their time. In the mid-2000s there were a whole array of bands trying to sound like Coldplay, Doves and Snow Patrol, who had all become popular singing their emotional anthems. This theme influenced the bands Wojtek was in, and the rest of the band would occasionally have to 'have a word' when his backing vocals started to echo his rock background and became like untamed hogweed, rising above the surrounding pretty meadow flowers and making their presence felt, bringing discomfort to passing dog walkers. He was led by the bands he was in, and apologised frequently for trying to put his own stamp on their sound. None of the bands really came to anything, and the answer was staring him in the face. It was time to say "Well, this whole music thing's been fun, but it's time to get a proper job"...... right, Wojtek?

"Not for a second," he sighs, "That's just not what I'm about. I love music and it's what I'm meant to be doing. I just couldn't picture myself doing anything else."

I have friends who feel the same but haven't been able to

make a living from music and so remain perpetually unfulfilled in that way. Whether they just haven't had the break they need, they haven't pursued it wholeheartedly enough for long enough or whatever the reason, Wojtek has found a way, and in doing so has proved it can happen. For years though he was doing what he really wanted to be doing and yet not. He was playing music for a living but not in the way he imagined he would. In 2008 he was working on his first solo album for Tigertrap Records. When he walked past the word 'Hope' graffitied on a wall it epitomised all he was feeling at the time.

"It was a very hopeful time for me," he reflects, "A lot of hopes came to pass. My album had glowing reviews, it got into the shops and I played a headline show at the 100 club, which closed a circle for me of sorts."

He felt like he had wasted a lot of time and money in the intervening years between the end of Symposium and the eventual start of his solo career, but during the recording of his first solo album he would walk by the canal every day. He took a hand-held video camera everywhere, and a huge montage of the images he filmed at the time became the video for his song 'Rosette Nebula.' 'Hope' and 'Progress' were very much the key words of the time, and with the music he was making he was finally doing what he set out to do all along.

Ironically, considering that I first contacted him because I remembered Symposium being an optimistic-sounding 90s band, he doesn't remember the 90s as being a particularly optimistic time, and apart from there obviously being more technology nowadays he doesn't see many differences.

"I've no idea if it's harder making a living from music in the 'digital age," he says, "I can only give a pat, empty and wholly inadequate answer about it being better for some and worse for others. I never wanted to be in PR, or work in a record company, or have management skills. Now it seems without those essential skills you can't get by as a musician."

Wojtek only ever really wanted to write and record and tour around the world, which he did in Symposium but not really on his own terms. In around 2008 I was reviewing CDs for a website and was intrigued when something by 'Wojtek Godzisz' came through my letterbox. It was so different to what I'd heard from Symposium that I couldn't tell if it was new music from Wojtek or a band who had named themselves after him. He found this hilarious when I told him.

"My early solo material wasn't too far removed from Symposium," he asserts, "Those songs had pop structures and some of them had quite a similar sound."

Wojtek was the main songwriter in Symposium to begin with, and the band's name was his idea. The rest of them weren't too keen on the name at first but they accepted it when he persisted. The only song that they kept from before Wojtek had joined was named 'Eddie Vedder ate my Walkman.' They said Wojtek's songs were better than the ones they had written up to that point, so they should probably just play them instead. By the time the second album was in the works the other members were contributing more; 'Peshwari Nan' and 'To the Lighthouse' were based around riffs Will had written and in fact were re-recorded by him with different musicians in the future. Wojtek believes that his wanting to be a frontman contributed significantly to the demise of the band.

"I struggled in the early days of Symposium to put my 'frontman' dreams aside, let Ross take on the role, and make the decision about 'the band' being successful, rather than just myself."

Wojtek's two solo albums to date have received critical acclaim, and his third will no doubt be on a par. He has really taken his time over the albums, partly because of touring with other bands to make money, including as Benny in part of an ABBA tribute band; ABBA Gold.

"Those are probably the biggest crowds I've played in front of post-Symposium," he admits, "Some of them have probably been bigger than I ever had before, for instance Hyde Park a couple of times, arenas, the Royal Albert Hall and even some crazy stuff like playing for the Queen at Buckingham Palace."

The following exchange between Wojtek and E-Win (Elizabeth Windsor) on the day, suggests she may not have actually been present for their performance: -

"Are you going to watch us, your majesty?"

"I don't know. What time are you on?"

"About 9pm I think."

"Oh no, I shall be fast asleep by then!"

At least she was honest. Wojtek is going on a substantial tour with Abba Gold in November, which he explains will hopefully mean he doesn't have to worry about his finances for the immediate future.

"A friend of mined lived with a clairvoyant once," he says, "I met her and she told me I'd perform in front of huge audiences. If she was right then I wonder if it's already happened as part of Abba Gold or if it will be my own gigs."

I tell him that whatever the clairvoyant said, I'm saying this book will be a bestseller, people will rediscover his music and he will play the biggest gigs of his life.

"And my third album will be called 'Hope," he laughs.

Wojtek's solo music is steeped in folk tradition but still has definite echoes of the rock music of his early career. Basically it's in stark contrast to the bands he found himself in after Symposium split, and sounds more like him. He is a musician as an artist, rather than as a shrewd businessman. Much of the lyrical content of his solo material looks to the past to paint a picture of the present. So what would happen if one of his band members started singing emotional, falsetto, Coldplay-esque backing vocals in rehearsal?

"I guess I would let them express themselves as much as they liked, and then explore how I felt about it afterwards," he muses, "If I thought it was horrible and out of place then I would say something as gently as possible I suppose. I don't know. I hope I wouldn't be unfeeling and cursory and hurtful without realising. It might be amazing and revelatory and lead to a new epiphany. New album title idea: 'New Epipanies' – sounds like Leonard Cohen."

Whether 'New Epiphanies' sees the light of day remains to be seen; watch this space. We will pick up Wojtek's story again another ten years on later. The intervening years between Symposium and then were all about continuing to make music his living; he says that the opposite would be an anathema to him. Although being in Symposium didn't allow him to be the frontman, in a roundabout kind of way you could say it did. His work with Symposium perhaps allowed a foot in the door when it came to making his own music and singing the songs himself. This could be true of any job; whatever you want to make your living from you just have to get your foot in the door to begin with. I've found this with writing. All the years I spent putting my first book together, even though it's not really the kind of book I would want to write now, enabled me to get work as a ghostwriter later on, and hopefully will help this one have a readership to begin with.

Wojtek's story, for me, is a lesson in how persistence, hard work and unwavering belief can and do bring results. They may not be instantaneous, but they do come.

CONNER'S STORY PART 8

Seeing Conner itching his nose was the seed of hope they needed. There was still something of him left, and from that starting point they could believe he might show further signs of improvement. Having said that, he was still very poorly, and it was the only sign they had seen so far that he was going to be anything like his normal self. He kept being sick throughout the morning, and every time he was Mark and Emma had to leave the room while the nurses cleaned up. Mark estimates that they lost 3 or 4 hours of visiting time over the whole day because of this. There were further positives during the morning though. At one point they were convinced they'd seen Conner move his toes.

At around 2pm that day Mark was stunned to receive a message from his brother Paul, saying he was at the hospital with his wife, Karen.

"His boss told him to go home, which looking back was superb. I don't know if my company would give me time off if my nephew was in hospital," says Mark, "Paul was off for around two weeks with full pay, and they even sent a £100 box of chocolates and a card. We'd never even met them!"

After buzzing Paul and Karen in to the locked ward, Mark and Emma tried to explain the whole situation, but just broke down.

"He's showing some signs of improvement," managed Mark, "He itched his nose at one point, and we saw his toes move."

Karen saw how distraught Emma was and so she called her workplace to explain what was happening. They said to take as long as she needed. Mark had messaged his work too, and they had replied saying he should focus on getting Conner better, and to just let them know when he was ready to return. Their ordeal had begun around 24 hours earlier. It had just been a normal day at work until Emma had received the call from Conner and then Mark had received the call from her. The world was a different place for them now, but everyone else at their workplaces would just be getting on with things. Everyone else outside the hospital too. It was just a normal day for most people, but how could it be? They weren't sure when, or if, they would be able to get back to normal again. Was their definition of normal going to be different from now on?

Only two visitors were allowed at each bed at once and so they took it in turns to spend time with Conner. News was starting to spread of what had happened, and Emma told Mark that one of Conner's best friends was asking to come and visit. Mark wasn't sure if this was a good idea because he only wanted positivity around Conner and wasn't sure if his friends, who were teenagers themselves, would be able to hold back their shock and sadness.

"Looking back now I was probably a bit of an arse about it," he reflects, "But I just wanted my boy to have the best chance of getting better, and I thought he would pick up on it if people were scared or upset around him."

It turned out that Conner's friend was already on her way with Viv and Gary, and Mark got a text from his niece, who showed up too. Before anyone went in to visit Conner, Mark would walk them down the corridor to see him through the glass, and if they were able to stay composed they were sent in to see him. If not, they had to get everything out of their system first. He was convinced that Conner could hear everything and so he only wanted him to hear what would be calming and reassuring.

Conner's friend did go in to see him. She held his hand, his right hand, which was said to be paralysed, but when she let go the fingers on his hand moved.

"Did you see that?" said Emma, stunned.

"Aye," replied Conner's friend. They told one of the nurses what had happened but she just couldn't accept it because the tests indicated that he was still paralysed down his right-hand side. Mark believed it though, and this was another huge positive to cling on to. When they were still on a high from this later in the evening they were taken aside by one of the nurses.

"The surgeon wanted to see you," she told them, "Shall I take you through?"

Mark and Emma stepped into a side room, and before long the man who saved Conner's life walked in.

"I'm Nick Ross," he said, "I operated on Conner last night and I wanted to see how you were."

They were somewhat speechless to meet the man who'd performed life-saving surgery on their son. He started to explain what had happened.

"As you will have heard, Conner had what we call AVMs on his brain. Their full name is Arteriovenous Malformations; they're a tangle of abnormal and poorly formed blood vessels that can cause a lot of damage if they bleed. I have no doubt that if Conner had been brought into theatre two minutes later he would have died.

Mark and Emma both started to cry.

"Having said that, the operation went well. After looking at the scans we've taken I'm confident that we've removed 90% of the AVM. I've only seen AVMs in one person younger than

Conner in my career. She was a five-year-old girl. I do believe it's possible that because of his age Conner could make a full recovery."

They looked at each other, their eyes still filled with tears.

"They said he was paralysed down his right side," sobbed Emma.

"I still feel it's possible he could recover fully," smiled Dr Ross, "It may take over two years, but I think he will be able to recover around 80% in the first 18-24 months, then from there it will just take time."

This was the first time any of the doctors had expressed optimism about Conner's recovery, and it was a massive source of hope on a day when they'd really had to cling on to any shred of it they could find.

"Dr Ross never calls himself Dr in any correspondence – it's always 'Mr Ross," says Mark now, "It's unbelievable if you ask me, considering what he does on a daily basis. He was so unassuming and laid back, and what he said lifted us massively. I know you have to be advised of the worst case scenario, but it helped us so much to hear someone being positive."

As Dr Ross got up to leave Mark stopped him.

"Can I shake the hand of the man who saved my son?"

Dr Ross smiled and shook Mark's hand firmly. He went to shake Emma's hand too.

"Forget shaking your hand," she wept, "I want a hug."

Dr Ross laughed and hugged Emma. They were given a real lift after speaking to him. They were both absolutely exhausted, but the adrenalin was helping to keep them going, even more so when Conner opened his eyes slightly just as they were getting ready to leave. He looked in their direction and his eyes shut again almost straight away, but he was starting to wake up. Emma didn't want Mark to drive, as he'd barely slept, so

CONNER'S STORY PART 8

Gary stepped up once again as chauffeur extraordinaire.

When they got back, having left around 9.30pm, they told Jayden that his brother was still poorly and that if he woke up fully he might be different to how he was before. They didn't tell him everything, but wanted to be as honest and upfront as possible in order to prepare him for what lay ahead. Mark explained that Conner might not be able to walk again, but they wouldn't know for sure until he was fully awake. Tomorrow was going to be another long, long day but they were able to go to sleep more soundly than they would ever have been able to the night before. There was a sense that even though he might not be the same again his life wasn't hanging in the balance.

GUILTY UNTIL PROVEN INNOCENT – THE ABOLITION OF THE WELFARE STATE?

When the ConLib government came to power in 2010 they spoke of the mess the Labour government had left the country in and what they planned to do in order to clean up. Leading up to this had been widespread talk of the 'credit crunch,' which was the perfect ammunition for austerity measures to begin. The most vulnerable people in society were targeted; David Cameron explained that the welfare state, originally set up to protect the people in society who needed support, would be one of the main areas they would be looking at. Since then life has been nothing short of a waking nightmare for thousands of people. There has been a lot of propaganda about 'benefit scroungers', and the Conservative attitude seems to be that helping people who are struggling dulls their ambition, creating a culture of laziness. Most who hold this view are people who have never had to live on the receiving end of these 'austerity measures.'

Not so long ago people had to work very hard to survive, but at least they knew exactly what they had to do to get by, and the way of life was more community-based, so in ordinary circumstances people who needed support were able to receive it. At least that's my perception. I could be wrong. Even ten to fifteen years ago I don't believe vulnerable people were criminalised in the same way they are now. We're supposed to be living in such tolerant times nowadays, but surely this should mean nobody who needs support has to fight tooth and nail for it?

Dan is one man who has recently been on trial, and has been stripped of the financial support he had been receiving for the chronic pain that prevents him from holding down a regular job. He worked as an electrician, then did a Btec in IT and has worked in a local factory. In his early twenties, he developed nerve pain from a slipped disc that impinged on the nerves in his back. It got worse over time and then he developed pain in the facet joints in his lower back.

"It derailed everything I wanted in life," he explains, "The pain got worse and eventually led to me developing depression, which contributed to the end of a long relationship. Over time it stopped me from being able to do a lot of the things I wanted to do."

For a while he was able to manage the pain to some degree. He did swimming and retook exams, then developed excruciating chest, back and neck pain with nerve sensations in his fingers as a result of some back intervention surgery. He visited Rheumatologists privately, who diagnosed `chronic pain syndrome`. All of this combined eventually caused the depression to get worse and made it harder to work. He helped a friend with his business and bought and sold on ebay, but was forced to seek financial support. The nature of most physical and mental conditions is that those who suffer them have good and bad days. Most workplaces can't afford to have someone on their staff who regularly needs to take time off, and so those with chronic conditions find it hard to hold down a job. Dan doesn't lack ambition; he wants to have work that he can hold down, he wants to rebuild the good level of fitness he once had, to do the things he enjoys, such as photography, but everything is dictated by his pain. At its worst the pain is so intense that it stops him from doing pretty much everything. At times there is respite, but it's always short-lived. He has had many injections into his facet joints, ribs and shoulders to try and help with the pain, often at great personal expense, having to sell possessions to be able to pay for them. Despite hating to take pills he has been trying many different medications and over the last year has been taking antidepressants combined with pain medicatio. He has also seen a psychiatrist. He has not been able to focus on trying to recover and to solve the problem once-and-for-all, because he has been subject to constant benefit reassessments. His financial support was stopped without warning last summer.

"Despite everything I can't fit myself into a single descriptor on the claim form," he sighs, "I have lots of paperwork from specialists, doctors, pain management, physiotherapists, psychologists, psychiatric help etc... A previous local MP put me in touch with a CAB representative. They help with advice but are themselves struggling with funding and so I don't know how long that support will remain.

Despite a vast portfolio of medical evidence, Dan is no longer able to claim the relevant benefits because his condition is complex and doesn't fit into the simplistic categorisation of the DWP. Along with the increasing digitalisation of many jobs nowadays, peoples' eligibility for support has been reduced to this. Dan is one of many who faces the ongoing nightmare of trying to prove to others who have never spent any time with him what he knows to be true. He spends every day wishing more than anything it wasn't.

He has been forced to apply for Universal Credit, which replaces the ESA that he has previously claimed. It means he will potentially have less money and be subject to constant sanctions, leading to worries that he might have the support taken away at any moment. He will be constantly on trial, even if his application is successful. He wants nothing more than to be able to live a full and independent life, but this is something he won't be able to do until such a time as he can finally break free of the pain that has blighted him for many years. His pain is his own kind of IPP sentence – he doesn't know when or if he might be free and is facing opposition from those who should be helping him to find ways to rehabilitate.

"There are people out there who are far worse off than me, although I cannot cope with the pain and don't deserve this"

What's happened to Dan is not new to me. When I worked for a mental health charity earlier this decade I would frequently speak to people with long-term psychological conditions who were subject to barbaric assessments that most described as being 'more stressful even than the condition.' Again, these peoples' outward appearances can often hide the debilitating illnesses that make everyday activities, let alone holding down a job, a challenge. A family member of mine has been subject to assessments for long-term pain, and most people probably know someone who has been through this ordeal. Austerity is not confined to the welfare state exclusively, but those who have taken the worst hits are people who were already struggling. There have also been massive cuts to much that is seen as non-essential, such as the arts, the countryside and there has even been a lot of talk of cuts to the NHS. When I walked through an area of countryside last summer that I used to walk through all the time I found overgrown paths, broken stiles and rotting signs where once the footpaths seemed lovingly tended and welcoming. This was because the local council are given no funding in order to maintain these areas, where once they were seen as a high priority. That walk, and the atmosphere it created, made me think forlornly of the vulnerable people who are being thrown to the wolves.

Around the same time Dan's pain became excruciating, Dom's nightmare was beginning. His wife, Jenny, explains: -

"Dom woke up on New Year's Day 2010 in agony and things were never the same again. At the time, diagnosing what was wrong wasn't a simple matter. He was back and forth to doctors and hospital for over a year before he was eventually diagnosed with Crohn's Disease. Crohn's is horrific; it's something you wouldn't wish on your worst enemy. I'll leave you to look up the symptoms at a time when you're not potentially eating!"

The parallels with Dan's life are striking. Prior to his illness, Dom did Mixed Martial Arts and plenty of other exercise, had friends, hobbies, a good job and everything but when he got ill he lost nearly all of it. Fortunately he didn't lose Jenny.

"If it wasn't for the care he received under QMC in Nottingham he would have died," she states, "Over the last seven years the quality of his treatment has declined because the treatment centre was taken over by a French company who made a lot of changes and at this point cuts were made."

Dom was part of the patient/staff panel for the centre, and was able to give valuable insights both as a patient and as a former A&E nurse. The panel was stopped, but not before Dom had discovered that the entire budget was heading towards being target-driven and that everything, including medication, was part of the budget.

"As an example, one particular treatment for Crohn's disease – an injection called Humira – costs around £900 a time," says Jenny, "Dom has just one consultant now, where he used to have a consultant plus access to two specialist IBD nurses. We can never get through to the consultant. We can never get advice."

The nurses were replaced by an administrator, who takes messages, and they are now worried that his medication might become too expensive, admitting they have no idea what will happen if it does.

Like Dan, Dom has faced pressure from the DWP and is subject to reassessments. Jenny echoes Dan's sentiments about the reassessment process: -

"The assessments for PIP and ESA are a joke. They are stressful and cause additional suffering. Only once have we gone through an assessment and passed without issue. The questions have changed now so that nothing is asked in relation to night time and sleeping. It doesn't matter that his colostomy bag often bursts at night and he has to be up and showered while I'm cleaning up the bed, floors and walls from where faecal matter has sprayed. Because of his medication he's often incredibly groggy and needs help getting into the shower. Dom's not a small chap. He's 6ft and 15 stone; it's hard work."

Dom and Jenny are full of praise for the QMC centre. Their problem is with the government. Like me they were no doubt up most of the night for last year's election wanting to see Jeremy Corbyn become Prime Minister, and the prospect of five more years of Tory rule were just as welcome to them as to me, i.e. not even remotely. For the first time I can remember I believe a man would have been Prime Minister who would actually have the interests of the many, rather than the few, at heart, just as he claimed. Corbyn gets a lot of flak, and I don't think he'd be perfect as Prime Minister, but could he really be worse than Theresa May for vulnerable people? People like Dan, Dom and Jenny would have had plenty of hope that someone who could change their lives was in a position to do so. Austerity runs deep and has impacted on Jenny's working life as well as her home life. She had to quit her career as a teacher to assist with Dom's care, which she didn't regret for a second, but was able to get a job through her mother-in-law holding humanist funerals, and is also a writer.

"While many of the people I hold funerals for are coming towards the end of their lives, they are also people who could easily have five or ten years left. They are being sent home from hospital because there is no room or ability to look after them and they are simply dying when there is no need. I am seeing suffering. I am seeing people struggling with affording care for their families, struggling with affording their funerals, struggling with everything and not seeing a bright future for their children."

Indeed, when I reached working age there seemed to be hope everywhere, even if my life was turbulent at the time. Nowadays life seems to be a constant struggle for everyone who is not already well-off financially. Austerity hasn't been aimed at people who can afford to take the hit, and as a result many are losing hope.

"I work with grieving families," explains Jenny, "These are from all strata of society. Some are very wealthy, some are very poor, but all deserve to be able to say goodbye to their loved ones and all receive the same quality of service from me regardless of their background or income level."

Does every family deserve to live without constant terror about their financial situation? Does every child deserve the same opportunities? Does every person deserve food, warmth and shelter as basic human rights? If this current government believe so then it is not a belief backed up by their actions. A scene from bestselling author Peter May's novel 'Runaway' sees an elderly gentleman and his grandson discussing the evidence of austerity they see in front of them and the older man is saying how he can't believe that people aren't even able to earn enough money to pay for what they need to survive. The cost of living is high, and one Tory MP said there was nothing to complain about because a bag of porridge is cheap, probably having tucked into an expensive dinner the night before. I don't know of anyone responsible for setting austerity measures who is living a thrifty life in a humble residence. These people may exist but from what I've seen it appears that austerity measures are aimed at those who are barely getting by. Those who already have comfortable lives have nothing to complain about because they are unaffected, and so they don't see a problem.

David Cameron repeatedly assured everyone he wanted all children to have the opportunity for a great education like his, and for people to be able to gain higher education. The reality is very different. Take the case of Ursula, who has two grown up children in higher education. There used to be an Education Maintenance Allowance of £20 per week available, which doesn't sound like a lot but £20 per week is £80 per month – a fairly substantial contribution. Ursula nearly had to withdraw her son from college because the loss of that allowance took her closer to the cusp of what she could afford. She found a way, and he was able to go to Plymouth University, but funding his studies is a massive challenge.

"He's running on empty all the time and is constantly overdrawn," Ursula explains, "In contrast, my daughter is studying her Masters in the Netherlands with her boyfriend. Both courses are free. They are moving into a small apartment soon and can claim about 350 euros (£310) per month towards their rent. They can also claim hardship grants and apply for student finance, paid back at a much lower rate than in England."

The theory would be that Ursula's son will be able to get a well-paid job on completion of his degree and clear his debts, but with the cost of living being what it is will this be realistic? What incentive would this be for anyone to study hard and go for a well-paid job when getting to that point can nearly ruin all but those who are already rich?

"I really do feel that this government wants us all to be living in debt," continues Ursula, "Someone in debt will work for peanuts. So sad, seeing as 'we' are supposedly the sixth richest country in the world."

Luckily Ursula is able to help to a degree with the huge cost of her children's education, but she isn't rich and so it's still a massive struggle. You might ask why go to University if it's so difficult to afford, but the job market is not much easier. Minimum wage, zero hour contracts, redundancies and debts are the realities of life for many. I know several couples where either both work or one has a reasonably well-paid job but they still need to claim some form of benefit to get by, which is becoming harder and harder to do. Both of Ursula's children are likely to have debts of over £50,000 when they've finished their studies. How are they meant to pay them off unless they spend years with their lives on hold working themselves into the ground? Even then who knows how long it might take?

So what hope is there for these people? Especially when it seems the welfare state is on the way to being abolished altogether.

"I did go and see someone at the CAB for advice at one stage," recalls Dan, "And she said it seemed like people were being targeted one by one, and the plan was to do away with benefits altogether eventually. Obviously the welfare system isn't there to be abused, but what are you meant to do if you need benefits? You have to fight."

Dan was accepted for ESA in 2011 and 2015 after going through reassessments, but just recently he was rejected, and he knows it was because the government want to do away with this kind of support. He is planning to go through the Community Mental Health Team to appeal again but in the meantime he continues to suffer enormously. At his recent tribunal he got six points out of the required fifteen. How can people who have been through the amount of suffering Dan has be subjected to a trial where points must be scored in ways that don't allow for the subtleties and complexities of their conditions? How is this allowed to happen?

Hope lies in the fact that there are people who think it is wrong and want to see change. There are countless families who have seen their loved ones have to go through this, and I've yet to meet anyone who thinks it is fair, or at least will admit to the fact. Do you think it's fair? If not then please don't stop thinking about it, don't stop talking about it. Pray if you do, write to your MP or bring it up in conversation whether you pray or not. Along with IPP this is one of the biggest injustices I know of that is currently taking place in the UK. People with long-term illnesses and disabilities, single mothers, low-income families and a whole host of other vulnerable people are all being targeted. Don't believe the propaganda; the vast majority of people who claim benefits do so because they have to, not because they want to. Don't let this go unnoticed. Don't allow it to keep happening without a fight.

TODAY IS A TIME OF INSTANT GRATIFICATION

"Recently my mum and I were driving through a housing estate near us on a Saturday around midday. There were no children playing outside. Each Saturday we passed the same thing, and around ten years before the estate would have been full of kids playing. Where were they? Inside on their phones or computers, snapchatting etc. A pretty good example of the negative effects of the digital age."

A reflection from Declan O'Shea, singer of late '90s Irish-French-Italian rock band Cyclefly, and one I'm sure many of us can relate to. I met Declan at a gig he played in Bristol way back in 1998; I was a teenager, and he went and got my brother Joe and I a beer each from his dressing room when we'd been chatting after their set. It was a bottle of Becks. Doesn't seem like much but I thought it was pretty much the coolest thing that had ever happened to me at the time. Bands meant the world to me then because their music offered escapism and gave me hope. I met French bass player Christian Montagne as well but I was too shy to talk to him beyond answering his question about whether or not I lived in Bristol. Listening to their music, which was a peculiar kind of rock with a heavy dose of atmosphere and Declan's unmistakable vocals, I would have expected them to be very urban individuals who thought the internet was better than reality, but talking to them now they seem to be pretty much the opposite. There was always a thoughtful, intelligent side to their music and that's what comes across.

"Today is a time of instant gratification," continues Declan, "A lot of this has to do with the rise of the digital age. It's not a good thing; people are addicted to their phones and computers, which are their new reality. People are becoming more desensitised today. The internet is definitely feeding this, and you wonder how far it could go."

Christian agrees that people are becoming more desensitised, and that it's blinding a lot of people to the injustices of life.

"The world is not fair for everyone," he outlines, "There are a huge number of homeless families around the world, through no fault of their own. At the same time the rich are getting richer, and it doesn't make sense to me. I believe that everyone should be entitled to have a roof over their heads."

Cyclefly were a band a select number of people loved in the 90s (many hadn't heard of them) and like Symposium they had some early success before hitting problems and ultimately splitting. Declan and Christian are both content enough in life now, but see the chaos and injustice around them and definitely hope for change. So how did their musical career, which brought them to my attention, come about?

"Our hope of getting signed was starting to fade a little," admits Christian, "We'd already done a lot of touring around Ireland and the UK and written a lot of songs. Anxiety took over but we kept going and continued our belief in the band. We got our break when Noise Management from London heard our demo and within the space of three months we had two record labels fighting over us. We decided, along with our management, to sign with US label Radioactive Records."

They were relieved to get signed, and recorded their first

album 'Generation Sap' in Los Angeles in 1999. Once it was released they saw a difference straight away, with people asking for autographs.

"It was truly humbling to be told what we were doing made people happy," adds Declan, "I always felt privileged to be doing something I loved and having a positive effect on others. I still feel this way."

Cyclefly would only record one more album, and their members have not had the same level of commercial success since, but Declan and Christian both consider themselves extremely lucky to live in areas that they find tranquil and inspiring.

"I live near Killarney National Park in the Kerry Mountains," explains Declan, "It's one of the most beautiful places I've ever been. I'm so lucky to live here and to be surrounded by scenery that truly takes my breath away. It definitely makes you stop and be in the present moment, and from this moment there is hope for everything."

I've always found that scenery makes a huge difference to the amount of hope I feel in the moment. When surrounded by concrete, traffic, noise and pollution I tend to feel less hopeful than when surrounded by stunning natural scenery, quiet and clean air. Funny that. Each time I've been to the Isles of Scilly, where there is noticeably clean and nature abounds in a palette of colours, I've returned as a different person. The air is so clean that I always try and gulp down gallons of it before returning to the mainland. Stress evaporates, inspiration flourishes and the desire for good health dominates. To experience this on a daily basis is a hope of mine for the future.

"I live by the sea in East Cork," says Christian, "I could literally fish from my balcony if I wanted to; that's how close I am to the sea. I'll never go hungry. I really think if I didn't live here, surrounded by nature, I would have lost it at some stage."

Christian and Declan both know how fortunate they are to live in such surroundings, and perhaps very judgementally, when I first met these guys in a Bristolian pub and saw them playfighting as they sank beers, I never imagined them being nature-loving types. They are twenty years older now, so it follows that they might want a little more peace and quiet than they once might have, but they're still making music together in new band Mako DC. Christian is learning about recording and mixing music so he can "Help other songwriters and bands realise their dreams," but they have plenty of musical ambitions of their own remaining.

"Christian and I will be releasing the second Mako DC album this year," says Declan, "I also have a new project called Vultures. We have a single out already and there will be an album by the end of the year. Next year I have a solo record planned, another Mako DC album and maybe a new Cyclefly record."

In order to keep making a living out of music, Declan has had to diversify. He writes scores for films as well as editing and doing video work.

"Everything revolves around being creative," he enthuses, "I always have albums on the go."

Deland and Christian agree that it's become a lot harder to make a living from music in the digital age, due to almost everything being available for free, but that the internet has enabled more people to reach an audience with their music, which is a positive thing.

Mindfulness is an important concept for Declan, and he finds plenty of inspiration from others: -

"I try to stay rooted in the present moment best I can," he explains, "I find there's rarely any problem when you're rooted in the now – most problems are in the past or future. I find that thinking less and being present more opens up more creativity too. To see or hear of someone doing something others thought was impossible is inspiring also, and is a catalyst for others to believe in themselves against the odds."

When I saw Cyclefly having success with their creativity as an aspiring writer in my teens it did feel truly motivating to me. They seemed so down to earth, and basically like people I'd have been friends with if we'd lived in the same area. Getting signed or getting published was the impossible dream, and they showed that with dedication and belief it could happen. Like Symposium, Cyclefly disappeared within a few years but there was no acrimonious split as far as I'm aware. Nowadays they seem full of hope despite their anxieties about the state of the world.

"I just want to be able to provide for my family, as situations may become uncertain at times," ponders Christian, "I hope that in the near future my daughter will be able to travel and to enjoy all the things I did when I was younger. I think that says it all."

Christian's hopes are the hopes of so many, and it seems it's becoming harder and harder to get by and to give your family the kind of life a lot of us enjoyed in the 90s. Declan would echo Christian's sentiments on this score.

"There's a huge divide between rich and poor that doesn't need to exist," he sighs, "My hope is that things will change before it's too late and that starts with us – "Be the change you want to see in the world," as Ghandi said."

Other phrases come to mind that people might use to describe how they want the world to change: -

"Don't put off until tomorrow what can be done today."

"What would Jesus do?"

"Actions speak louder than words."

"One can make a difference."

There's no point in me writing this book and highlighting a lot of things I see as being wrong with the world if I'm not doing anything to try and change them day to day. I guess writing the book and trying to encourage others to keep considering these things is the first step. What else does Declan consider to be wrong with the world?

"I don't like the emphasis on wealth, consumerism and the manufacture of so much stuff we don't need, and how it's gradually eating away at our freedom and our planet," he continues, "We're chained to stuff that isn't important at all, and it usually takes death for us to finally realise, when it's too late."

It takes constant focus to avoid being swamped in the mindless and artificial, which takes our attention away from what's happening right under our noses. I've heard people argue that there have always been distractions and today is really no different to any other era in history in those terms, but I have to disagree. When I think back to the 90s, when I saw Cyclefly perform live on several occasions, it seems like there was so much more time to think, people actually talked to each other so much more, and people did so much more. The internet was mostly too slow to be all that much of a distraction, and it wasn't anything like it is today because of the absence of social media. Anyone remember Friends Reunited? Seemed revolutionary at the time, but when compared with Facebook or even Myspace it seems so archaic.

"In the 90s a band would need to tour, record demos, find a manager etc. in order to get signed by a label, who would provide funding for tour support, distribution, marketing etc," recalls Christian, "Basically you had a team of people who would do the background work for you so that you could focus on the music and your live performance. If you were dedicated and willing to work hard your dream could become a reality. Everyone had the same chance."

As with many jobs, music is far more digitised than it used to be, and because it is so easily accessible the record labels have less of a budget to sign and promote bands, so it would be a lot harder for anyone wishing to make it their living nowadays. Declan and Christian found a way to make music their life, and both feel cautiously optimistic about the future. They see plenty wrong with modern life, but retain plenty of hope. For me this sums up how life is. I think we have a fair amount of common ground; suspicious of the internet, seeing gross imbalances in the world that don't need to be there and recognising the amazing power of nature to inspire. I've sometimes wondered over the years what they are doing nowadays, and now I have the answer I'm pleased I made the effort to find out.

CONNER'S STORY PART 9

"What's happening?" Mark tried to ask with urgency, but he could only croak the words because his voice was almost gone. You may have forgotten that he was ill himself the day Conner was taken to hospital, and now it was catching up with him. He had been trying to ignore the way he was feeling physically, but it was getting harder. Now he was anxious to hear what Emma had to say.

"The nurse said Conner's taken a turn for the worse in the night," she began, "The pressure in his brain has increased."

Emma had been calling the hospital each night before they went to bed, to check on him, then she would do the same every morning. After everything Dr Ross had said the night before they'd been on a high, but the gravity of the situation was hitting home once again.

"What if I've passed something on to him?" said Mark, his voice cracking with every word, "I'm making an emergency appointment with the doctor."

They now had to keep to normal visiting hours. For the first couple of days the nurses had allowed them to stay for as long as they wanted, but now they felt they had to start enforcing the rules. Going to the doctor, as well as providing reassurance when Mark was told he wasn't showing any signs of infection, used up plenty of time before 11.30am when visiting hours began.

They had taken Jayden to school that morning but on the

understanding that if he wasn't able to concentrate or got too upset he would be picked up. Most of Conner's old teachers were still at the school and they all asked after him. They wanted Jayden to try and get back to his normal routine as quickly as possible, but understood that it might be too soon.

Conner was more stable again when they arrived at the hospital, and showed further signs of activity throughout the day, kneeing Viv in the head at one point. Can many people ever have been so pleased to be kneed in the head? The bolt was removed from his brain, and he kept trying to take the tubes from his nose, leading to a splint being placed on his arm. He managed to remove this as well. He'd also opened his eyes a couple of times, seemingly in response to Emma saying his name, but it appeared that just the effort of opening his eyes exhausted him, as he would close them again straight away each time. He seemed to recognise Mark and Emma when he opened his eyes but he just couldn't stay awake long enough to confirm it.

The next day he was becoming quite a handful! As soon as Mark and Emma arrived he thrusted his arm out, pulling out his cannula and creating a mild bloodbath in the process. Mark, not being one who relishes the sight of blood, felt ill just looking at this, but he did his best to help by grabbing the cannula. They were asked to leave while the nurses sorted Conner out and cleaned up his bed. While out of the room they reflected on what they'd been told the night before. A nurse had told them to expect ups and downs, explaining that there may be days when Conner showed plenty of signs of improvement but then there could be a whole week during which he would show nothing further. They would have to try and be patient and focus on what Dr Ross had said, plus the signs of activity they'd seen. On what Conner had done, rather than what he hadn't done.

When they were allowed back into the room they showed Conner a note that Jayden had written for him. Obviously without him speaking they didn't know for sure but he did seem to be trying to read it. He had to wear a boxing glove to stop him from pulling his tubes out. Remembering how he'd kneed Viv in the head before, I'd have kept my distance if I'd been there, thinking maybe he'd catch me with a right hook when he had the gloves on! The nurse had said some of the things Conner had done could have been flukes, and they shouldn't build their hopes up too much at this stage. Mark wanted to take every positive he could, but he felt he had to be realistic at the same time, and so when Conner held his hand out he said it was probably a fluke, taking it and putting it back on his chest.

"Is it heck?!" Conner didn't actually say out loud, but he reached out his hand again straight away as if he was trying to tell them otherwise. Emma leant over to give him a kiss and he put his arm around her neck. He would do this several times, and was seemingly trying to kiss her on the cheek.

"Your lips are looking chapped, son. You need some lip balm" said Emma. Conner chewed the chapped skin and stuck his tongue out. It was like he was trying to talk to them without actually being able to speak. Mark took his phone out straight away and took a picture. The nurse had requested he didn't until Conner said he could, but this was his son. All the same he'd tried to be subtle, but he'd left the flash on and the whole ward seemed to be briefly illuminated. The nurse had definitely seen, but kept quiet.

On the way home that night they decided to tell Jayden everything that Conner had done during the day. Jayden laughed as they told him, and they were so happy to see him in good spirits during what must have been an incredibly difficult time. They still felt it was too early for him to visit the hospital, but that day was getting closer. It must have been so hard on Jayden, who had been used to having his parents around all of his life, and was very close to his big brother, but suddenly all three of them were barely there. Mark and Emma felt guilty about all the time they were spending away from Jayden, but they knew Conner needed them to be there.

There was further good news the next morning, although it was mixed news in a sense. Conner was considered to have made enough progress so he would no longer be on the Intensive Care ward. He would even bypass the High Dependency Unit.

"The normal procedure would be to move from ITU (Intensive Treatment Unit) to HDU (High Dependency Unit)," explains Mark, "But we were told that because of the progress he'd made he would be bypassing the HDU altogether. Now I wonder if there were beds available or not. Regardless, it was a positive sign and he was moved to the ward later that day."

Their minds were blown when Conner managed to pull his full arm splint off using his good leg. It was like he was trying to resist the fact he was so ill, and just wanted to be back to himself again. His young Geordie mind was tough as nails. Masonry nails I mean; not the generic ones you can get a big pack of for a quid in Poundland. Other pound shops are available. Any lingering doubts Mark and Emma had this day about whether Conner had any self-awareness were smashed into a million pieces when he pushed himself onto his front with one arm and then used that single arm to perform a press-up. He then turned his head right round to look them straight in the eye. All that was missing was a raised eyebrow and "Well?"

They told the nurse what had happened, and I am reminded of a scene from the cult classic TV show Lost at this stage. In the final episode when the characters are trapped in a subconscious world between this life and the afterlife, Jack Shephard has performed experimental surgery on Jon Locke, who had been paralysed below the waist. Jon is coming round far quicker than expected.

"Hello, Jon. You've just had major surgery," begins Jack.

"It worked" says Jon calmly.

"It went well," smiles Jack after a momentary pause. Jon interrupts him before he can continue.

"No, Dr Shephard. It worked. I can feel my legs."

"Jon, I really think it would be too soon for you to have regained sensation..." asserts Jack, but then he is struck speechless when Jon wiggles his toes as stirring music, composed by Michael Giacchino, begins. Much of the soundtrack of Lost epitomises hope for me, and Michael says it was one of his favourite ever projects. I was hoping to speak more to him about it, but being a very sought after composer he is very short on free time and so it wasn't possible before the book was done.

Anyway, when the nurse was told about what Conner had done, he basically said it couldn't have happened. He relied on his medical training and rational thought rather than listening to what Mark and Emma knew to be true about their own son. They didn't even have to be his parents to have observed what had happened and know what it could mean. The nurse just wouldn't accept it, but luckily Conner seemed determined that he should, so he repeated what he'd done three more times throughout the day. On the third occasion the nurse was there to see it with his own eyes. He was stunned into silence at first, but Michael Giacchino wasn't there to soundtrack the moment and so it wasn't long before he spoke.

"I've never seen anything like that before" he stammered.

At this stage it almost seemed like Dr Ross had been cautious in what he told them might be possible. Conner was annihilating expectations each day. The whole morning was packed with activity, and he even seemed to move towards Emma when she asked him for a kiss.

After this peak came a trough. In the afternoon he moved wards, which brought complications straight away because there were different nurses who hadn't been with him up until this point. They still had a lot to learn about him.

"The nurse in the new ward started to put his meds down his feeding tube with a load of water," says Mark, "This was despite him still being sick off his food all the time. We tried to warn him but he didn't listen, and sure enough Conner projectile vomited everywhere."

Emma was right next to his head at this point, but somehow he managed to miss her. Emma was feeling upset that he wasn't getting the 24 hour care anymore. They had taken this as a positive, because it meant he was no longer considered to be in immediate danger, but he was still a long way from being himself, and in their minds he was still incredibly poorly. He still needed a lot of care. Everything was still so raw. As the day went on it seemed like his body couldn't keep up with the progress his fighting spirit wanted him to make. He was still very ill, and his body was exhausted from battling it all the time. He was getting worn out, and it had a chilling effect.

After the amazing signs of progress he'd made, Conner had hit a wall. He hardly moved during the evening, and the looks of recognition had been replaced with a blank stare. It was almost like he was no longer there and he was staring straight through them. Like the signs they'd seen over the past few days were the last flickers of his personality leaving. Embers briefly igniting back into life before being extinguished. Now their worst fears about how he would be seemed to be confirmed. Mark tried once again to keep things positive, remembering that the doctors had said there may be periods of inactivity after he'd shown signs of improvement. He hadn't been unresponsive all day. Maybe tomorrow would be better. They agreed not to bring Jayden to the hospital yet, as they weren't sure how he would cope with Conner's blank stare.

Tomorrow. Tomorrow was another day. Conner needed them to be well rested so they could be there for him again, and Jayden needed to have some time with them as well. If they rested tonight they could be fully present tomorrow, whatever it may bring. Emma kissed him goodnight, and Mark saw his eyes flicker just momentarily. They didn't want to leave him after this, but they had to. He'd been fighting, and so would they. They'd never give up on him.

IN ONE SINGLE MOMENT

One night in April 2007, around 21 months before I had what I believe will be my last ever alcoholic drink, I was leaving Café Mamba bar in Taunton with my friend Bob. We chatted to some people on the way out, at least one of whom we might have antagonised in some way, because as we were walking towards another friend's flat we suddenly woke up on the ground. I had a gash above my right eyebrow which blood was pretty much pouring from, and Bob's front teeth were chipped. One walk to our friend's flat, one drive to hospital (by our friend's brother, who was sober I hasten to add), a few stitches for me, a bit of emergency dentistry work for Bob, a cooked breakfast in a café the next morning and we were basically fine. When I think back to that night I still don't remember what happened. I guess our attackers were cowards, because they must have just struck us out of nowhere. I also think what lucky, lucky men we were. How did I work that one out? Well not so long before this happened a seventeen-year-old lad had been in a similar situation just a mile away and he wasn't so lucky. He never turned 18. I was 26 when I was attacked, and I'm 37 now.

"Lloyd was attending a friend's 18th birthday party at Taunton Vale Sports Centre," begins his brother Adam Fouracre, telling the story to the best of his knowledge and understanding, "Him and his friends stayed on to help the parents tidy up, so left later than they intended. He was walking back to his friend's house with the others when their group met another group walking in the other direction. The other group had been drinking all day, were aggressive and had been kicked out of the pubs they were drinking in. Before leaving the Staplegrove Inn they'd smashed a window and were fighting amongst themselves as they left."

Further research into what happened that night, through a couple of blog posts Adam has written, would suggest that two of the other group had been involved in an argument and one of them was determined that he was going to get into a fight; it didn't matter who with. He had a troubled upbringing, with a violent stepfather, and was seething with rage. He had nobody to help steer him in a more positive direction, or at least didn't accept any help there may have been. He was so young, and he didn't know any different. Only 18 years old himself, he'd had more to deal with than many do by his age, but his anger combined with the alcohol made him volatile. The argument with his friend had been the tipping point, and he was out to hurt someone.

"One of Lloyd's friends shouted across to the other group, asking them if they'd been/were going to the party. One of the offending group (the guy previously spoken about) approached Lloyd's friend and punched him in the face. He was able to break free, and shouted to Lloyd's group to run. Everyone ran, while the guy who punched Lloyd's friend called his friends back."

This is one of several parts of the story that really gets to me. Lloyd and his friends wanted no part in any violence. They were trying to get away, but the other group, or at least some of them, were determined that somebody was going to get hurt. Lloyd Fouracre was the unlucky one.

"Lloyd was the slowest to run," explains Adam, "One of the

offenders picked up a wooden parking sign that had been discarded in the grass verge and used it to hit Lloyd over the head. He was unconscious with the first blow (we understand and hope.) He was then hit again with the sign. The court heard it described as like an axe being brought down on his head. He was kicked in the face 'like a footballer taking a penalty shot,' had his head stamped on, was kicked to the abdomen and torso, hit with a bike seat. He died in hospital from multiple brain haemorrhages and suffered multiple facial and skull fractures. There was no history between Lloyd's group and the offenders, which was confirmed by one of them who I met recently."

This wasn't a chance meeting between Adam and one of Lloyd's attackers. After Lloyd's death, which he describes as a pointless waste of life, Adam knew that it was going to be something that would always affect him, and so he figured he wanted to use Lloyd's story to help prevent the same thing from happening to others. To this end he set up the Stand Against Violence charity, which is still going to this day.

"I wanted to make Lloyd's death mean something, and to create a bit of a legacy and memory for him," says Adam, "I also didn't want other families and friends to go through similar, or other young people to continue to lose their lives to mindless violence."

Stand Against Violence connect with around 18,000 young people each year from Birmingham, Cornwall and many places in between. They run educational workshops through schools, prisons, youth offending and other places where young people who are at risk of finding themselves in similar situations can find out what the consequences may be. It's clear from the extreme level of violence on display that night that Lloyd's attackers meant to harm him, but I don't believe their intention that day was to kill someone. Things just went way too far, and they learnt the hard way how fragile life is. They ended a young man's life, and the two main attackers were charged with murder. One has recently been released from prison after serving twelve years, the other is due to be released in a couple of years' time. They will have a second chance at life, whereas Lloyd's life ended before their prison sentences had even begun. So how do Stand Against Violence try to help young people not to make the same catastrophic mistakes?

"We use Lloyd's story and other real life examples to educate, and the workshops focus on empathy-based exercises to create an emotional connection," explains Adam, "We use the same approach to address bullying, alcohol and substance use and also work with partners to do personal safety and first aid. Our own evaluations show an 84% attitude change among the young people we teach, and 96% state that they are against violence following our delivery. Our aim for the future is to become a sustainable charity that can grow and reach as many young people as we can. We want to deliver consistently to each new generation, with the hope that this will eventually create a generational change within our society."

It's clear that the work Adam and his charity are doing is really connecting with young people. One thing startles me, which is the 4% who don't state they are against violence after attending one of the workshops. I wonder if these are people who would argue that in some extreme cases violence can be justified for self-defence, or if they are people who could watch the reconstruction of what happened to Lloyd that is shown in the workshops and still think violence is acceptable. I really hope it's not the latter.

What happened to Lloyd Fouracre, it goes without saying, should not happen to any young man. One of the things that impressed me most about Adam is that he met with one of Lloyd's attackers on two separate occasions, has tried to understand what happened from his side, and without perhaps being able to forgive him for ending his brother's life, has tried to urge him to make the most of his second chance. Jay, the man in question, is now in his early thirties. He has just recently been released from prison and has started to work as a personal trainer. Adam believes he is truly sorry for what happened. Jay feels responsible despite not being the one who struck the blows with the wooden sign, as it was he who first punched one of Lloyd's friends and then called his friends back when they ran. He has expressed how it was his intention to get into a fight that night. He didn't mean to kill anyone though, and was truly shocked when he found out Lloyd was dead. Good further reading to help understand why young lads become the way Jay did is the novel 'Knifer', by former prisoner officer Ronnie Thompson. It's based on real life events from a number of different young people he met in prison, and tells the story of how a young lad has a troubled upbringing and falls in with a crowd who are violent and apathetic. After a disagreement with one of his friends he accidentally kills him in a fight and goes to prison, slowly rehabilitating over the years but struggling to let go of his old life completely. I'm not sure if Jay is feeling similar pressures, if there's anything of the angry young man he was left in his current personality. Adam seems to think he has moved forward.

"Jay has worked hard to rehabilitate," urges Adam, "He seems to be a typical example of someone who has made a catastrophic mistake and a poor decision. In this instance it resulted in the death of my brother, and has destroyed his life. When I met Jay the first time, when he was still in prison, he explained to me how he felt he doesn't deserve to be happy or to have any success in life because of what he did. I want him to live a meaningful life, because if he didn't then what would the work I've been doing all be about? Andrew (the other main attacker) still maintains his defence from the trial that he was too drunk to recall what happened. I don't believe this, but there we go."

Alcohol can impair the memory, but to forget such an extreme act of violence completely? If someone had been drunk enough to forget everything, surely they wouldn't have the co-ordination to chase after someone else and strike them over the head with a wooden sign. That's the way I see it as well, but until he admits anything different to what he's already claimed then we can never truly know. It's not particularly helpful to speculate too much on this, but if Jay makes a success of his second chance and can help others to not make the same mistake he did then some good can come of this truly awful situation. That's why Adam wanted to meet Jay, and was pleased that he agreed to it. Obviously he had a lot of anxiety surrounding the meeting, and explained how when his dad called him the night before to check if he was Ok he cried uncontrollably. He was meeting the man who had jointly caused his brother injuries that would end his life, but was able to look beyond this one tragic and always regrettable incident to see Jay as a man who would always be haunted by what had happened too, albeit in a different way.

The first time they met was in the prison chapel. Jay was nervous about the meeting, as you may well imagine, and although obviously what he did cannot be excused, it must have taken a huge amount of bravery to come face to face with the brother of the lad whose death he'd played a significant role in causing. Jay fully explained to Adam what he'd done, the events that preceded the incident and the aftermath. Adam listened, and got the answers he'd been seeking. He didn't feel he could say he forgave Jay for what he did, but he was able to recognise that the man sitting in front of him was different to the lad he'd seen in court all those years ago.

Adam met Jay again after he was released, and even gave him a hug before he left, telling him "Have a good life." It may be a step too far for them to become close friends, but they do seem to have a mutual respect, and surely that's a better outcome than for them to be burning with hatred. Adam has not met Andrew, and doesn't particularly want to unless he is willing to admit responsibility for what he did. Which one of the two is more to blame for what happened is neither here nor there. The fact is that somebody died, and by meeting one of the men responsible Adam has been better able to manage his feelings surrounding what happened.

As with all charities, Stand Against Violence rely on funding to survive, and this is a constant challenge. Being a former PR & fundraising co-ordinator for a mental health charity, I know first-hand how hard it is. There are so many excellent causes and nobody can support each and every one of them at the same time. Therefore Adam needs to reach people who have a personal connection with his cause and are in a position to help.

"Funding is always a challenge," admits Adam, "We have a mix of grants, internet fundraising and corporate support. We also get a few donations and generate a small income from delivering talks and workshops."

As with so many things, the future of Stand Against Violence is dependent on being able to continue to secure funding. Adam remains hopeful that they will be able to expand on the excellent work they've already done.

"My hope is that we have a breakthrough with funding or are

able to launch our corporate training programme to generate enough income to sustain ourselves and get our message, unhindered by finance, to every young person. Also to have our work recognised by the powers that be and to have it backed and put into all educational organisations to help us create that generational change."

Sadly, what happened to Lloyd is not an isolated incident. Some of the highest profile cases other than Lloyd's are those of Stephen Lawrence and Sophie Lancaster. To think that anyone can attack another person so viciously, and in such an uncontrolled manner, that it will end their life, doesn't bear thinking about. People like Adam have no choice but to think about it every day though, because in one single moment his whole life was turned upside down. We should not forget the potential for history repeating itself, and the work of Stand Against Violence should be able to not just continue but become a staple part of education for young people nationwide, and even around the world.

As I wrote this chapter I wondered about the impact of violent films, games and TV shows on young people. There seemed to be a trend in the last decade of films that depicted extreme violence by groups of young people. Kidulthood and Adulthood were about UK gang culture, and although the overall message was similar to that which Adam is trying to put across, there were a number of graphic scenes of violence where youths would kick each other unconscious, and even one in which a youth died after being hit with a baseball bat. I wondered if the scenes went some way towards glorifying violence. Similarly, there were a bunch of football hooligan films, including Green Street and Football Factory, which again had a sombre message of where this kind of violence can lead, but also featured a lot of graphic scenes. I wondered if the audience would remember these images more than the overall message. I asked Adam what his take on it was.

"There's very limited evidence to support the theory that violent films and games increase societal violence. However, there is some longitudinal evidence to suggest that long-term repeated exposure to programmes depicting violence cannot only normalise it but skew peoples' perception of the world."

I can definitely see his point. An old friend's mum who worked in a local doctors' surgery told us about a nurse over from Kenya whose family had been terrified for her to come to the UK because of what they'd seen on the news, thinking England was some kind of war zone. That's for starters, but the theory is more that if young people are portrayed in the media as being mostly violent, disrespectful thugs then that's the general attitude people will have towards them, which will fan the flames. Also, if a young person with a troubled mind sees nothing but violence and negativity on TV they might be influenced over time by all the darkness of these images.

"Despite the lack of evidence I do feel that the media in general, from the news producers to the Hollywood film makers, have a responsibility to ensure well-balanced stories from negative to positive to ensure a balanced perception of the world. Ultimately, a normal person with a healthy childhood will generally appreciate a fictional film for what it is but someone who may have a difficult childhood or may be more vulnerable might not be so balanced and so is more likely to skew the boundaries of fiction and non-fiction."

Balance is key, as is understanding. I say in the following chapter that behind everyone focused on their next fix is all that happened to make them that way. Behind every violent youth is all that happened to make them that way too. What Stand Against Violence are trying to do is show both these people and their potential victims how to stay safe. Many violent young men and women have a difficult past lacking in warmth, empathy or guidance. Of course this doesn't excuse the violence, but if a young person is heading down this path they need to be made aware of the possible consequences of their actions, and for someone to believe in their potential for change is a massive help. One of Lloyd's attackers has taken responsibility for what happened and continues to put a lot of effort into moving forward. He described himself as being like a ticking timebomb when he was 18, full of anger at the world. With negative influences, the lack of a mentor and too much alcohol he ultimately became involved in a moment that would tear not just his own life apart but a number of others. If troubled young men are demonised and shunned then what happened that night remains nothing but a pointless waste of life. If they are educated and shown that there is another way, then maybe there is hope for them to change before another tragedy occurs. Maybe that generational change Adam and his organisation are trying to bring about can one day become a reality.

SELF-MEDICATION IN THE FACE OF REJECTION

"I was just leaning forward one morning to grab me baccy and 'pop'; my femoral artery had burst. Blood was hitting the wall and the ceiling. Every time me heart beat it was shooting out metres up in the air."

Rewind around 24 years and a young Danny McCormack, bass player in popular Geordie rock band The Wildhearts, was in a doctor's surgery trying to get help for the mental health issues that had plagued him for over a year. After a bad LSD trip he'd never truly come down from he'd been experiencing psychosis, mood swings and anxiety. He knew there was something wrong, but couldn't diagnose it by himself and so he went to see the doctor in the hope of help and understanding.

"I could see it in his eyes," Danny recalls, "He just thought 'druggie' – get him out of here. Next!"

In a scene that is all too familiar, Danny was just given some anti-depressants without a single question about the circumstances that had led to this point, and sent on his way. The doctor couldn't see past this troubled young man's drug use, and refused to see him as a complex human being who desperately needed help. People take drugs for a variety of reasons – escapism, curiosity, peer pressure, despair. Nobody sits down with a clear head and comes to the conclusion, after making spider diagrams and lists of bullet points, that becoming a drug addict is the best way forward. However, so many still hold the view that people who take drugs deserve no sympathy and have given up their right to be a respected member of society. Predictably, the anti-depressants did nothing for Danny, and the psychosis he'd been haunted by kept raging on, so he decided to self-medicate. This is when his heroin addiction began.

"Sounds strange that it took one drug to repair the damage done by another drug," says Danny, "But heroin was what made me feel like Danny again. It was the only thing that let us think clearly and balanced everything out. I couldn't get any other help, and I was going out of my mind, so of course I was gonna keep doing it."

This wasn't the first time he'd tried heroin. Growing up in South Shields, Danny had tried boxing and football in his youth and shown some promise in both, but music was the one thing that stuck. Inspired by the punk scene, his band Energetic Krusher signed a deal with the Vinyl Solution label when he was just 16 or 17. At such a formative time in his life, a desire for experimentation and escapism meant that he would naturally gravitate towards the drugs that came his way through the company he kept.

"We'd go down to the caves at Marsden Rock and take magic mushrooms," he laughs, "We'd watch the tide come in and go out, light a fire and play Anti-Nowhere League on a ghetto blaster. I have to be honest, at the time it was bloody brilliant."

Many will have done similar in their late teens, but for many this is just a phase, and no lasting damage is done. In a touring rock band with a reputation for intoxication, temptation will never be far away. Danny first tried heroin after he'd joined The Wildhearts aged 19 and they were supporting the Manic Street Preachers.

"It felt bloody lovely," he admits, "If it didn't feel good nobody would do it, would they?"

Many things that feel good are bad for us. The number of people who will rebuke those who take drugs whilst pouring gallons of alcohol down their necks or tucking into their fourth greasy kebab of the week? Whether you can't stop eating chocolate, smoking cigarettes, chasing meaningless sexual encounters, playing computer games or taking heroin you're seeking something to compensate for what's missing. "I play computer games all day because I enjoy it. What's wrong with that?" Someone might say. So you're absorbed in that screen because it feels pleasant to you and it offers escapism from your problems? That's what heroin did for Danny and so many others. Yes, it's dangerous, but so can all the other things be that I mentioned. Sugar can cause health problems, as can smoking, casual sex can lead to STDs amongst other things, staring at a screen all day? Well that's a relatively new phenomenon and so research is limited, but there seems to have been a massive increase in depression and anxiety since the digital revolution kicked in – is this a coincidence? This is most definitely not a suggestion to take heroin to escape your problems; this whole story should act as a deterrent, but it should also offer understanding of why people fall into the trap.

"My life was all about highs and lows for years," Danny continues, "When we signed our first record deal we got £10,000 each. I'd never seen that much money before. I bought a gigantic block of hash and a bass guitar straight away."

Danny explained that he never got rich being in the band, but he definitely got by.

"You can't spend your money. People give you free drinks, free drugs, free everything. You can save the money you make for what you really need."

The rock 'n' roll lifestyle seems glamorous to so many, but

it costs some people their lives. Danny could easily have been one of them.

"It was a crazy life," he recalls now, "I would be on Top of the Pops one minute and then the next I'd be hanging out with my homeless mates in King's Cross shooting up heroin. I was their best mate because I'd bring them clothes, food... and drugs of course. Sadly a lot of them have died since because they weren't as lucky as me."

His addiction went on for years, and at times he would get clean for a while but then fall back into the cycle as soon as he put himself in the way of temptation. He was kicked out of the Wildhearts on a couple of occasions, the unreliability that went hand in hand with heroin addiction causing tension with singer, and one of his closest friends, Ginger. Danny recalls: -

"I'd be going round the dealer's place and inside my head I'd be saying 'Don't do it! Don't do it!' but there'd be a louder internal voice saying 'Do it. You'll feel great."

Despite the fraught times, Danny loved being in the band. Music, rather than drugs, was his first love. He has extremely fond memories of touring around Europe with AC/DC, who he describes as being very down to earth.

"They've got nothing to prove, so they're just really nice guys," he explains, "Touring with them was like a dream come true for a lad from South Shields. We supported Guns 'n' Roses once as well, and I got £10,000 for that gig. Not bad for 40 minutes' work! Slash was a great guy too."

Apart from being in The Wildhearts, Danny formed his own band The Yo-Yos, who signed with the Sub Pop label in America, previously home to infamous grunge bands Nirvana and Soundgarden. They toured extensively around the USA, playing in 42 states over 5 months. He describes this as a wonderful time as well, and it's clear from talking to him that he genuinely loves playing music. This is why he wanted to be in a band. The drugs were an unfortunate by-product of this lifestyle.

Living the dream definitely came at a price, and earning the kind of money he did now and again meant he was considered a good customer by his dealer, who would deliver to him wherever he was, and let him pay when he had the money, making it all too easy to stray back onto this path after getting clean. When he was on heroin, life would just be about his next score. It became like a full-time job, and was all he really cared about when he was high. He was lucky that his status afforded him liberties that others wouldn't have.

"People get their faces cut because they owe £20," he sighs, "I got into loads of debt when I was an addict, don't know how I survived really, but my dealer knew I was good for it and so he'd let me off."

Years would pass and the cycle would continue, but then one morning three years ago was the incident first described in this chapter.

"It's frightening thinking of it now," he admits, "But at the time I was pretty calm. I just thought 'right, I'm bleeding' and my girlfriend was there. She knew what to do."

Blood was shooting out of his femoral artery at a horrifying rate, and his girlfriend put a credit card over the wound as she called an ambulance. Ironically, the state of his veins from his years of injecting heroin meant the aneurysm he had suffered led to his artery bursting outwards through his skin. He was losing a lot of blood, and if nothing had been done he would have bled out and died within minutes, but if he hadn't taken heroin all those years it's most probable that he would have bled internally and died almost straight away.

"Man, I was so lucky. There was an ambulance just four

minutes away. They got to me really quickly and rushed me to hospital. What my girlfriend had done to stem the flow of blood saved me life too."

The extent of his heroin addiction meant that to give him an anaesthetic the doctors had to turn him upside down on the operating table and inject into his jugular.

"It was pretty embarrassing, mate," he laughs, "I'd run out of veins to shoot up into over the years, so I'd had to shoot up into my neck before, and even a place I won't mention. They were struggling to find a vein and I had to explain to them it was all because of drugs. I didn't feel proud. I knew it was pretty serious though what I was going through, and I remember as I went under I was thinking 'Fight, Danny. Fight!'"

This was just the beginning of his ordeal, but he showed the same fighting spirit a number of my family, also Geordies, have in fighting their own ailments. When he woke the doctors explained that they'd have to amputate his leg below the knee. They'd had to cut off the flow of blood to his leg to stop an infection from spreading, and had inserted a stent to do a bypass, but his toes had gone black and three of them had fallen off. They believed they could save his life, but they couldn't save his leg.

"That's what it took to finally break the cycle," he says, "After the operation when I was on one leg I just thought 'That's it.' I haven't injected for over two years now."

He was recovering in hospital for five months, putting a lot of weight on due to his inactivity. After he'd got out and started to ease back into his life the overwhelming feeling was not of sorrow for what he'd lost, but of joy for what he'd gained. He lives with his girlfriend, and is a step-dad to her three children, who are 26, 25 and 21. One is a carer, one works in an electronics shop and the other in a café. Danny has talked to all of them about his addictions, has been honest and is delighted that none of them have followed the same path, as many of his friends have over the years.

"Man, that's where I get my hope from. Striving to be a better person, making sure the kids are alright and that my girlfriend's alright. Every day I stay off heroin gives me hope too. You have to take it one day at a time, and then when you do that the weeks soon stack up, then months. I'm not gonna lie, I still have a smoke now and then. I still get high once in a while, but I'm not doing heroin any more. I don't drink at home, I won't do any drugs at home. It's under control."

Danny has a new band, The Main Grains, and is back in the Wildhearts, having made up with Ginger again. He has a prosthetic leg after the horrors of his hospitalisation, but…. here I find myself writing 'has taken it all in his stride' and definitely didn't intend that pun. Having talked to Danny I can imagine him taking that in good humour. I also told him on the phone how much he sounds like my Uncle Chris. This is the point. I remember reading about Danny McCormack in magazines twenty years ago, about his heroin addiction and his rock 'n' roll antics, and it was easy to forget that he wasn't some character who was there for peoples' entertainment but is a lad from South Shields, just like my dad and my uncle. Unlike them, he ended up addicted to heroin. This happened because he was ill and couldn't get help. He has now been diagnosed as bi-polar, and has found an anti-psychotic medication that keeps him feeling balanced.

"I've never looked back since then," he seems very pleased to say, "For years I'd have these massive highs and lows, I called my band the Yo-Yos of course, and all that time there was a reason for it. Things could have been so different if I'd known sooner."

SELF-MEDICATION IN THE FACE OF REJECTION

Who knows what might have been had the first doctor he saw taken the time to work out what was truly wrong and offered further pathways to help rather than rushing him out of the door because he thought he didn't deserve the time of day. Danny is happy with his life now though, and seems to be heading in the right direction. Like many I have spoken to he describes the internet as being 'brilliant', but has his qualms with it also.

"Man, it's taken away your privacy," he sighs, "The Wildhearts tours would have been very different back in the day if they'd happened now. It was ridiculous what went on, but nowadays there would be pictures and videos all over the internet within minutes. Man, you can't even fart nowadays without it being on social media."

I get the feeling Danny sees the whole thing as being humorous rather than sinister though.

"I'm a sociable guy. Some people in bands are like 'I'm an artist, I want to be alone' but I'm not like that. I love it when people come and talk to us who recognise us. Mind you, there's one thing I hate about the internet and that's cyber-bullying."

For the first time in the whole conversation his cheerful mood seems to break.

"I hate bullies, man," he scowls, "I think it's maybe worse on the internet too 'cause it sticks with you. You can't see the person who's doing the bullying so it's more of a psychological thing. It's horrible."

Anyone who looks at someone like Danny and thinks 'junkie', just know that he wants nothing more in life than to look after his family, the thought of people being bullied was the one thing that seemed to make him angry in the whole 40 minutes I spoke to him, and he was seeking help for his problems before his addiction even became a thing but was turned away by someone who should have treated him with understanding. You might say he could have gone for help elsewhere, but when you're already in a fragile state of mind being rejected can have huge implications. A reminder as always that you never know what someone is going through, and just because someone has made bad decisions doesn't mean they don't deserve your help and understanding. Danny's on top of his addiction nowadays, and is looking forward to touring with The Main Grains and The Wildhearts. He could so easily have not been here to talk to me for this chapter, and to give hope to others who have been in his position. People might disappoint you sometimes but they need understanding, because inside every person out there looking for their next score is all that happened to take them there.

At the time of finishing the book, Danny has just begun recording the new Wildhearts album and has enthused about the songs a lot. With everything that's happened since the last one they have sure had a whole heap of experience to inspire the writing, and with the original line-up back together there's going to be a lot of excitement, which will no doubt come across in the recordings. Danny has had some great personal success too, in that he's been able to stand and to walk more without the aid of his crutches in recent times. When I read this chapter back to him he laughed "It sounds like a train wreck doesn't it?!!" but the overriding feeling for me is about survival against the odds, and how he's been through a lot in life but has managed to keep going, and things are possibly better now than they've ever been.

CONNER'S STORY PART 10

What was behind those eyes? Conner now just stared blankly. Mark and Emma had felt the closest they could to euphoria in the circumstances when the nurse had seen Conner do a press-up before turning round to look at them. Now they just didn't know what to feel. The fight seemed to have faded from him, and their feeling of helplessness was exacerbated by the song 'Faded', which never seemed to be off the radio. The haunting refrain of "Where are you now?" burrowed into their heads; harrowingly appropriate in the moment. It had been one of Conner's favourite songs, and it was as if the track had been a startling prediction of his future. Mark and Emma couldn't hear the song without tears falling, and they still find it hard to listen to now. Emma says it gets her every time, and takes her right back to the hospital. Conner's favourite Ellie Goulding song seemed to always be playing too, but he would just stare into space. He'd show nothing upon hearing these songs he'd enjoyed listening to just a couple of weeks before. This was one of the hardest things of all. He was seventeen, and should be doing the things he enjoyed. Now it seemed he wasn't able to enjoy anything. Would he ever again?

It was a long day. The clock seemed to tick in slow motion, echoing through the gaps in sound when a song on the radio would finish and the DJ was about to speak. There were still glimmers of hope, but nothing like the flurry of activity from 24 hours previously. At one point during the day Conner reached up and lightly felt the tube in his nose. He hadn't given up completely. He didn't want the tube to be there. It didn't feel quite right. Another time he lifted his hand and put his thumb up, but he did this without a flicker of emotion on his face, and so they didn't think it meant anything.

As the day wore on they felt flat, and very tired. This was when two of Conner's friends, Caitlin and Olivia, came to visit. Would they be able to cope with seeing him like this?

"Are you tired?" said Caitlin as soon as she saw him. Her voice had the effect of a defibrillator, jolting him out of his trance. He sat up and looked right at her, raising his hand and putting his thumb up again. Maybe it hadn't been for nothing before. Had he been trying to tell them he was Ok? Hearing a familiar voice that he'd not heard in a while seemed to give him a push. The effort seemed to exhaust him again though, because he was fast asleep when they left him that evening. Again there had been something to keep their optimism in place. That's what mattered. Because Conner was lying down, Mark could see the wound on his head properly, and he took a photo. There were 30 staples forming a 'C' on the top of his head. 'C' for Conner.

The next day he did a lot more staring into space, but again there were moments when he showed he was still in there somewhere. He had to have his boxing gloves on whenever nobody was there to keep an eye on him because during the night he'd managed to remove his feeding tube. Maybe in his head he was thinking he could murder a burger and chips, and what was this rubbish they were giving him? He was moving his right arm more, and when staring into space he was making a face like he was trying to get rid of an itch by moving his mouth and nose. Again his eyes shot open just as they were about to leave, which was becoming a real struggle. Why couldn't he have done this sooner?

Another day went by and he had his first speech therapy session. The news wasn't what they wanted to hear. Conner wasn't able to talk, and the therapist considered him to still be a long way off this, or eating independently. In fact he wasn't following a single command. Not unusual for a teenager you might think, but Mark and Emma were struggling to stay upbeat about things. They'd felt like he was making progress, but the speech therapist's findings seemed to suggest he was still right on the first rung of the ladder. However, earlier that day his staples had been removed, along with the stitch from where the bolt in his brain had been. There was a little bleeding but nothing too significant. The physio team had visited him that morning and had sat him in a chair for an hour. Something didn't look quite right.

"He looks like he's in a prison outfit," sighed Emma, "It's time he wore his own clothes."

When he was back in his bed she thought back to when his friends had visited.

"He's hardly moved his head since Caitlin and Olivia were here," she said to Mark. Mark's mouth fell open and he pointed at Conner, who was moving his head. Later on he started to adjust his own pillows and blanket to make himself more comfortable.

When they took a step back and thought about all that had happened there were plenty of reasons to take heart. There were more complications appearing all the time though.

"He started to develop a rash every time he woke up," remembers Mark, "They said this was probably a stress rash, and it seemed to go again as quickly as it came, but it was distressing seeing it appear all over him the first time. It was like he was aware we were there and he was getting very stressed as he couldn't talk or do much and then his eyes would glaze over and it would go. Was very strange to see."

Conner also developed a twitch in his left hand, which got worse as the day went on. He'd had an EEG scan too, because there was concern that the faces he kept pulling might actually be down to seizures. This scan ruled this out, to everyones' relief. Further reaching consequences were beginning to occur as well though, as Jayden's teachers had said he wasn't himself at school. They were still cautious about letting Jayden visit the hospital because they knew Conner was so different to how he had known him. They found the staring hard enough to cope with, so were scared it would really unsettle Jayden. They made sure they explained everything to him though, as they felt he might hear rumours at school and believe them. If he was kept fully in the loop he'd know what to believe. They did show him pictures of Conner, asking first if he was ready to see them, and he seemed to deal with it Ok.

It was time to bring in the big guns again. Caitlin and Olivia had inspired a reaction in Conner before, so they returned, and again he responded. This time he was stroking Caitlin's hair and seemed to try to cuddle her. He managed to sit in the physio's chair for around four hours too. Completely on a roll at this stage, he confounded the expectations of the speech therapist the next day by eating three quarters of a pot of yoghurt. Not sure what was wrong with the other quarter, but just a few days after hearing he was weeks away from eating real food that's exactly what he'd done. He still wouldn't do anything else the speech therapist told him to, but the devouring of the yoghurt softened this blow. His head did swell during the day, which of course worried Mark and Emma. The doctors didn't seem too concerned, but said they'd do a precautionary CT scan. When they examined his head he kept moving around, which surprised them. A couple of the nurses said they'd come into the room just to look at him while he was resting because they loved his eyelashes.

"Even in a virtual comatose state he still gets the girls" laughs Mark.

Caitlyn and Olivia both remember well when they found out what had happened to Conner. Being so young themselves, they didn't realise the gravity of the situation straight away.

"I remember first reading our little group chat we had, and one of our friends had said Conner was in hospital," says Olivia, "Me and Caitlin just assumed it wasn't anything serious and that he'd been poorly, then Emma and Viv rang Caitlin's mam to explain what had happened and we couldn't believe it. We just sat for the whole night in her room crying."

It must have been so much for them to take in. There were absolutely no warnings for what would happen to Conner, and to suddenly hear how ill he truly was came as a complete shock to them both.

"I couldn't get my head round it until I'd actually seen him," says Caitlin, "So I got to go up to the RVI to visit him when he was in the Intensive Care Unit. I still remember walking in, and everything hit me then how serious it all was. I couldn't believe it."

Caitlin explained everything to Olivia before she visited for the first time, so she wasn't shocked when she went herself. At this stage he was unresponsive, and it was truly horrible for them to see their best friend like this but they were both determined to keep visiting.

"I remember him stroking my hair when we came to visit another time," continues Caitlin, "It was amazing, because then I could tell he was recognising me."

"Conner had been very unresponsive the first day when

they came to visit together," adds Mark, "And it was like someone switched a light on when he heard Caitlin's voice. He was suddenly very aware of us and he was looking for Caitlin. She was on his right side, so it makes sense now why he was struggling to see her."

Over the next few days his activity increased. His boxing gloves had to go back on again because he was scratching the wounds on his head so hard that scabs fell from them like autumn leaves in a gale. Although the doctor had to stop him from scratching he said it was a good sign because itchy wounds mean the healing process is beginning, and Conner wanted to do something about it.

Two weeks to the day from the start of the whole nightmare, Paul was telling Conner jokes whilst walking around his bed. He wasn't laughing. Not sure if this was because of the quality of the jokes or because he just couldn't, but his eyes followed his uncle around. Emma was wearing a necklace Conner had bought her, and he held it in his hand at one point, feeling the 'E' initial as if he remembered he'd seen it before. Further good news was that he'd been lifting his arms to help the nurses put his clothes on, and that they'd asked him to lift his arm if he wanted more yoghurt, which was still the only thing he could eat, and his arm had been going up a lot.

When Mark was writing a message on his phone the evening before, Conner sat bolt upright and gave him a look as if to say "Put that down while you're here to see me." When Mark put the phone down Conner laid back down on his bed.

"He's still in there isn't he?" Mark said to Emma on the way home.

"Aye. But he can't tell us yet. Do you think he will?"

"He will when he's ready. Talking of which, do you reckon Jayden's ready to see him now?"

They agreed that he was, so two weeks after he'd last seen his brother he finally looked upon him again. It was the longest they'd ever been apart.

"Do you want to give him a kiss?" asked Mark.

Jayden couldn't reach Conner on the bed so Mark lifted him, and then the most incredible thing happened. A moment none of them will ever forget. Jayden slipped and made an involuntary squealing noise, then Conner gave half a smile and laughed. Maybe Paul does need to work on his jokes after all. All joking aside though, this was the first real emotion Conner had shown since he'd woken up. He was coming back to them.

'YOU DON'T GET OLD IF YOU KEEP MOVING'

"Something is better than nothing."

These five words, spoken by one teenager to another in a classroom in South-West England way back in the mid '90s were never intended to be profound. They were simply designed to take the edge off my geography teacher's disappointment that I hadn't done my homework. We'd been asked to write some facts about New York; I hadn't written any but my friend Dan suggested it wasn't too late to write down everything I already knew about 'The Big Apple'…. Oh! There's something. As it happens, my geography teacher was probably not too impressed by my handful of generic New York facts, but Dan made a point that can be applied to so many situations in life and can be a great starting point for moving in the right direction. One of the main ones is exercise, and health in general.

One of the harsh truths about exercise is that you get out what you put in. If you want to be super fit it doesn't happen overnight, and once you get there you have to maintain it. It's a constant process, just like most things. If you slip up it doesn't mean you have to stop altogether, and if you don't have time to stay super fit it doesn't mean you shouldn't still do what you can. The internet is both a plus and a minus in that there are absolute mountains of resources to inspire and plan your fitness goals but it's easy to just spend all your time planning and researching, whereby if you didn't have the internet you might actually get on and do it. This has been true for me at times for sure. It's no coincidence that some of the fittest people in the world are prisoners. When you spend most of your day in a tiny confined space, one of the best ways to pass the time is to exercise. Without vast expanses of nature to explore you have to be pretty inventive about the way you exercise, but some of the most effective ones are those you can do using no equipment and your own bodyweight in a very small space. Planks, push-ups, star jumps and all of that stuff comprise the bulk of the workout plans of 'The body coach' Joe Wicks, prisoner Charles Bronson (I think still the world record holder for the most press-ups in a minute) and a whole host of other super-fit individuals. If you don't get on with any of those exercises there are so many options – yoga, tai-chi, weights, dancing, pilates, a whole range of sports... the list is pretty much never ending. Of course there are factors that get in the way of exercise, such as injury, illness, insult and old age. Does age have to be such a barrier though?

If you're over 70 it's very unlikely you'll be able to run as fast as you could when you were under 30, but that doesn't mean you should stop being active. Modern life is becoming more and more geared towards inactivity. Machines are slowly being programmed to do just about everything for us. Despite the importance of health and fitness being pushed in a big way, the general direction of society is moving away from what promotes good health and fitness the most, i.e. doing what our bodies are designed for. We don't need machines and technology to do what we are perfectly capable of doing ourselves. Everything is aimed at speed and convenience, which may seem wonderful in the short term, but in the long term is having a detrimental effect. Patience is something it's becoming harder to have, because we live in a culture of instant gratification and are bombarded with information. I could write a vast chapter on this topic alone, but I'll just let you think it all over because I'm sure it's something you may have considered already. I'm not saying anything revolutionary here. The way I currently live my life doesn't reflect the way I know I should, so it would be hypocritical of me to tell you what to do about it. Instead let's explore some stories of what's possible when you stay active, as well as what can stand in the way.

The title of this chapter is a quote from Karl Meltzer, who has always lived an active life and as a result is still able to do pretty much all he could as a much younger man. His son, Karl Meltzer, is pretty active himself, having been inspired by Karl Meltzer to love the outdoors. Keeping up? Ok, so Karl Meltzer senior is in his mid-seventies, still runs, is always working on some building project or other and is generally living a full and active life. He may be a little slower than he used to be but he doesn't say he's too old for running because he can still do it. He can still do it because he's looked after himself and stayed active. His son, Karl Meltzer, has won more 100 mile trail races than anyone else ever, with at least one win over each of the last eighteen years. He's 50 now and is still winning a few. He loves running as much now as when he first discovered it as a child, having tagged along with his dad. The Meltzers may be a fairly extreme example, but if you apply the 'something is better than nothing' logic and just make sure you're active in any way you can be every day you'll invariably find that you can do more in general for longer, as long as you retain your health of course. Even if you don't, anything you can do will still make a difference. There are so many factors, but if you look at the attributes believed to make Kenyans the best marathon runners, most of them are related to living a natural and nonsedentary lifestyle.

Several years back I spoke to a selection of national marathon record holders from mostly obscure nations for a book project I was working on at the time. The book didn't take off, but some of the stories really stayed with me. Two of the main ones related to athletes who have got older but didn't stop moving, and are still competing at a high level within their age categories. Both are from tiny European nations. Justin Gloden, of Luxembourg, became a professional runner aged 57, competing in veteran athletics championships. In the male 60+ category at the European Masters in 2014 he won a gold medal for 10,000 metres on the track. He runs in around fifteen competitions per year, and spent seven months injured with a fissured tendon in his foot before training for twelve weeks to run in the Masters World Championships in Malaga. He finished 8th out of 44 runners, which he says didn't satisfy his ambitions but wasn't bad considering all the time he was injured. He's running pain-free again now.

"I've always tried to live a healthy life," he explains, "This includes no smoking, no drugs, not many alcoholic drinks, workouts, enough sleep... all of this makes me hope to get older in good shape with a strong mind. Always staying active is important to me, and this has helped me to keep my aim for 'lifelong running' alive."

His running career overall didn't start when he was 57, as his professional running career did. In fact he has been the national record holder over many distances, including the marathon, for most of his adult life. He ran 2:14:03 at Frankfurt Marathon in 1985, and remembers it very well.

"It was my first marathon," he recalls, "From around the 15k mark I was running alone until the finish line. I was 4th place of around 8,000 finishers. Herbert Steffny of Germany won in

2:12:12. At one stage I was hopeful of finishing in 3rd but a muscle cramp at around 40k made me stop a few times and I had to run my first marathon more defensively."

His PE teachers saw his talent for running, but he began his sporting career as a footballer. He played for the Luxembourg national team on one occasion in 1976, losing 1-0 to Germany. After attending New York City Marathon as a journalist with some runners from his country, and meeting several famous runners there, including Ron Hill, he decided that he would one day run one himself. His national record still stands more than 30 years after he set it.

"It's a really great feeling," he says, "The record is often compared to other performances of national marathoners. I think it may have helped the 'running boom' to happen in Luxembourg, and it's still going higher."

Indeed, if Justin had run his fastest time as a Kenyan he probably wouldn't have had the same impact. As it is, he is the most successful runner from his country ever, and may be slowing down literally but definitely not metaphorically.

"I've never really had any major psychological problems in my life," he states, "Maybe this is because I never totally stopped running. I know during a running session I can often find a solution to problems in my job or private life. If I can carry on my running uninjured then I will be among the happiest men in the world."

Justin was working at a bank for 37 years, which included the time when he set the national record. It makes me wonder if he could have gone even faster had he been able to focus solely on his training. I'm not sure it matters too much to him though; what's far more important is that he is able to still run and not get old because he keeps moving. Like many I've spoken to for this book, he sees the digital age as being problematic.

"It's a computer world nowadays; you have to live with the new technologies and help from specialists is often required. The digital age can make people stressed. Human contact fades, and burnout is the modern illness. There's also too much air pollution caused by cars, planes, industry and man."

He's not wrong. It's no coincidence that the summers in the UK, notwithstanding this year's heatwave, were far sunnier back in the 90s. Nowadays clouds fill the sky more often than not, and it must be to do with all the planes, don't you think?

Justin's dedication to fitness should be all the inspiration I need to get well and truly back on the case myself, but I feel I may need further persuasion. Step forward Toni Bernado of Andorra. His national marathon record was set in 2003, and was just 22 seconds behind Justin's fastest time.

"Be sure I am not a talented runner," he says with a colossal slice of modesty, "When I saw Dennis Kimetto break the world record I saw a really talented runner. He's been running and training seriously since only about 2008 and he ran a marathon in under 2 hours, 3 minutes. Now that's real talent."

Obviously a man who has run a marathon in less than two-and-a-quarter hours can't be too shabby at it, but if Bernado and Kimetto at their best were to have raced then the Andorran champion would have been made to look fairly ordinary. Only one man in history, Eliud Kipchoge, has beaten Kimetto's best effort at the time of writing. Bernado finds it hard to fathom how someone could get so good so quickly when he'd been training from a very early age and hadn't got close to the Kenyans. Until he was 18 years old Toni played and competed in tennis and skiing and did a lot of sports in general. Having a solid fitness base from his lifelong active lifestyle served him well when it came to running marathons, which had been his dream since he was a small child.

Perhaps another advantage Kimetto would have is that he can train all year round in a pretty similar way. Toni did all of his 85-130 miles of training per week in Andorra, which has a hugely different climate depending on the season. This wasn't ideal.

"It's very difficult training in Andorra," he says, "We have very cold winters with a lot of snow. I do my training here, but it's very mountainous; it's good for getting some tough training in over the summer but winter is very hard."

He's not such a fan of running in the mountains, preferring to run fast on the road or track. When running a race he focuses on his pace, which he has learnt to keep at the optimum level by being in tune with his body sensations. If he's breathing too hard too early, overheating or feeling especially sore he will know that he's going too fast, and over time this becomes almost instinctive. He describes his record setting run, which happened at Barcelona in 2003, as 'the perfect race.' If you look at the statistics, he ran the first half in 1:07:14 and the second half in 1:07:10 – to be fair, can you get much more perfect than that? Interestingly, the race was at the exact half way point of his marathon career, being the 14th of 27 marathons he has run. You could call it one for each of the 26 miles of the marathon, then the one representing the additional .2 was the race where everything fell into place. He did run very close to the same time on another couple of occasions, but that day in Barcelona 2003 was the peak.

"What I had was a lot of determination, intense dedication and discipline; the three D's," he reflects, and I can imagine him being completely in the zone during a marathon. His mind would be empty of any particularly philosophical thoughts, and he would just be putting one foot in front of the other. Locked into the groove as the miles, or the kilometres for him being a mainland European, kept ticking on by. I picture him snapping out of his trance at the finish line, almost feeling like the race had only just begun and yet having run for nearly two-and-a-quarter hours at a pace I couldn't sustain for a mile. He didn't have a single low point during his best ever run. To me that is talent.

Toni, like Justin, is still running competitively long after many athletes would have retired. He's in his 50s now, and is going after world records for his age group; it's good to aim high.

"Last year I ran 31:23 for the 10,000 metres, and the M50 world record is 30:55," he states, "Many years ago I beat the M40 world record for 3,000 metres, running 8:03. Aged 45 I got the M45 European record and second best world time of 30:16 for 10,000 metres. There's a way to maintain competitive spirit!"

He's absolutely right, and is feeling inspired currently because he's training for Valencia Marathon next December. Again, he's proving that age alone is no excuse to stop striving for a decent level of fitness. He may not challenge his best marathon time, but I'm sure he'll be researching the best M50 times, and will have a decent crack at them. He's another very optimistic guy, perhaps in part due to the truckloads of endorphins flowing around his veins from all the running he still does, and his active lifestyle in general. Shortly before the manuscript was submitted for this book he broke the M50 3,000 metre world record, running 8:37. The previous record had been set by a French runner in 2004, and was 8:41. Toni also ran 14:56 for the 5,000 metres, which was just three seconds off the M50 world record.

"I'm living in Andorra and doing the two things that give me life," he explains, "I'm working with large animals and I'm training daily. I feel very lucky to be able to live, run and work out of town. I'm living in a very small country in the middle of the Pyrenees mountains, and since I was a child I always preferred the countryside to the city."

Had Toni been forced to live in the city perhaps things could have worked out very differently, but I'm guessing the three Ds helped him to secure the veterinary career that allowed him to stay out of the urban environments that stress him out. He knew what he wanted to do from a very young age and he went after it with everything he had. Being able to do the things that make you feel alive on a daily basis is considered a luxury to many. Toni doesn't mind a bit of hard work, in fact it seems to be what he likes best, and maybe that, along with his competitive spirit and daily training, is why at 50 he's still way fitter than most men half his age. He's certainly a lot fitter than I am right now.

Now, picture the scene; you're in the final mile of a marathon. When you reach the finish line you will have demolished your national marathon record by four minutes as long as you can hold your pace until you get there. The metres tick down. 1 kilometre to go – you can feel the enormity of the effort catching up with you, but you're going to make it... 900 metres... 800 metres... not feeling great now, but it's less than half a mile to go. You got this.... 700 metres... and then nothing. The next thing you remember is waking up in the back of an ambulance and not knowing where you are. What happened with the race? Did you make the finish line? The doctors tell you that you collapsed 700 metres from the line and passed out. You didn't finish the race. You didn't break the record. Sorry.

Do you know how that feels? Softly spoken gentle giant Janus Eigaard from Greenland does. One winter's evening in early 2015 he called me shortly before I was going out to meet some friends at Pizza Hut. His accent was like none I'd ever heard, and his story captivated me. In him I saw something of a maverick, and someone whose life could have turned out very differently if certain things hadn't happened at certain times.

"I started too fast," he explains of the run where he passed out, and this will become a recurring theme when he talks about his races, "My parents didn't do sports and so it was something I had to learn myself. When I was about ten I asked my father if he thought I should do running in the summer while I was doing cross country skiing in the winter. He looked at me and after a few moments said 'Yes, I think it probably would be a good idea.' I had a route of roughly 3k that I'd run every day, and I would always run it fast. If you want to run fast in a race you have to train fast; if you're not worried about the time you can relax, but if you want to run a good time you have to train at high intensity."

The blistering pace he gained from his high intensity training as a child would one day allow him to become the first man from Greenland to run a sub 2:25 marathon, breaking the national record set by Kim Gotfredsen, who now works for Greenland Athletics and was the one who put me in touch with Janus. However, perhaps only being used to running fast meant he would always start a race at a pace he couldn't sustain until the finish. This happened during his record setting run too.

"I was in third place, but I had started too fast and was overtaken by a Polish runner, who was also named Janus, with around 5k to go," he reflects, "I slowed up during the last 5k, but I still finished in record time. I am very proud of my record, which hasn't been beaten for a number of years."

It's as if the Polish Janus was a vision of where he might have been had he started just a little more conservatively, but of course this can never be known. You can never be sure over a race of marathon distance. He set the national record at Copenhagen marathon, which he chose because Greenland is a mountainous country that doesn't have any flat marathons, but he wanted to choose somewhere that was still reasonably cold, this being what he was used to in his homeland. The race in which he lost consciousness was in Lanzarote, and he explains that he's never been good at running in the heat.

So did he always want to run a marathon?

"Well, I was more into cross-country skiing but then I started working as a policeman and would travel a lot, so I needed a sport where less kit was required. For running you don't need a lot of equipment, so it was ideal. I did most of my training in Greenland too. It's hard to train there in the winter because of all the snow and ice, so I still did a lot of skiing in the winter, but I was lucky to have a friend who owned an indoor sports complex, so I'd get a key from him and then I could go and get some quality running sessions in over the winter by running indoors. In the summer I would run outdoors on the roads, and then would head into the mountains with friends. I love running in the mountains because our nature is stunning."

The nature is something I was hoping to talk to Janus about, because I'd heard there were polar bears in Greenland. Has he ever seen one?

"I have seen polar bears before, but never when running. Sometimes when a polar bear arrives on an ice floe people go out in a boat to see it, and I did this once. I also had to go out and shoot one when working as a policeman. If they get close to the towns we have to shoot them to protect people, because they're so dangerous."

Wow! When I think of an elite marathon runner I think of someone running endless loops around a track before eating and resting all day. I don't think of someone stalking a polar bear through an expanse of ice and snow to protect the civilians. From what I know of polar bears, if one did get into a town people wouldn't be able to frighten it away by shouting and waving their arms, as you might be able to with an escaped cow in the UK, or even with a larger beast in Africa depending on what it was. Polar bears are aggressive. I've heard they can run fast too?

"Yes, they can run very fast," explains Janus.

But they wouldn't be so good over marathon distance?

"No," he laughs, "I'd say they're more sprinters really. I'm not worried about seeing one when I'm out running though. Some people are afraid of encountering a polar bear when they go to the mountains, but I don't worry about it, because the chances of seeing one are one in a million. Besides, they always arrive from the south, and if one is our country we get to hear about it and usually know where it is."

It seems to me that Janus was more of a threat to himself than polar bears ever were to him. Nothing is certain, but I did feel like there could have been a darker undercurrent to the run in Lanzarote as we talked more. Subconsciously, Janus perhaps knew that by pushing himself so hard he was risking serious injury, or worse, but as a young man it seems like it was a price he was willing to pay in order to see how far he could go. Everything was to change when suddenly he was forced to stop thinking in these terms.

"A while after that race in Lanzarote I got divorced," he explains, "And I was on my own with two tiny children. Suddenly I didn't have time to run much anymore, and so I lost a lot of fitness. For my record setting race I was 80kg. I'm not a small guy, but I was over 100kg at one point, and I couldn't run anywhere near as fast."

His children might have cost him a lot of his fitness, but paradoxically it seems they may have saved his life. He now has six children and a second wife. He hasn't challenged his record setting run since, but has started to train more again, and is trying to instil a love of outdoor activity in his children.

"They all live health lifestyles," he smiles, "My oldest son is a very good boxer. I don't know if any of them will run a marathon, but I'm hoping one of them will one day. I don't get to run a lot now because I have so many kids, but I do what I can because I want to stay young and strong. I think I will always have an active lifestyle."

He reflects on how having children changed his mindset.

"A doctor friend of mine once said to me "Janus, you know you can push yourself too hard with exercise and you could even kill yourself," he recalls, "He told me he would advise me to stop running. I said he must be crazy, because running was my life, but then having two children to bring up forced that decision anyway. They were far more important."

Karl Meltzer has spoken of how perhaps a big factor in being able to achieve what he has in running was that he doesn't have kids. To be the very best at something requires a whole lot of time and effort, and having someone who needs your care and attention all of the time doesn't lend itself well to this. With that in mind, is it a selfish pursuit trying to break a national marathon record, or even to be an elite athlete, if you have children? Being a single father certainly ended Janus' athletic ambitions, but he's found in recent years it doesn't have to end his pursuit of fitness completely. He has just had to set himself new goals based on his circumstances, just as everyone does when they get older and no longer have the speed they once did. The point is that there will always be obstacles to fitness, but in the end it's a choice to be made. Do you want to be as fit as you can by doing what you have time for? Even if you can shoehorn a few 20-30 minute workouts somewhere into your week it's far better than nothing. If you see your obstacles as barriers that prevent you from exercising at all then your health and fitness will inevitably decline. If you see them as obstacles only and still do what you can then there's hope for you even if you find yourself in a poor state of fitness at 40, 50, 60 or beyond. There's always something you can do. If you keep moving you will literally still get old, but getting old won't mean you stop moving. Something is better than nothing.

IF JESUS CAME TO WESTON ON A SATURDAY NIGHT

"If Jesus came to Weston-Super-Mare on a Saturday night would he go and have dinner with the mayor or would he be with the homeless and vulnerable?"

Would he have dinner with Weston's super mayor? I'm sure the mayor might be a nice man, but I believe, as James Wotton does, that he would far more likely be spending time with the homeless and those who need support. James is a gas fitter by day and an occasional Street Pastor by night. He first became a Christian when his parents tricked him into going to a Christian summer camp aged 17, believing he was going to a sports camp. You might be sitting and reading this thinking his parents were dishonest and that what they did was, ironically, not particularly Christian, but when you consider the number of vulnerable people who James has helped in Weston on a Saturday night you can't argue with the end result.

"I don't usually go around broadcasting the fact that I'm a Christian, although I do wear a massive jacket with 'Street Pastor' all over it," he says, "I find you don't need to wave a bible at people to make a difference, just try and act like Jesus would to start with and see where it gets you."

So what does a street pastor actually do? Well, I pretty shamefully have to admit that when I was still drinking alcohol, but not too long before I finally quit, I was horrifically intoxicated in Taunton one night and interrupted some street pastors who were talking to a homeless man. They were probably having a meaningful conversation with him but I blundered on over like a bull in a china shop and got them all to sing Kumbaya. To be fair they did join in, and the homeless guy did too.... I fact he LOVED it! Everyone joined in the group hug afterwards too, but then I gave the guy a little bit of money and in a dreadful display of hypocrisy I told him not to spend it on booze! I don't know what I was thinking. I wasn't thinking. The alcohol had got in the way of any kind of rational thought. That is one of hundreds of reasons I don't drink now and haven't for nearly ten years. The point is, the street pastors had been doing what street pastors do. They were out at night engaging people in conversations and helping them in any way they could. They don't wave bibles at people; they talk, they listen, they assist. They treat everyone with kindness. If they see someone struggling in any way they try to do what they can to help ease that struggle.

"The best part of being a street pastor for me is working as a team to help vulnerable people on a Saturday night," enthuses James, "We have built up amazing relationships with Weston's homeless and try to help where we can, but it's a privilege to get to know them and just be there like Jesus would have done."

It's not just the homeless James and others are there to help. Those street pastors I met in Taunton that night were there to help people like me too. They want to do what they can to help anyone who is out at night to be safe, and can often be seen chatting with groups of young people on other nights. Just by showing willingness to engage, friendliness, understanding and compassion they are having a positive impact and perhaps helping to instil a sense of calm where trouble may flare up. It's brave to be out there, but James and others who feel called to do what they do have faith, which gives them courage. Usually a team of four head out onto the streets whilst two others stay behind and pray over any situation that they hear about from the street pastors. James has seen some amazing answers to prayer during nights on the town.

"There have been lots of answered prayers," says James, "We were with a very drunk guy for hours once and couldn't get him any better. We prayed for an answer. He was unresponsive the whole time we were with him, and was on his own. We prayed again, and the guy suddenly came round as a group of men wandered past. It turned out they were his friends, and within five minutes he was walking off with them in safety and heading for home. The turnaround was incredible."

They have prayed for calm when violence has broken out on a number of occasions, and many times it has calmly come to a stop afterwards. There have also been a lot of situations where they have encountered very drunk people who are unable to get home safely, but through prayer something has come up that has enabled them to.

"There was a young girl once who was missing," James recalls, "Her friends and parents came back out to look for her. We prayed a lot over the situation and she was safely found miles from town."

Were these answers to prayer just coincidence? As previously said, many people will turn to prayer when they find themselves in a desperate situation. Do you believe prayer can work? I do. I've had a number of prayers that have gone unanswered, or at least so it looked, but some have been answered in ways that I don't believe could have been coincidence. When my best friend's dad was in hospital a few years back there were at least two occasions when the doctors said he had taken a turn for the worse and that she should come to the hospital as soon as she could, with the implication that it would be her chance to say goodbye. On both occasions people from all over the world prayed after requests to do so, and on both occasions he made a remarkable and ridiculously speedy recovery. He went from looking like he wasn't going to pull through to seeming like his usual self within an hour or less. He has been out of hospital since apart from when he's had to go in for check-ups etc.

When I did counselling training a few years ago the general consensus on the course and with the theories explored was that God is not real. However, when I spoke of how I believed in God during one session the lecturer revealed how he did believe prayer worked, and spoke of a situation where he was feeling the onset of hypothermia when outdoors, having been cut off from the group he was with, but after prayer he found a way to get warm until morning, when he found his friends again. In the bible we are told to worry about nothing and pray about everything, which is very hard to do, but it's all about having trust. This is what James and his fellow street pastors rely on, and he's still here despite being out on the streets of what can be a rough town many nights, and going right to where the danger is.

I think a lot of people respond to street pastors, even many you wouldn't expect to, purely because someone is showing an interest in them and not judging, just engaging them in conversation. Many a time when heading to the local shop in the evening I've seen street pastors chatting away with young people who are clearly out up to no good if they're anything like I was at their age. Many of these young people just need a bit of focus, a bit of guidance, a bit of understanding. Being a street pastor is largely about being able to provide this in the moment, in the hope that it will have a lasting impact over time.

"I have a simple faith," explains James, "If God tells me to do something I just get on with it and He will sort the rest out. If people are shown hope through my faith it's because I look at it as 'Helping One Person Everyday."

If someone is willing to help there is great hope already. Having to face something alone or having someone who is willing to stand alongside you during times of difficulty? It's obvious which is preferable. James tries to give people hope on a daily basis in this way. Even with his faith though he's not immune to the attractions of the digital age.

"I don't like how we (me included) are addicted to our phones and technology," he admits, "We could quite easily lose hours in the day reading or watching rubbish on social media but don't give God, or our families, enough time."

A familiar scene nowadays is people being gathered together but all being lost in their own worlds. The heartening thing about it is that judging by the answers given in this book, from a whole range of different people, we are aware that it's a problem.

James runs a lot in his spare time. He has come close to winning races before, and has also been last in one, somewhere in between on other occasions. When he runs a race though he always enjoys himself, and has the same approach he has as a street pastor, always mindful of opportunities to help others. He tries to show compassion and kindness in his day to day life as a way of living out his faith, and in this way reminds me of another Christian long-distance runner.

Billy Isherwood is the author of 'From Alcohol to Atacama,' which documents his troubled childhood and the resultant battles with drugs and alcohol, followed by completing the Atacama Desert Marathon (actually multiple days of racing, including one day of 50 miles) in Chile and discovering his faith. Billy has had a lot of struggles in life but embraces them now, as getting through them continues to build resilience.

"It gives me hope to know that many have trodden these dark paths lost, confused and tired," explains Billy, "Digging deep within myself to find the mental strength by reaffirming that myself and others have got through similar helps me to do so again. My message to anyone who may be struggling would be that the struggle is part and parcel of your dilemma – overcome that and you're a winner. You can't expect life not to be a struggle, but sometimes you have to go through the struggle and strife of life in order to help someone else, so I embrace it and learn from it. I want to reach the rainbow, because somewhere over the rainbow...."

Billy knows as well as most just how hard life can be, but the hope for everyone who is going through a struggle is that it will ultimately lead to something better. Also, having your own difficulties can help you to empathise with others. Billy says that since he was seventeen years old he has thought the world was a little insane, which suits him, but seeing a lot of the harsher side of life has allowed him to empathise.

"Since I was seventeen everyone I met was either messed up, fighting, arguing... the leaders of the world were starting wars, multi billion pound satellite dishes were sent up into space yet over a third of the world's population, our fellow human beings, were starving literally to death. It's hard to live in a world like that sometimes, and I had no real desire for anything but then God saved me and the rest fell into place. It took a while, because I'm a stubborn so and so, and still am, but I don't beat myself up about it and neither does God."

If you read the book of Jonah in the bible you will read about another stubborn so and so who God didn't beat up. Jonah went through quite a lot, but God knew that he'd come good in the end, which is just how Billy sees his own struggles.

I got in contact with Billy after I'd read his book, and it always makes me smile to see what he posts online – he's a fantastic character, and like me has a slightly unusual sense of humour. Basically, like James he's living out his faith by showing kindness to others, making them smile and not slapping them down. Billy knows what it's like to struggle, and how hard it can be to remain positive when you look around you and don't see a lot of hope, but he's also living proof that people can come back from the point of almost every kind of collapse and things can and do get better. At the time of writing I'm most definitely one the stubborn so and so end of things, and I need people like Billy to remind me what happens when you put your mind to something, and have unwavering faith. His motto is NFS (No 'Flipping' Surrender), and it's one I have lost sight of at times, but is the only way. He highlights a verse from Corinthians (Cor 4:8-9)...

"We are troubled on every side, yet not distressed; we are perplexed, but not in despair. Persecuted but not forsaken, cast down but not destroyed."

This brings to mind the story of Richard Wurmbrand; a Romanian pastor who was imprisoned by Russian communists last century and tortured daily for fourteen years, but never wavered from his faith. He was finally ransomed and moved to safety in America after spending time in Norway and England, dedicating the rest of his life to helping and encouraging persecuted Christians around the world. The bible has many stories of extreme persecution of Christians during those times, but to think it is a thing of the past couldn't be further from the truth. In some countries around the world (a Google search of 'persecuted Christians' will quickly lead you to a wealth of information) today Christians are still killed, imprisoned, tortured and ridiculed for their beliefs. In what are supposedly ultra-liberal times it seems that this liberalism doesn't extend to Christians for many. To believe in the bible is seen by a lot of people nowadays as being akin to believing in Santa Claus or the Tooth Fairy, whilst having a biblical worldview is seen as outdated, judgemental, even hateful. Christians are the ones seen as doing the persecuting, when actually they have been some of the most persecuted people throughout history. In Tudor times many were burnt alive for going against the Catholic faith of Henry VIII and his daughter Mary Queen of Scots. What happened to Richard Wurmbrand was not an isolated incident; many Christians have been horrifically tortured for their faith around the world, and continue to be today. Largely, those of us in the UK might get a few harsh words on Facebook now and again but at least we are not usually prone to the treatment we would be in other countries.

To talk about the opposition to Christianity in the modern day, and to give an adequate response, is a whole other book in itself. If I have left out or not fully explored a topic that is relevant to the theme of this book it's either because it's not relevant to my life or because there simply wasn't room. To my mind, any true Christian may not agree with you on everything but will not be hateful towards you. Could you be friends with a Christian even if they didn't agree with you on what might seem like some crucial points? If you were to go through all of your friends and compare views and beliefs would they all tie in? A Christian like James wouldn't think drinking until you lose control and getting into a fight would be a good way to live, but if you do these things he'd still want to talk to you and hear what you had to say. A Christian like Billy would probably make you shudder with some of the stories of his past, no matter how un-Christian you consider yourself to be. If you were willing to engage with them they'd be delighted to. To disagree with someone is not to hate them. That goes both ways.

"When things go a bit haywire in my life," concludes Billy, "I try to remember that God is in control. When you give your life to God that should be a done deal, but you and I know we have to do what we can. When we've done all we can and it hasn't worked we're ready to surrender everything to God. That's what He's waiting for."

CONNER'S STORY PART 11

"Yeah"

That one word was all it took. That single word was like the clouds parting and sunlight streaming through. Not many parents have to wait for their child's first word when the child is seventeen years old. That's what this was though; his first word for the second time. For fourteen days not a single word had passed Conner's lips, but on the fifteenth he had turned over on to his front and seemed to be trying to turn back around.

"Do you want to be turned around?" asked Emma, hoping he could respond in some way.

"Yeah."

She looked at Mark to make sure she'd not imagined it. She hadn't. He was aware. He could communicate. The "Where are you now?" refrain from the song they couldn't stop hearing now had an answer.

"I'm right here."

He didn't actually say that, but he didn't have to. Now they had complete confirmation that he understood them. Absolute irrefutable proof. They wanted to have a full conversation with him. Had he been having them on this whole time? Could he have spoken earlier? How was he feeling? They had to be patient though. For now that one word was enough. What's more, it was the culmination of a day when his progress had accelerated almost faster than they could process. When they'd first arrived that morning he'd been sweating, meaning his body was working, so Emma cleaned him with some wipes. He'd been eating so much yoghurt that he was now allowed to move on the pureed food. They'd been asking him questions and getting him to lift his arm or blink a few times if he wanted to say yes. He'd been doing both, but he still hadn't spoken. They asked him if he wanted a drink, which they were allowed to give him. He raised his arm. Emma gave him tiny sips, terrified of giving him more than he could handle and choking him. After humouring her for a few minutes Conner decided enough was enough. He made a noise, pulled a face and snatched the drink from Emma's hand, downing it in one! He restrained himself from slamming the cup down on the table beside his bed afterwards or throwing it over his shoulder. He'd made his point; he wasn't an invalid. He was going to be himself again.

Just a few weeks ago Emma would have told Conner off for being so rude had he snatched a drink from her, but today it meant something completely different and she couldn't have been happier. At least not until what happened when they were leaving that day. She asked him if he wanted a kiss.

"It was a rhetorical question," explains Mark, "He was getting one whether he wanted it or not, but he lifted his head towards Emma and muttered something."

"Love you, mam," Emma is certain he said. This was by far the happiest they'd been since the whole nightmare began.

Jayden hadn't shared in their euphoria and they hadn't really been able to do anything with him for two weeks, so Mark took him to the pictures the next day while Emma stayed with Conner. Mark needed the time out anyway to recover from seeing the brain scans Dr Ross had shown them that morning. Just the sight of them had nearly made him pass out, which Emma found hilarious.

"The scans are consistent with him being paralysed down one side," Dr Ross had said, "And with his lack of speech."

They told him about Conner speaking the day before, and about what happened with the drink, which stunned him. Conner was making amazing progress, but not enough for his own liking. He hated the pureed food he was being given for a start.

"The pictures of the food are weird – they kind of mould the food to make it look like what you're meant to be eating," laughs Mark, "He didn't like it anyways!"

When Conner woke that morning he was really trying to talk to them. He was ready. Once again though his body wasn't responding as quickly as he needed it to. Mark had been alert enough to start filming, but Conner wasn't able to say what he wanted to and his words were unintelligible, apart from when he suddenly said "Eeee, for 'f...'s' sake, man!"

Mark and Emma couldn't help laughing. They had always tried to stop him from swearing, but right now they'd much rather he did then say nothing at all. At least he was training himself to speak again. They just hoped he wouldn't say it too much when the nurses were around. Dr Ross had said he would struggle with speech, and this proved to be true today unless he was swearing. He could curse for England right now, and for now that was enough.

After the film Mark tried to explain to Jayden what might change from now on, but that they loved him as much as Conner. He seemed to understand, but they were becoming more and more conscious of how difficult it had become for them to be equally good parents to both of their children. If Conner always needed as much care as he did now they just weren't sure how they would manage to be there for Jayden as much as they needed him to be, and to be able to give him a normal childhood. They'd have to find a way. It was impossible to be in two places at once but they'd have to do what they could.

Mark hadn't shown the video of Conner talking to Jayden; not because of his bad language, but because he wanted it to be a surprise when they went to the hospital. He had shown Viv and Chris, who couldn't believe it. He dropped in on Paul and Karen too. Paul was away but Karen burst into tears of joy when she saw Conner speaking. He was so far ahead of where the doctors has said he'd be, and everyone found it overwhelming. When they got back to the hospital there were a number of visitors. Conner was managing to get a few more words out but most of what he said they couldn't understand. Obviously it wasn't just his Geordie accent, because it was also their mother tongue. He really wasn't able to form the words the way he could see them in his mind. They showed him some pictures on Instagram and he took an interest but couldn't focus on the screen for long before he started rubbing his eyes and head.

On the next day his frustrations were beginning to show again. He was desperately trying to communicate with them but couldn't make any sense, and the effort was exhausting him. For a long time he'd been trying to explain something but couldn't, and he started to look angry with himself. He wouldn't have really know what had happened to him at this point, so he didn't understand why he was unable to get his point across. Eventually they worked out it was a particular t-shirt he was asking for. Mark tried to explain to him what had happened, why he was in hospital and why he was struggling to do things. He kept feeling his wound as he listened, but didn't show much in the way of emotion.

Another day had gone by and he was due to have his

angiogram, for which he was supposed to be nil by mouth. Mark and Emma had forgotten about this. The physio had been with him when he arrived, and when they were able to go in he was far from calm. He couldn't stay still, and appeared to be reaching for something. They realised it was a drink he was after, and he had one before they realised he wasn't meant to. They let the nurse know what had happened and she said it wouldn't be a problem, just to make sure he didn't have anything else.

At around 1.45pm a team of doctors and anaesthetists arrived. Trying to put myself in Conner's shoes, not that he was wearing any in bed I'm sure, I think I would have been pretty freaked out by all the people in surgical clobber milling around me if I wasn't fully aware of what had happened. They spoke to everyone, including Conner, about what would be happening, and then took him away. They said he would be back in around an hour or so. 2.45pm came and went, then 3.45 did, and he still hadn't returned. Mark and Emma had got used to things sometimes taking longer than they expected, but after everything that had happened it really wasn't pleasant having to wait, and wondering how much longer it would be. They'd felt so euphoric when Conner had started speaking again, and wanted to keep focusing on this to try and keep him upbeat as well as themselves. He was getting tired again, and with this came a lot of frustration. They were worried that he might take a step back again, having come so far.

When he finally got back it was almost 4.30pm. He seemed exhausted and just wanted to sleep, perhaps because of the anaesthetic, but before he did he tested Mark's constitution again by somehow pulling one of his tubes out and leaving blood all over the floor. The nurses had to clean up the blood again, and Mark and Emma left while they did. When they came back Conner had fallen asleep. He did wake up when visitors arrived later that night, but he didn't seem in the mood to see them.

"Conner was acting really strange," recalls Mark, "He kept unintentionally flashing his bits to everyone, and his general behaviour was off. We were reading out some of the messages that people were sending but he was tired and asked us to leave in a roundabout way."

At the time Mark and Emma were concerned, but they later found out what was happening.

"We found out it was a combination of his anaesthetic and a water infection that made him act strange. Water infections can send people loopy – we saw a few when he was moved to Sunderland and when Emma was in hospital too (Emma later had to have an operation of her own to correct the position of her brain; what a year!) – one woman went nuts because she thought this guy had a gun!"

Their emotions were up and down like a yo-yo during these days. The next day was better again; when they arrived Conner was with the speech therapist, who explained to them that she was clearing him to eat solid foods. Just four days ago she'd said it would be weeks before he might be able to. He kept wanting to prove everyone wrong, and she couldn't believe how quickly he was improving.

Dr Ross had been to see him again and was similarly amazed. His body was still getting exhausted quickly though. He had a hydrotherapy session in the pool, which had to be cut short after twenty minutes because it was wearing him out, and then he slept for most of the afternoon. The physio left a wheelchair with them and said if they wanted to take Conner off the ward over the weekend they could.

"Looking back, it annoyed me that the physios were only

available Monday to Friday," says Mark, "You'd think they could alternate shifts so patients could get a session every day."

Conner's food was delivered that evening and it was pureed again rather than the solid food they'd asked for. They decided to take matters into their own hands. Conner deserved a treat, so Emma rang Viv and asked her to bring a McDonalds! Conner devoured the chicken nuggets, fries and strawberry milkshake like he'd been stranded in the wilderness with no food for days. He probably could have eaten another right there and then, and he would have a plain cheeseburger later in the week, but having something tasty to eat after endless yoghurts followed by an array of slop really left him buzzing. Paul and Karen came to see him that evening too, and of course were just as amazed as the doctors had been by the change they saw in him.

The next day they took him out in his wheelchair. They did a tour of the RVI, taking in the Costa Coffee, the café and shop, then Mark asked him if he'd like to go out and get some fresh air. He did, and so for the first time in nearly three weeks he saw the outside world. Out into the light after being in the confines of the hospital ward for all that time. He might have felt a little like a vampire at first, and Mark expresses how gaunt and frail he looked in the pictures he took at the time, which is quite harrowing to see now. He soon tired, and wanted to go back to his room, but on the way back he showed how much better his speech was getting. Sometimes he would say the wrong words, for example he said "For f...'s snakes"" instead of "For f...'s sake!" and would laugh about it. Mark laughed with him, but was careful to explain that he was laughing with him rather than at him, because he did still get frustrated when he couldn't say what he wanted to sometimes.

When they got him back to his room he stunned them once more when he tried to get up out of his chair and walk to the bed. He'd seemed to forget that he was paralysed down his right side, and so they had to hold him down and explain to him again what had happened. They also had to correct him when he said he was in South Shields hospital.

They arrived a little late on Sunday, and the nurse took them to one side. She explained that Conner had an accident during the night. They'd found him on the floor next to the bottom of his bed. He couldn't stop laughing, but didn't tell anyone how he'd got there. Perhaps he'd tried to get up and walk again. It was strange how he was going through all the stages of development he had as a tiny child again, but this time was reminding himself how to do everything rather than learning it for the first time. He was also trying to remember fully who he was, although he did have some awareness. It was like he had to start again from square one, but each time he managed something new a part of the old Conner came back.

The rest of the morning went well. Some of Conner's friends – the lads this time – came to see him, and he perked up at their presence. He was laughing and joking with them, but unlike Caitlin they didn't get their hair stroked. Sure they didn't mind! The visit seemed to do him a lot of good, and everyone began to relax again after the recent difficulties. This was short-lived though as Conner became stressed in the afternoon. Mark thinks it was because the lads were talking about what they'd been up to and Conner became aware of how he should be out enjoying life with them rather than being stuck in hospital. He wanted to be out riding his bike and playing football, and just hanging out with his friends rather than lying in this bed day in, day out. It all got too much for him and he was visibly upset.

"He's getting tired, lads," said Mark, "I think you'd better let him rest now, hey? Thanks for coming; he loved it that you did"

Conner's friends left, and he reflected on what he couldn't

do. They would later find out he had aphasia, which was responsible for his difficulties with his speech, and his vision was severely compromised. His right side visual field has gone.

"It's very tough to describe," says Mark, "Think of two circles next to each other. Colour the left half of both circles in white and the right half of both in black. That is basically his eyes looking straight ahead – the black section is where he is now blind."

This coupled with everything he realised he was missing out on meant he became really quite frustrated. Around this time he started pushing Mark and Emma away when he felt this way. Emma found this especially tough; after everything she just wanted to be with her son all the time, and didn't like it when she couldn't see him. Mark found it tough as well, but tried to rationalise things and remember that Conner was getting more and more aware of how different his life was now to how it was just a few weeks previously, and that it was bound to take a bit of getting used to.

Mark and Emma's approaches were different in some ways. Emma was constantly researching things on Google to do with what was happening to Conner, because she wanted to be prepared for everything. Mark didn't know how she could live like that, worrying about every possible thing that could take place. He preferred to stay in the here and now. Mindful Mark and Educational Emma. They were a team despite their different ways of dealing with things, and although they had so much to be pleased about there was still such a long road ahead of them. Just how long would it be, and how much more progress would Conner make? Would he always need the wheelchair? Would he be able to talk fluently again? Would he ever be able to hang out with his mates outside of this place?

All of these questions they had no answer to. So far he'd

done so much better than the doctors expected him to, but he was still so different to the lad he had been. He was talking a little bit, eating solid food and trying to get up and walk, but this was far less than he'd been able to do before, and it was starting to have an impact on him emotionally. Would the negativity of what he couldn't do creep in and hold him back, or would he be able to focus on what he could do and keep building on it?

PS4 OR PSL?

Games consoles have been around since I was a small child. Back then it was different consoles to those you will find now, but the premise is the same. I never owned one – my parents wouldn't let me – and instead, around the same time a number of my friends were getting obsessed with them I was getting obsessed with nature. My dad was very knowledgeable on the subject and inspired me to discover nature in the same way Karl Meltzer Senior inspired Karl Meltzer Junior to discover skiing and running. He showed me a world that existed far beyond the parameters of the computer screen, and it blew my mind. Birds were fascinating to me, and there was literally nothing I liked more in my early teens that spending a whole day from dawn until dusk trying to see as many different species as I could. It meant I had a focus for the whole day, would be active, would be using my brain and would be appreciating the natural world around me. One of the biggest tragedies of my life was that I didn't pursue this as far as I could and make a career out of it in some way. Instead I tried to please people by becoming a party monster and have been paying the price for it ever since. Anyway, that's a different story for another day.

In my birding days I had something of an interest in butterflies, moths and dragonflies but I only scratched the surface of the vast scope of nature that was all around me. A niche hobby in the UK that you may well have never heard of is Pan Species Listing (PSL.) Basically every observable species counts, and by its very nature – pun intended a bit – this becomes quite all-encompassing. The most dedicated Pan Species Lister will build up a vast library of identification guides along with a powerful microscope, binoculars, telescope and various other pieces of equipment that will help them locate and study a vast array of life. Everything from the birds of the air, the fish of the sea, the bugs that crawl along the ground to the plants that grow wild, the mosses and lichens on rocks and walls and even the mould on untouched satsumas in the depths of a fruit bowl. There's enough nature out there to occupy all of the spare time you have remaining on this earth. If you stick to one category of species and are dedicated to your hobby then the opportunity to see new ones tends to dry up after a few years or so, but if you don't specialise then you'll wish you had an extra 24 hours in the day just to try and figure out what they all are, and to study their intricacies. That's if you enjoy it of course; if you don't then you won't want to spend another minute looking. I don't understand on a personal level how anyone could not be blown away by nature, no matter where they believe it came from, but I do accept that some would rather stare at a screen for 8 hours than spend the same amount of time outdoors. That's just the way it is, no matter how wrong I may consider it to be.

So….. think Pan Species Listers are a bit crazy? Let's talk to some of them and then you can decide, having heard what they have to say. First of all, meet Tom…

"When I was a child I was obsessed with animals," he begins, "I learnt facts about wildlife in a similar way to how some boys would learn about football. As I got old enough to wander on my own I would find interesting things, and as I got older still I got into birds in particular."

"Yeah! Me too, mate!" – I can almost hear the chorus of lads making a not in any way predictable joke. Think he meant the feathered kind, chaps. All joking aside though, Tom could basically be explaining my childhood. I learnt facts about football too, but I did get into birdwatching in a huge way as a teenager. It's basically all I wanted to do for a long time.

"I had a few years off while I pretended to be too cool for such things, but in my mid 20s I started birding again," he continues, "When I got to the point where I'd seen nearly all birds you could see without 'twitching' I started getting more into natural history, and eventually PSL."

Yeah, that pretty much sums up my life in terms of PSL too. I'm not Tom though, I promise. He does exist. By the way, for those who don't speak the lingo yet, 'twitching' basically means going to see a rare bird someone else has found on UK shores which has arrived here by accident, having been blown off course during migration. Or maybe these rare birds are just here on vacation. We don't know for sure, do we? Nobody knows the mind of a bird. Rare birds that only a few people manage to twitch, or nobody does, and are very rarely seen in the UK, are known as 'blockers.' Not sure if I have anything that would be considered a blocker on my list – perhaps some to those who have only just started twitching in recent years. A lot of the rarest birds I've seen were in the 90s. Anyway, sorry Tom, you carry on.....

"You have to enjoy PSL," he says, "If you're not enjoying it then you're going about it the wrong way. Find your own stuff – it's more rewarding than 'twitching', but twitch stuff if you want to and don't let anyone tell you otherwise."

Basically there's no right or wrong way to do PSL. There isn't one overall list – some people count human as a species, some don't. Some count the sheep that live around Cheddar Gorge as wild, some don't. It goes on and on, but it can all get too overwhelming if you try to identify everything at once, plus some things are a nightmare to identify even when you've been doing the whole PSL thing for some time. You could spend hours staring at mosses through a microscope and only really scratch the surface of what they might be. Does it matter? Well if you want to build up your moss list then yes it does. Besides, it can be fun to try. You might learn something. Many a time I've Googled purple spots I've found on a leaf and excitedly posted on the PSL Facebook page about what I believe them to be, only to be told there are three other things it could potentially be and it'll take some serious microscope work to figure it out… or possibly figure it out. Personally I prefer species that I could potentially identify using just my eyes, or a pair of binoculars, and a book. If you're new to PSL that's probably the best way to start. I mean you wouldn't learn piano by going straight for a Chopin piece. How about Tom though, what are his favourites?

"Moths are one of my favourites because of the variety of what will come to a trap (A box with a powerful bulb – nothing barbaric; no moths are harmed) that you would never know was there otherwise. I like birds for old times' sake but the ticks have dried up, and I like fungi because it's such a fascinating group. It's a strange mix of being accessible but baffling at the same time."

So where would you start looking?

"Many 'lifers' (species you've never seen before), including some good species, have been found in inauspicious places – walls, rough ground, places I pass on the way to work, local parks, places I can get to on my lunch hour. Yes, a dedicated trip to a nature reserve will deliver the goods, but there's stuff everywhere to find. It's a fun game in a way, and gets important records in less watched places, but it also keeps you rooted in the present (which is the foundation of mindfulness) wherever you are."

This is an excellent point about PSL. If I spend an hour glued to a screen my mind will dart between a vast range of topics, few of which I will even remember later on that day. If I spend an hour in nature my mind will be in sharp focus and I will feel calm and inspired afterwards. If I'm staring at a screen for any length of time it usually increases my stress levels and leaves me with an unhealthy vibe. Another superb point is that pretty much every time you go to a new place, or even when you fully explore the place you're in, there's always something to find. The most successful Pan Species Lister of them all, a man named Jonty, said in an interview that the next place he'd be looking for new species would be his local pond, as there were probably stacks of things in there he'd never seen that he could find with the help of his trusty microscope. If none of this sounds cool enough for you then you might surprise yourself with how fascinating it is if you just give it a try. Or you might not. There are tens of thousands of different species out there to find if you're willing to look. Makes Pokemon seem pretty limited.

For some, PSL represents an escape from the trials, pains, confusion and difficulties that go along with life. Meet Bill (not my dad for anyone who knows me, although he is into PSL in a big way.) He started by birdwatching as a child, like Tom, then expanded his interest as he got older. When working in Australia as a young man he was absolutely spoilt in terms of the diversity of nature he had to explore.

"I'd ended up in Oz, a long way from my home and family. Work wasn't what I was promised, and I was depressed and lonely," he begins, "At work I'd be looking forward all day to going home and seeing the lizards at the place I was staying. I started looking for poisonous spiders and snakes, seeing how many I could find. I spent hours watching the gala, lorikeets and cockatoos, feeding the pelicans."

He remembers his time in Australia as being isolating and lonely, but being able to share this with a myriad of nature really took the edge off things. Later on he got married and now has a daughter, but being something of an insomniac, he still feels lonely when they go to bed.

"I hate my job. What I do was never what I intended to do, or want to do now," he explains, "My wife leaves to do her dream job every day. She comes home satisfied. I come home empty, longing for something I can't obtain. Then daughter, dinner, smiles, laughs, stories, games…. silence! She goes to bed and my wife goes too. I don't; I can't. I feel too full of resentment of my day up until the smile my daughter gives me."

It's the opposite of the stereotypical image there can be of blokes working late or heading to the pub to avoid spending time with their families. Time with his family is clearly what gives Bill what was missing from his life before, but when his family are not with him he still feels the emptiness he always did.

"So when everyone's sleeping I've discovered a passion," he continues, "Something I enjoy, something I'm good at. I identify little things down a microscope. It's a puzzle with so many small pieces. It's not easy, and I like the challenge. It keeps my brain alive, my heart warm."

This isn't escapism for Bill. It's a part of the day he looks forward to, and he waits until his family are going to sleep before he starts staring down the microscope. 'Peering at things while the family sleep' conjures up untoward images, but what Bill does is a world away from such pursuits. He gives his family his full attention first, because trying to identify a tricky moss needs a level of focus you can't reach with any distractions.

It's kinda like a cryptic crossword, or a hard Sudoku puzzle, but with something from nature. Fungi, flies, beetles, mosses, lichens and a whole host of others can be just as challenging as each other. It has to be good for the brain to be fascinated by something so intricate and thought-provoking. It's probably the last thing a lot of people would want to do after a hard day at work; they'd rather do something mindless. Not Bill. He's completely in his element, and it's getting to be a bigger and bigger focus outside of family life.

"I love LotR type books," he enthuses, "Magicians flying around on dragons; that kind of thing. I've not read a book like that for six years though, since my daughter was born. Instead I read nature-inspired books like Dave Goulson's 'Bee Quest', 'Sting in the Meadow' or 'Feral.' I haven't felt the need to escape because when I've felt like I might I've had something worthwhile to do instead. It doesn't really take me away; it puts me right there and gives me focus. It challenges and inspires me. I like the kudos of getting it right, and of helping others, because now I can."

Bill is a deep thinker, and so the challenging aspect of a species that can only be identified using a microscope gives his mind somewhere to go when it could wander to dark places. He finds it hard to be optimistic about the future, but discovering PSL has given him hope.

"I have no hope for mankind, or for the environment," he sighs, "I think both are doomed. My only hope is that we can prolong the good and stave off the end for as long as possible. People are too selfish and destructive. I have a daughter. I hope that I can instil in her an appreciation of the world around us. I hope that future generations can start to enjoy simple life; fresh air, bird song, crickets chirping, and to love the world and the environment."

When I think about the difference between life now and life twenty years ago it has to be said that Bill has a point. Even the bible doesn't disagree with his prophecy for the future; that the world will ultimately be destroyed by the greed and selfishness of humans, and if you look around you the signs are already there. I don't think I'm just gazing through rose-tinted spectacles when I recall my teens and picture there being so much more wildlife around than there is now.

Discussions on bird forums confirm that many species have declined dramatically in number since the 90s. You could say it's swings and roundabouts because there are a number of bird species that were virtually non-existent in the South-West that now have strongholds on the Somerset Levels and elsewhere. Bitterns and Marsh Harriers breed in good numbers, Great White Egrets are often around whereas Little Egrets, which first started arriving in numbers when I was a teenager, are getting more common all the time. However, there are so many species you would have sure-fire sites for back then you would be hard pressed to see down this way now. It used to be virtually impossible to drive past Dorchester in the daytime without seeing Corn Buntings on the fences. There used to be plenty of Ring Ouzels on Exmoor in the spring. Turtle Doves would always be in Haldon Forest in the summer. Little Owls would be all over the place. There seemed to be nearly as many Swallows and Swifts in the summer sky by day as there were stars at night. Lady Amherst's Pheasants were in forests in the Home Counties if you knew where to look. Greenfinches were as common then as Goldfinches are now, if not more so. All of these things have changed. That's just the birds. Destruction of habitat and perhaps changing climate has led to the disappearance or diminishing in numbers of hundreds of species from across the PSL palette.

In 2007 my friend Sergio and me spoke to a lady in a bookshop in Ilminster who told us how she used to take lovely photos of sunsets from her window but wasn't able to any more due to so many houses being built in the surrounding countryside. I remember learning about 'urban sprawl' in Geography lessons at school, and now it seems to be getting out of control. Habitat is being built over all the time, people on the whole seem more stressed and paranoid than they ever were, hardly anyone seems to be able to afford to live without getting into debt and life is slowly turning into virtual reality.

"I hate that I'm depressed and sometimes escape into a virtual world," Bill bemoans, "I have all these friends there but am lonely and never see them or talk to them. I hate that every day is a rush – get here, do that, go there again. I hate that people are so self-absorbed; no 'hello, good morning, it's a beautiful day' etc. I hate the way every tree seems to be cut down, and how chemicals are sprayed everywhere willy-nilly. There's no thought, and no conscience."

Bill might come across as a doom monger to some, but the fact is he's highlighting truths that many would like to sweep under the carpet. He's not choosing to ignore them for the sake of an easier life. He doesn't feel he is able to. It's good to focus on positives in life – when I focus on nothing but the negative I get too despondent to have any motivation, but if I focus on nothing but the positive too many important things pass me by that I would otherwise ignore. It's all about balance. Bill feels conflicted by the modern world and his place in it.

"I love the internet, and my IPhone. They keep me sane," he admits, "Being connected to nature through Facebook or Twitter. If I can't see a beetle then someone, somewhere will, and I will see the photo, sharing their joy. I hate my dependency on the phone and the connection. I used to be out every night talking and laughing. I love my car too, and the freedom it provides. The ability to go to places I wouldn't otherwise go to. The chance to see things; nature, landscapes, the sea. I feel guilty though for loving my car and for using it."

I think the points he makes here are so telling about the modern world. Motorised transport, the internet, increased air travel and so many other modern changes have made the world seem far smaller as horizons grow broader. To me this is a curse as much, if not much more, than a blessing. I remember the comedian Dave Gorman talking about how he couldn't seem to write a novel because he writes it on his computer, which is connected to the internet. The internet contains everything in the whole world ever, which can be a little bit distracting. I'm not sure I've heard it put better. So many things seem possible nowadays, and are at the touch of a button, so if you don't have instant success it's easy to feel like a failure. With social media everyone else's lives seem to be in your face the whole time, and again it's easy to get very despondent if they all seem to be doing better than you are. I don't remember life seeming so competitive back in the day. Of course part of it has to do with being an adult and feeling more of a sense of responsibility, but it seems like back then there was so much more time, and although I felt a sense of incompetence and underachievement I reasoned that I would be able to put things right, and had room to breathe while I worked out how. Now I feel a constant sense of pressure from all angles, and I believe that the internet is largely to blame. So why not just come off it?... Come off it! See what I did there?

I've digressed a little. What does this have to do with PSL? Well to me, PSL is about stopping, breathing, looking and discovering what's right under your nose. From that place things don't seem quite so daunting. This is the appeal of fishing for many too, which is a way of combining two hobbies when you fish to broaden your pan species list. It's all about refocusing on your connection with nature. It also shows you how much more there is to the world around you than you realised, which can help you to believe in more possibilities. At least it does for me.

There's something almost spiritual about PSL; literally if you believe in creation. I remember just after I'd got into it and I saw a tiny fly buzzing around the bushes. It was like time froze, and I thought of the first flies at the beginning of the world.... but PSL is so scientific. It's incompatible with belief in God. Right?

Enter Simon Davey. His fascination with PSL began before it even had a name. Before the internet was even a thing. Before my dad was born. He didn't call what he was doing Pan Species Listing back then, but there's no doubt that's exactly what was going on.

"My mother told me that when I was still in the pram I used to get her to pick flowers for me, which I would arrange into colours," he begins, "One of my earliest memories was discovering that there was a yellow dead nettle, as well as a red and a white."

Like me, Simon had a father who was fascinated by nature and perhaps lit the spark of his interest.

"I can still remember in 1947 the excitement of seeing Clouded Yellow butterflies and Hummingbird Hawkmoths being attracted to a buddleia bush, and the great excitement when the shout of "Swallowtail!" came up, which would cause us to grab our nets."

He doesn't remember being so excited by the sight of Large Tortoiseshell butterflies, which are now long extinct in the UK and so would lead to huge excitement if found by any PSL enthusiasts. Back then Collared Doves had never been seen in Britain. The first ones were seen in 1955, and now they are one of the UK's commonest birds. Times have changed, but Simon's appreciation of nature has remained undiluted. It's always been a huge part of who he is.

"When I was eight I was awarded a choristership at Ely Cathedral," he recalls, "I got into birds in a big way around that time but I remember reading a book about wild flowers, and when I was sixteen I became passionately interested in botany again. Being interested in birds seemed more acceptable to other eight-year-old boys than flowers. During the holidays I spent time in the Botany Department at Leicester University with Professor Tom Tutin. He told me about a site for Military Orchid near Barton Mills in Suffolk. I spent the early summer cycling over to Barton Mills in search of that mythical plant."

Can you imagine a 16-year-old doing such a thing nowadays? Of course it would be a totally different experience, because he'd probably already be aware of it from the internet, and he might be tweeting about his expedition, or even broadcasting it live over Facebook. The mysticism would not be there. Simon's early forays proved fruitless, although he was able to enjoy a lunch of a pie and pint in a pub in Barton Mills. He would later discover that the pub was owned by the headmaster's secretary, and so he nearly got found out, especially as he would hear that the headmaster would have his lunch there fairly often. It's hardly the same level of rebellion as some of the stories we've heard, but I get the impression that finding a hobby he was so immersed in right from the pushchair helped Simon to have focus in life and to keep away from many of the unsavoury aspects. For the record, he did get to see the Military Orchid eventually when a friend from the university took him.

Simon pursued a career in ecology, being Keeper of Biology in the Hampshire County Museum Service to begin with, as he thought it would mean concentrating on the New Forest. It turns out he was wrong, but he was able to run the Curtis Museum in Alton, which was concerned with the botanist William Curtis, and so he was able to devote some of his time to his passion still. In 1971 he met Dr Francis Rose, who died in 2006 and he describes as his 'natural history guru' right up until then.

"Francis would dedicate his time and enthusiasm to anyone showing an interest in botany," Simon explains, and I get the feeling he is just the same. He was very helpful when I was struggling to identify some lichens and mosses a few years back, giving me plenty of pointers.

"I made a collection of lichens for the museum, largely in my own time, which luckily is now appreciated by many. In 1987, following a terrible time under a bullying director, I left museums and became a freelance ecological consultant. Being freelance, I was able to have the incredible privilege of taking natural history tours to many parts of the world."

Sounds like an amazing job to me. Simon describes himself as primarily an ecologist, and he gets the greatest inspiration from seeing plants and animals living together in an ecosystem, although he does keep numerous lists and loves seeing new species. His job enabled him to turn his passion into a way of assisting others and educating them about nature, hopefully inspiring them in the process to discover more about the world around them. Now we move on to his spiritual beliefs.

"My appreciation of nature is closely bound up in my spiritual beliefs," he says, "Ecology and the intricate and complex relationship between all aspects of life is just incredible. To delve into it is, I believe, a way of exploring the nature of God. Humans are all spiritual as well as physical beings, and to explore the nature of the spiritual side of life is so bound up with hope. Frankly, I find it rather difficult to see hope without it."

Why are so many people certain that God doesn't exist, and that looking at nature has to disprove the idea of creation? Simon admits that Darwinian theory did sadden him to begin with because it seemed to go against everything he'd believed up until that point. However, nowadays he sees his belief in God as going hand in hand with his appreciation of nature. Darwinian theory is a theory, and has not been categorically proven to me any more than creation has to an atheist.

"The perfection of the relationship between water, oxygen, DNA, the sun and a million other aspects of the environment is all a bit illogical," continues Simon, "Most explosions lead to chaos rather than the order we experience here on Earth. I see God being just as essential today as He ever was. Science cannot explain how these perfect relationships exist, even though it can explain a lot. For God to be a creator whose creation obeys the complex laws of science to me is far more impressive than seeing Him as a being with a magic wand saying "Let there be elephants" and elephants just appearing."

Something to consider. But the aim of this chapter was not to cause a theological debate, more to explain how a diverse range of characters inhabit the PSL rankings, and so why not give it a try? You might find your mind is blown. You might not, if you don't then I don't need to hear about it. Your energy would be far better spent doing something you enjoy. It blows my mind though to know that there are thousands upon thousands of different species out there just waiting to be discovered. Yesterday, for example, during a walk on the edge of Exmoor I saw fly agaric mushrooms, various mosses and lichens that Simon would have been able to identify instantly but I didn't have a clue about, a number of bird species, a large black beetle, wild whortleberries, rowan trees, sycamore trees, birch trees (with Birch Polypore fungus growing on one), an ants' nest, which was fascinating in itself. I could go on and on, but the point is that it adds a whole new vast dimension to life when you start to appreciate what's around you in this way. I feel somehow sad for the people who can't appreciate it, in the same way they might feel sad for me because I can't appreciate something else. The bottom line is that no matter what you believe about how it began, nature is awesome and you know it. That's something everyone should be able to agree on instantly.

WHAT IS AMBITION?

"Ambition is a word that's relative," argues Charlie Carroll, author of 'No Fixed Abode,' which documents his experiences of becoming voluntarily homeless for a while to try and better understand the lives of rough sleepers, "An MP who wanted to close soup kitchens because he believes it dulls the ambition of homeless people might have an ambition to become a party leader. This is so far out of reach for most of us that it seems ridiculous, and somebody like that could have no comprehension of what ambition even means to someone who might visit a soup kitchen."

I remember reading a few years back about a plan by a London council to close soup kitchens locally because they believed that giving rough sleepers handouts meant they would have no ambition to get off the streets. At the time I thought it must be a fake article, as surely nobody could truly believe this. Since then though I've seen numerous people with long-term injuries and illnesses having to fight tooth and nail to be entitled to keep their financial support when they should be able to focus on their recovery, or at least managing their conditions, without having the additional stress of having everything taken away. This is just the way of our current government it would seem. I remember David Cameron making a speech on TV maybe five years ago. With a stony face he said "Would I want everyone to have an education like mine? Yes I would, because I went to a bloody good school!" All of his supporters cheered as he gave a steely, self-righteous glare, but they clearly didn't teach him anything in the way of compassion at this wonderful school of his. Observe a couple of years later when Jeremy Corbyn repeatedly asked him during Prime Minister's Question Time if anyone would be made worse off by the upcoming tax credit reforms, and he refused to give a straight answer to the question each time, knowing that many would indeed be made worse off.

"To those who are forced to exist within the most unfortunate of circumstances, average and every day pursuits can be all-consuming," continues Charlie, "In response to that awful, awful comment, feeding the homeless is not dulling their ambition. It's satisfying one ambition so that they might use the energy and headspace they'd expend looking for their next meal pursuing other ambitions."

Charlie's observation makes perfect sense to me, and brings to mind Maslow's Hierarchy of Needs, which has been mentioned in several places I've worked. It basically states that if you're lacking in any of the fundamental human needs such as food, warmth or shelter, or if you're particularly stressed about something, you probably aren't going to be very focused on your work. In the context of homelessness it follows that if someone's food, warmth and shelter are not a given each day and are something they have to invest energy into finding, that will be where their daily ambition lies. It is far easier for someone who wants for none of these things and has money and time to invest in ambition to have it then it is for someone who is mostly just focused on survival. Despite this, not everyone has always thought that Charlie understands the situation well.

"I was doing a book reading once," he recalls, "When somebody in the audience asked me if I'd ever had a drug addiction. 'No,' I replied. Then he asked me if I'd ever had literally no money at all and been forced to beg for it. 'No,' I admitted. Finally he asked me if I'd ever had to run from the police just because I was hungry and so I nicked a loaf of bread. 'No,' I replied again. "Then you haven't had a proper homeless experience," he said, at which point he walked out, being sure to call me 'Jackanory' as he left."

While these experiences reflect the realities of homelessness for a number of people, there are so many more who would also answer 'no' to these questions, or at least some of them.

"Rough sleepers account for about 15% of the homeless people in the UK," explains Charlie, "The other 85% are composed of those we know less about because they are less visible. Those in shelters and halfway houses, those who sleep on their friends' couches because they can't afford rent, those who are crowded into temporary accommodation because their houses were repossessed and their lives destroyed. We must of course consider rough sleepers when we consider the homeless, but to ignore the vast plethora of others who exist in different states and are still homeless nonetheless is both ignorant and exclusive."

By definition, anyone who doesn't have a home is homeless, and this is ever on the rise in what, as you may remember Ursula identifying in a previous chapter, is supposedly the sixth richest country in the world. Nobody 'needs' to be rich, people just need to be able to feel a degree of comfort, and quite a percentage of the population don't feel any comfort in a country many people move to believing it to be one of the best places in the world to live. Undoubtedly there are some things about this country that are far better than elsewhere, such as the NHS and the relative peace. I won't say that there's no privilege involved with living in England. However, this is still a nation where so many fear for their future every single day, and if this is one of the best places in the world to live then just how bad is the worst?

"I have two friends, both teachers, a married couple with a child," Charlie expands, "Who in 2010 both lost their jobs as the education budget was cut and schools laid off thousands of staff across the country. With no income or savings, my friends could no longer afford to rent their house. For two years, while they both looked for work, they were forced to live at their parents' homes and then with various friends. At one time they were sleeping in a friend's garage for a week. Because of their child they couldn't stay in one place for long, and they moved often. Fortunately they have both found work again, and are renting a new flat, but for those two years they were without a doubt, in my mind, homeless."

Charlie used to work as a teacher himself, and it turns out we had a kind of mutual mentor in Elliott Furneaux. Elliott was head teacher of Heathfield School, where Charlie worked, and he had been head of Holyrood Community School Lower Site when I was a pupil there. This was pretty random to discover, and in fact is almost like something off the TV show Lost! We both remember Elliott as a genuinely kind man who had an impact on our lives. Charlie had the following to say about him: -

"Many of the headteachers I have worked for have been elusive and somewhat shadowy, hidden in closed offices negotiating who knows what for the good of the school (we can only hope), appearing once in a while to deliver a short assembly before retreating into the murk once more. Not Elliott Furneaux. He was as hands-on as it was possible to get. I often felt like I didn't work *for* Elliott, but *with* him.

One of his favourite ways to keep his presence in the school known and felt was to conduct lesson observations of the staff.

For many teachers, observations are at best a bore and at worst a constant source of stress, especially if it's a member of the Senior Management Team doing the observing. Meanwhile, Elliott had a way of enhancing a lesson observation simply by being there. Once, he observed a lesson of mine in which a group of 32 sixteen-year-old boys had to create on the spot role-plays as characters from 'An Inspector Calls.' While most of observers would have sat at the back of the classroom quietly taking notes, Elliott got involved, becoming a character from the play himself and acting out a role-play with one of the boys, thereby modelling not just good practice for me as a teacher but also good practice for the students. He showed them how it could be done. They loved it, and he did too. It was why he was in the job.

He once told me about his previous career as a rep for Penguin Books. He remembered driving an MG across Europe 'like James Bond' on his way to a book fair. He was successful, he was ludicrously well paid, and yet he felt empty. The following year he started a teacher training programme. "I remember going into my first school," he had said, "It was an all boys' school, and their behaviour was atrocious. All I could think was 'this is where I'm meant to be."

"These few memories sum up Elliott Furneaux for me," continues Charlie, "He was never afraid to get his hands dirty, so long as it meant he could have a positive impact, which he absolutely did."

I would agree. He had an impact on me. He made me believe I might actually be a half-decent writer, and I e-mailed him to tell him so about a year before he died. Sadly he became ill and deteriorated pretty quickly, losing his life and leaving big shoes to fill, both literally and metaphorically. I remember him having an imposing physical presence to go with his big heart and powerful mind. In fact he once told a story of how he'd grabbed a man in the theatre by the collar who kept interrupting a play they'd been to see for a school trip because he'd been so convinced by his performance; it turned out the man was an actor and was part of the play, but before he knew this Elliott had eventually decided enough was enough and it wasn't fair for him to spoil everyones' enjoyment. He wasn't a rough man, but he did have a strong sense of justice and wasn't afraid to muck in when the chips were down. I remember him once saying that he thought if someone was attacking his family he could murder them in self-defence. After the incident in the theatre his students would cower for comic effect when he walked past them in the hallway, and he would always laugh.

Elliott said he remembered me well when he replied to my e-mail, and that his wife found it annoying how he was useless at remembering everyday information but he could remember small details about nearly all of his old students. I can believe that he could; he made a point of knowing, and using, everybody's name. This wasn't to show us that he knew who we were and so we'd better behave. It was because he wanted us to see that he knew our names and we all mattered. During one assembly he was talking about how everyone has different talents and pointed out the individual talents of pretty much every student in the room. He knew.

In another assembly he spoke about the how impressed he was with the recent inter tutor-group rugby final he'd watched. I remember him enthusing about "Luke Bujniewicz breaking through the line, then Dave Hurley charging him down." He wasn't just trying to be down with the youth either. He genuinely loved his job, and when one of his students impressed him he always made a point of telling them. During one English lesson he praised many of the writing assignments we'd done. We'd had to write our own chapter of Goodnight Mr Tom, which we'd been reading through. He read bits out of a number of them that he'd liked, then I noticed there was one exercise book still in his hand. It was mine. Uh oh! "I have to say, there was one in particular that really moved me. This was a truly excellent piece of work." I can still remember the exact feeling when I realised he was talking about my work. To know he really believed in me is possibly a lot of the reason you're reading this now…. Well of course this bit in particular, because it's about him, but I meant the book as a whole. He said in his e-mail that he was amazed to hear he'd inspired me as a writer because he was useless at writing his own stuff. School was not a good time for me, because I didn't fit in, but Elliott Furneaux made me feel like I mattered.

He was a man who really put you at ease, unless you were in trouble of course. You felt bad for letting him down, because you knew he believed in you. When he did tell you off, and it did happen to me a few times, he did it in a firm but fair way. He explained why he was having to do it, and tried to get you to understand rather than just saying you were bad. He had a great sense of humour too. I remember once he was pretending to speak Russian in class, and he was convincing! He would finish a sentence with one of our names so we'd wonder what he was saying about us, but of course we found out he wasn't saying anything. Every one of us believed him until he told us otherwise. When we did a project where we all wrote a script in groups and then recorded them on tape at the end he was genuinely invested in all of them. When our lines got a laugh from him we felt proud on the inside.

Charlie recalls also that Elliott brought in a zero tolerance policy to swearing at teachers. This was about ensuring there was respect, and it's something I remember him bringing in at Holyrood also. He did make sure to explain there was a difference between someone swearing as a reflex action after taking a heavy tackle on the rugby pitch and swearing in a conversation with a teacher. He just wanted people to grow up to have respect for others.

I was very saddened to hear of his death. I was looking forward to speaking to him further and recommending books to him, hopefully getting a few recommendations back. That the world is carrying on without him in it seems somehow unfair. Luke Kennard, one of the UK's finest modern poets and creative writing lecturer, was in the year above me at the school and was similarly complimentary about Elliott when I asked him casually on Facebook if he remembered him.

So why have I spoken so much about Elliott Furneaux in a chapter about homelessness, apart from the connection with the man who has written a book about it? Well here was someone in a position of authority and influence who genuinely cared. I'm sure Elliott would have cared deeply about homeless people, and if politicians were more like him then I'm certain more could and would be done to help. I really don't get the feeling the current government are invested in trying to help homeless people in a genuine way. Meanwhile Gideon Amos, the Lib Dem Prospective Parliamentary Candidate in Taunton, cares deeply. When living in Oxford in 1987 he became one of the main organisers for Shelter's International Year of Shelter for the Homeless.

"A few short years earlier backbencher Stephen Ross MP had managed to get his private members' bill through parliament," he recalls, "For the first time the law of the land, in the shape of the Homeless Persons' Act 1979, placed a duty on local authorities to house anyone presenting as homeless that night – no ifs, no buts."

So instead of closing soup kitchens, the local council would have to house people who had nowhere to go. Surely this would be a better foundation from which ambition could grow? Another big wheel in the Liberal Party, Des Wilson, was instrumental in setting up the Shelter Campaign. The Independent reported at the time: -

"Des Wilson was 25 years old when he wrote a report for the Church Housing Trusts urging that the campaign should aim to convince people that the housing situation 'was out of control', that Shelter would be a 'rescue operation' in a national emergency and that the homeless were innocent victims."

This was quite a few years ago, but it could almost describe our country in the modern day.

"Homelessness was then and is now one of the main spurs to me to continue the campaign for and to seek to change the lives on people in our midst who have become so disconnected from the comforts we take for granted," continues Gideon, "The Homeless Persons' Act has been so amended by subsequent governments (mainly Conservative) that a full obligation upon councils to house the homeless no longer exists, and is only provided in exceptional circumstances. Given that most of the council resources have been cut so severely and council houses sold off, these amendments were just cynical ways to reduce costs, dressed up in the political rhetoric of the day."

Gideon recognises that there are often a number of problems for rough sleepers that need to be addressed along with the problem of needing a roof over their heads, and that doing so properly will be expensive for service providers, but he sees this as being like a drop in the ocean compared to the impact of doing nothing.

"Above all, liberals like me believe the role of government (and local government) is to support and enable every citizen to lead happy, healthy lives with a meaningful place in our society," he explains, "These lives should matter to us and the costs of leading a life without a home to the people involved is incalculable. We need a government and a parliament of MPs willing to address it."

It's refreshing to me to hear a parliamentary candidate so passionate about helping the least fortunate members of society. He doesn't want anyone to live without a home, and I truly believe he means it. His wife, Caroline, hosts many of the local home education events, and during one of the recent events he came out to help retrieve a football from a tree, which is when I spoke to him about this book. I'd previously seen him talk on social media about food banks, and how shocked he was that so many families rely on them in a supposedly rich country, so I thought some insights from him would really add to this chapter. He seemed keen to help, and before long he'd sent me a lengthy e-mail with the personal reflections you've read and a whole lot more. I'd have loved to include them all; the only reason I didn't is the same reason I had to edit nearly everyones' responses to my questions.

Going back to Charlie's friends, they lost their home because they didn't have the money to pay the costs of living there. Isn't that essentially why most people who are homeless find themselves to be in the first place, although the details differ from situation to situation? It's telling that when I spoke to a number of different rough sleepers on the streets of Taunton and asked if there was anything in particular I could try and get them that would be of any help, the common answer was 'To be honest the thing that would be most helpful would be money.' The majority of people who are on the streets are there because they don't have the money not to be, because they don't have anyone who can put them up, or don't like to ask.

Most people can't afford their own home on one income, but many of them have family they can stay with, friends they can share with or partners who also work. However, nowadays it's a struggle to even get by on two incomes because the increase in wages doesn't come anywhere near matching the increase in the cost of living. Is it right that in such a supposedly civilised country it is such an all-consuming struggle just to keep a roof over your head? Of course it was a struggle in the times of yore when everyone worked their own land, but in those days everything was basically in your own hands. Now everything can so easily be taken away from you, when it doesn't have to be that way. Doesn't everyone have the right to at least have their basic survival needs met, or the means to be allowed to do so? Should anyone be made homeless?

Ok, so why don't I put my money where my mouth is? When I was asked for money by rough sleepers why didn't I give them everything I had? Well of course that's not a sustainable solution. If I was to give a homeless person a few hundred quid they might be Ok for a short time, but what about when that money runs out? Everyone needs their own income to be able to get by, and it needs to be enough to meet their living costs. The level of homelessness is rising every year; you don't need any statistics to prove this. The number of homeless people I have seen on the streets of my local town has kept rising in recent years, and everyone I've spoken to about it says the same. So if I, or you, can't solve the crisis then who can? Any ideas, Charlie?

"It goes without saying that there could and should be more – much more – support available to homeless people in the UK," he says, "But I don't like to naysay when it comes to the support currently available, because to do so downplays the wonderful and often selfless work done by so many organisations, institutions and individuals all over the UK."

Some of these organisations Charlie got a real insight into when he set out to investigate the situation first-hand.

"Take places like St. Petroc's in Cornwall, The Wild Goose in Bristol or St. Mungo's in London," he continues, "All of these are good and worthwhile, deeply noble enterprises, run not for profit but for purely altruistic purposes, and funded not by the state but by charitable donations from the public. I would further say for those who want to help, becoming involved with these organisations in whatever manner possible is the most useful way to do so. Give money to them if you have it to spare (they desperately need it), or if you don't have that then give belongings which you perhaps don't want any more – tinned food you're never going to eat to food banks, clothes you're never going to wear to shelters, those books and board games that sit on your shelves gathering dust. Most vitally, what you can give is time. By fundraising, by volunteering, or simply by visiting the organisations and lending a sympathetic ear to those who are rarely afforded such a simple luxury."

I can't argue with the fact that there is quite a bit of support available for homeless people. A few of the churches in Taunton run homeless outreaches, and the Open Doors organisation do some excellent work, as do Taunton Association for the Homeless. I have met some enterprising people who are living on the streets of Taunton. One man was selling his artwork, another was trying to start a car washing business. Of course there are also a number of Big Issue sellers; a business that has been prominent in the town since I was a teenager in the 90s. This would all count as ambition, but these same people still need the support that is offered in the town. Many families who have homes and wages still rely on food banks some of the time, and so it follows that keeping soup kitchens open does not dull ambition, rather it makes a challenging situation far more so than it has to be, and makes 'ambition' purely about survival.

If money is given to the voluntary organisations who help homeless people then perhaps it leads to a more sustainable kind of support for as many people as possible than if a bit of money is given directly to different rough sleepers every now and then. Not everyone on the streets might access the support though, and it shouldn't be assumed that they all do. It only takes a couple of minutes to ask someone what support they are aware of locally and what help they are receiving. Often, being given the time of day seems like a big thing to a rough sleeper, but why is anyone sleeping rough in the first place if they don't want to be? There are hostels, but they cost money, and there is only so much room.

I am reminded of a time earlier this decade when a campaign was started on social media to get an old Rage Against the Machine single, rather than the latest X-Factor winner's single, to be the Christmas number 1. The campaign spread and achieved its goal, and the people who'd made it happen really felt like they'd won. I remember thinking at the time, what if all of those same people got together put the same amount of energy into achieving something that truly mattered? If people power can alter the course of the music charts then can it alter the plight of the UK's rough sleepers? The criminal justice system? The fairness of the welfare state? What else could it have a bearing on? Well here's the starting point – if you feel a sense of injustice at any of the issues highlighted in this book and want to see what we can do about them then please message me via my Dave Urwin Author page on Facebook or e-mail daveurwinauthor@hotmail.com and let's talk. I've wanted to start something for years but have never really known how to go about it, so here's a humble beginning, like an acorn. Will it turn into a mighty oak?

So in summary, many, many people in what is supposedly the sixth richest country in the world are homeless; many visibly, many less so. Even more would be homeless if they weren't lucky enough to have family or friends who could help them, and have the means to do so. A problem this widespread surely cannot be down to a collective lack of ambition. Charlie knows it, I know it, hopefully you agree. Nobody can afford to give every rough sleeper enough money to change their life, or enough time to talk at length with every rough sleeper they see, but something is better than nothing, and many somethings add up to way more than you would think.

WOJTEK'S STORY PART 3 – POLISH RIDER

"Let's just stop for a minute."

"What are you talking about? The summit's right there!"

Just metres from the summit of Kilimanjiro, Wojtek and his brother are debating what to do next. Wojtek is desperate to press on to the very top before resting, his brother wants to get his breath back before the final push. I can see both of their points of view. Wojtek's brother has a point, because it's not like the summit is going anywhere any time soon. Wojtek has a point because with just a little more hard effort they can take all the rest they need, knowing that they only have to walk back down the mountain from that point onwards. An amateur psychologist might suggest that Wojtek was the one who felt he had something to prove, but I wouldn't say so necessarily, even though I would more likely take his approach and it might partly be because I felt I had something to prove. This was one of a number of physical challenges they did together in recent years, including London Triathlon, and Wojtek ran London Marathon alone another year. His brother was the one who enjoyed such activities to begin with, but Wojtek found he quite enjoyed them too once he got into them, and when we spoke on the phone he seemed intrigued by the idea of an ultramarathon.

Our man Wojtek is now in his early forties, which is a little strange to me, seeing as I remember him in magazines as a 21-year-old and it doesn't seem like twenty years ago. Music is still his living, but remember how Andy Hamilton said in an earlier chapter that you don't often keep making a self-employed living doing the same thing? Wojtek ploughs a diverse musical furrow when earning his crust. He drives his musical tractor into many fields.

"My third solo album will probably be called 'Polish Rider', after the enigmatic Rembrandt painting," he reveals, "I also plan on doing an English folk song album, sort of updated, revised and rewritten. At some point I'd like to write some serious classical music, chamber pieces and large scale works with voice and piano. There's a rich tradition of folk music down here in East Sussex, and I'd love to form a little group that could go round playing at pubs and festival type events, perhaps a fiddle, accordion, mandolin, close harmony singing. I'm also branching out into what is known as 'library' music, and film music, music for adverts and trailers... it'll hopefully enable me to stop travelling around as a hired hand piano player."

With so many musical ambitions still remaining you'd think it might be another twenty years before they're all realised. By that time Wojtek's daughters will be around the age he was when I became aware of his work with Symposium. He is now married to Michelle, who he describes as 'The first person I've been in a relationship with who hasn't tried to change me.' She is an artist herself. They have two very young daughters; Penelope and Beatrix, and being a father makes hiking towards the summit of Kilimanjiro, the oxygen growing ever thinner, seem easy in comparison.

"There was a time a while back when Beatrix wasn't sleeping and so we weren't either, and there were all sorts of other pressures going on at the same time," he sighs, "I was thinking to myself 'Ok, this is hard!' in a way I never had done when Symposium were unravelling and I had huge debts, or when I was climbing Kilimanjiro. It's just a totally different level of hard to anything else I've experienced, having someone who literally relies on you for survival."

He explains how he's become a lot more selfish in a way since becoming a father.

"Although looking after young children is a very selfless thing, when I do get time to myself I've found I have to give myself a huge break."

When I spoke to him on the phone a second time he was about to get a Thai takeaway, which is one instance of giving himself a break. Usually he would cook up a huge meal such as lentil stew. He also talks about being harder on himself nowadays because of having two very young children who rely on him. Sometimes things are tough financially, but he's managed to get by without having to do anything other than music for a living.

"Music was my first love and it will be my last," he asserts. Incidentally, the sun is shining on him in East Sussex when I speak to him as I am sat in all-encompassing gloom over in Somerset. He is certainly making hay while the sun shines, and I get the feeling he is resourceful enough to make sure it will continue.

As with many 90s bands in recent times, Symposium have been offered money to reform for some gigs. Some of the band were keener than others, and for the record Wojtek was up for it. He reiterates that he has some regrets about his time in Symposium and wishes he'd tried harder to make it work in retrospect.

"I've still never been to Australia or Japan," he reflects, "It would have been such a wonderful way to experience those places, touring with Blur."

He won't completely rule out a reunion in the future, but of course it depends on all of the members being on board, and you could say it would be a little strange for a band who split up in their early twenties to be playing songs that reflect this time in their life when they're now in their early forties. You get the feeling it would have to happen relatively soon if it was going to make sense. They were a band who really meant a lot to young people in the 90s, and it was something he always found confusing, being so young himself.

"Sometimes people would give us personal items of theirs and say we saved their lives," he recalls, "I never really knew what to do with that information, but I rationalised that if it hadn't been us it would have been Ash, or Mansun, or another band who were around at the same time. Young people look for hope in bands, and it's nice to think that we were one of them, even though I was somewhat uncomfortable with the idea."

It does seem strange when I think of it how people took such hope from what Wojtek was doing when put alongside the image of him crying on the tourbus late at night. He has explained though that his dissatisfaction with it all was nothing to do with the music, aside from the fact that he wasn't a frontman.

We move onto the subject of despair, which is the opposite of hope, and is something he's not sure he's ever truly experienced.

"I've always thought there could be hope even for someone who feels suicidal," he says, "Apart from the fact that they think death will take their pain away, it has to be the lowest point you can get to and so the only way from there is up."

It's a subject he's spent some time reflecting on despite never feeling suicidal himself.

"I watched a documentary called 'The Bridge' once," he

remembers, "It was about people who jumped off Golden Gate Bridge in San Francisco. Five of them survived, and were interviewed. All five of them said as soon they jumped they were filled with intense regret about what they'd done, and didn't want to die. I found that fascinating."

It's truly horrific to feel so devoid of hope that suicide is something to be contemplated. Wojtek is definitely a deep thinker, but not one prone to despair, as so many are. After all, how many philosophers can you name who present an overwhelmingly positive outlook? There aren't many, although Wojtek identifies that Bertrand Russell, of whom he is a fan, is one. So where does his hope lie?

"Cynically and prosaically, maybe I only hope for more money," he admits, although this was on a day when his daughters had kept him up most of the previous night and he wasn't feeling at his most positive, "I hope for continued security and health, but I can try and take better care of my health and then hope is no longer needed. I hope my children grow up to see beauty, satisfaction and fulfilment."

When they grow up you can bet their father will still be a musician, but looking at his life so far you can only guess what kind of music he might be playing by then. Perhaps a folk band touring the pubs of East Sussex playing a selection of Symposium songs rewritten for mandolin, harpsichord and close harmony singing? 'Farewell to Guitars' perhaps? He has revealed that Ross and him have plans to make music together in the future, and when we spoke for the second time he'd just been talking to a violinist friend of his about forming a band together. Perhaps we'll see more of the classical compositions he speaks of.

Either way, what is hopeful for me about Wojtek's story is that he has been able to earn a living from his talent through hard work, dedication, inventiveness and perseverance. These qualities are adaptable to so many things in life, and without them I can guarantee this book would not exist. This goes for the hard work, dedication and perseverance of those who have shared their stories with me as much, if not way more, than my own. The reason I have shared more of Wojtek's story than many is that his life explains how he succeeded ultimately in ways that weren't obvious to me when I first read about him back in the 90s. I thought the life he was living then was the epitome of what I should be aiming for, but the life he has now, although it would have seemed far less cool to my younger self, makes him far happier. It is a far more wholesome life. We are a fairly similar age, and I have had a conviction for much of my life, without the results to back it up most of the time, that I can actually one day earn a living through writing. Wojtek has shown, although it's music rather than writing for him, that it can be done. He had an early level of success that I definitely can't claim to have matched, but he has also had a level of debt I can't imagine and come out the other side. Besides, I enjoy talking to him. As well as the fact he's easy to get on with and seems to enjoy the conversation as much as I do, it's great to have the nostalgia.

"We can talk again – I don't care about the book, I just like talking about the old times!" he jokes. He has heaps of other stories as well. There's one about All Tomorrow's Parties festival, one that I actually attended at the same time as him, which I have insisted he saves for his own book as it would make the perfect opening. He also tells me he has heaps of other Symposium stories, and there's more about his meeting with E-Win, but these are different stories for another day.

I hope we will talk again, but look out for his book one day because I believe it will be a hugely entertaining read, whether it is written in collaboration with me as it obviously should be, or he decides to write it by himself for some strange reason. I mean, he must be FAR too busy with his music for such shenanigans as writing a book? Just look back at the list of things he wants to write/record in the future.

Anyway, now it's time to draw Wojtek's story to a close as part of this book. Let's move on to another story and leave him to dream up some more musical ideas as he walks his daughters around St. Leonard's. That humble man with the cardigan, the grizzly beard and the musical mind that many have enjoyed for twenty years. Farewell for now, Polish rider.

CONNER'S STORY PART 12

It was a sombre occasion on the day I met Conner for the first time. A cold day too. The kind of cold that bites your skin and makes a winter's day down south seem tropical by comparison. You have to be pretty tough to cope with a Geordie winter. Maybe that's why Geordies have that reputation, although they also have a great sense of humour. You need that when the fog on the Tyne's icy grip won't let go between late September and early May the following year.

All joking aside, the day had gone quickly and now it was time to say goodbye to Conner, Mark (who unbelievably I was also meeting for the first time), Emma, Jayden (another first-timer), Viv and Chris again. I was shaking Conner's hand. He looked confused – not a blank stare, but like he was struggling to recall. This lasted for a moment, and then the same grin that had been on his face for a lot of the day returned.

"I thought it was the other way round actually," he smiled, as I heard laughter erupting all around me. I'd just asked him if he had the fifty quid I'd lent him earlier, because he said he couldn't remember where he'd been. He saw the funny side. So did everyone else. Phew! My jokes don't always pay off. I recently made a friend's little girl cry by pretending to be really hurt for comedic effect when she hit me with a pencil.

I hadn't spoken a huge amount with him that day; it was the day of my grandad's funeral. Early in the morning we'd all spoken about a story in the local newspaper involving a lady who'd apparently bathed a fox that wandered into her house, thinking it was a dog. During the wake I asked Conner if he'd met that fox, because he was wearing a pair of those trousers with a whole load of rips in them, which seem to be in fashion with the youth nowadays. I met my cousin Amber for the first time that day too, who Conner seemed to get on really well with. He seemed to get on really well with everyone. Aside from forgetting about the money I lent him.....er, I mean forgetting where he'd been earlier that day, and showing signs of his impaired vision when he walked now and then, I would never have been able to tell something had happened to him if I hadn't known. What impressed me was that he was trying to live as normal a life as he could. He didn't want anyone to feel sorry for him, he just wanted to be the same 17-year-old lad he would have been had he never experienced all you've read.

Conner has very little recollection of being in hospital. Things are different for him now than before he was there, in that he can't play football or go out on his bike like he used to. These were the things he used to always enjoy, and that so many young people take for granted. Nothing should be taken for granted, but until something major happens to remind us of this, things always are. It can't be helped. Neither he nor his family are able to forget what happened; things have changed, and there's no denying it. He's alive though, and not just alive but living. He has a great sense of humour, and if Facebook is anything to go by he's a popular lad. People continue to be amazed when they find out what happened to him. An old teacher of his bumped into him on the beach and Conner explained about his time in hospital. The guy listened in silence and openly wept when he'd heard everything out loud. Conner felt a little awkward because he hated to see someone so upset. He didn't know what to say and so he just gave him a hug. Conner doesn't want to be treated differently, and apart from his eyesight and memory not being quite what they were, he's still basically the lad he was before.

Caitlin and Olivia both feel they've been changed by the whole experience. I didn't have anything like this happen to any of my best friends when I was 17, and can only imagine the shock and upset they felt.

"They whole thing really changed my perspective on everything," says Caitlin, "How much I love my best friends and how much you've got to be there for them, especially in times like this. It was hard to see Conner get himself all frustrated but he always fought back in the end and it really paid off all the hard effort he put into making himself well again, because he's amazing now and I'm so proud of him for what he's done."

Olivia echoes this, and remembers a hydrotherapy session of Conner's they went along to observe with Mark and Emma in the RVI.

"He was really pushing himself to try his best even with his weaker side, so I felt really proud of him," she recalls, "Was quite embarrassing for me that day though because the physios had asked us to take our shoes off to go and stand by the pool. I was like "Er...oh....really?" at first, because I had odd socks on. Not just odd; one of them was an ankle sock and one was a knee high!"

They all laugh now at the memory, and it was humorous moments such as these that helped keep them all going. Another time Caitlin and Olivia visited it was Valentine's Day. They'd made cards for Conner, complete with 'cringey words' on the inside, and he was laughing at what they'd written.

"That day when we went in Viv told us they had a surprise for us, but she couldn't keep it in and so she told us on the way there," laughs Olivia, "It was that he'd started talking, and we were amazed by how much he'd improved since the last time we'd seen him. He was trying to tell us something; he tried a few times and we finally understood him because he sounded quite clear. We realised he was actually trying to say our names. It was a relief that he remembered us, then every time we went after that we noticed how he kept making improvements. This helped us to keep positive even though some days were more upsetting than others."

Obviously it took a long time for Conner to get to where he is now in terms of his recovery. His speech came back over time, and it frustrated him immensely to not be able to get his point across, as it sometimes still does. Having learnt to talk years ago, it seemed unfair that he had to do it all over again. Also, his brain was working far quicker than he was able to keep up with. He called Mark every name under the sun before he called him 'Dad' again. I don't mean abusive names by the way. He called him Norris once though, which makes Mark laugh even to think of now.

After a while Conner left the RVI and was moved to Sunderland. He was sad to leave the RVI at first because he'd grown close to the nurses there, and I wonder if perhaps, already feeling a sense of loss of who he was before he'd been in hospital, it seemed too much to deal with to have more loss. When he got to Sunderland he had a choice to make, because what had happened to him was incredibly rare for someone of his age. He could either be in a ward full of small children, making him by far the oldest, or he could be in a ward full of old people and be by far the youngest. He chose to be the youngest. It took him some time to settle in to his new environment, but he was helped after a few weeks when a lad from the RVI who had been in a serious car accident moved over. Conner is still in touch with him now.

Despite struggling in Sunderland to begin with, Conner continued to make improvements. By May they had started to discuss the possibility of him coming home. Around a week before Jayden's birthday they had a meeting to discuss options. He had been allowed home for a weekend previously, but the therapist wondered if he was ready because he was still very confused, and obviously it was a big adjustment going back to where he knew so well but not being able to do everything he could the last time he was there. Having said that, he was feeling very unhappy in hospital because he wanted normality, even though currently it seemed beyond his reach, so they agreed during the meeting that it was in his best interests to go home. They decided he would come home on 16th May. Conner had to leave the meeting because it was upsetting him. Mark thinks it may have been due to hearing himself being talked about in such a clinical way.

Unbelievably, things were about to get far more complicated the weekend before the 16th. Emma collapsed, and was taken to hospital, as mentioned in a previous chapter. This was the beginning of a fairly lengthy spell of illness for her as well, and was to do with corrective surgery being needed to alter the position of her brain. Her condition wasn't life-threatening but did give her a lot of headaches and made her feel unwell. The timing was astonishingly ironic, and Mark was now spread pretty thinly. He was back at work by now, and when he wasn't there his time had to be split between Conner in Sunderland, Emma in South Shields Hospital and Jayden at home. I picture him with elasticated limbs being stretched out when I think of this. He must have been exhausted! Their friends John and Lynsey helped a lot during this time, including taking Conner back to hospital on that Sunday evening – he'd been allowed to come home for the weekend. What all of this meant for

Mark though was that when Conner was due to come home he couldn't guarantee there would be the constant care he needed. He dreaded breaking the news to the nurses in Sunderland because of what this might mean for Conner, having made so much progress. How would he react knowing that his homecoming would be delayed? They didn't know what was going to happen with Emma at this point, so if he wasn't coming home now they couldn't tell him when he would be. With another dose of perfect timing, not a minute after Mark had explained everything to the nurses, having psyched himself up, Emma called and said she would be allowed home later that night.

They went up together on the Tuesday to bring Conner home. The nurses were a little anxious about how Emma would cope, but she was determined that nothing would be delayed any further. Although he couldn't wait to come back, Conner was distraught to leave in a way because he would have to leave his beloved Rachel behind. Rachel was a nurse he'd become smitten with. There was another nurse named Leslie whose name he struggled to pronounce, and so she became 'Reslie', even when he would have been able to call her by her proper name. Conner had a good laugh with her. When he left there were tears – he'd gotten very close again to all of the nurses, but he had to leave. Not least because he had a big birthday surprise for Jayden, who didn't know he was coming home.

He'd been walking unaided, albeit with some difficulty, for a week or so leading up to this, having been in his wheelchair for some time. By the time I saw him in November he was walking without much difficulty, although his sight sometimes made it tricky. On the day he was due to leave hospital he stumbled whilst walking, and almost instantly there was a nurse right upon them who had been at the other end of the corridor and see what had happened.

"You scared us then, Conner! Don't do that again," she blasted, having been terrified that he was about to collapse.

Conner has been out of hospital since. He's been on holiday a couple of times with the family, and has only visited hospital again when it was something to do with his continuing recovery. There's been no relapse. He turned 18 in January 2018 and went to Turkey for three weeks with the family this summer. To think how close he was to never turning 18, the overriding feeling is of what he has gained rather than what he has lost. Of course there are times when he will think of what he'd be doing if none of this had ever happened to him, and may feel despondent and frustrated at times, but that he's still here is remarkable in itself. That he made such a recovery is a similar story of resilience and determination as his great grandad; my grandad William Urwin, who lived more than half as many years after his terminal cancer diagnosis as he did before it.

I'm amazed by how quickly he recovered, and could write paragraphs about it, but to do so here rather than telling him myself seems insincere. For now I will just say that when I was seventeen I was giving my parents as many sleepless nights as Conner did his, but for entirely different reasons. I was a complete twerp. Conner is not. He's a jolly good fellow. He seems like a much wiser 18-year-old than I was. I'm not sure if his parents would always agree, as you know what teenagers can be like, but his story I'm sure is going to inspire a lot of people and will be a source of hope for families who find themselves in situations nobody would want to be in.

Mark and Emma, it goes without saying, are proud of Conner for the way he has dealt with the whole nightmare, and of Jayden, who has been very unselfish despite coming second for a long time while Conner was recovering, and being passed from pillar to post. He understood. They are also very thankful to Caitlin, Olivia and all of his friends who came to visit in hospital, who probably aren't aware just how important a role they played in his recovery. The entire thanks list is long, but if you have been mentioned in the story consider that to be a thank you. If you haven't then hopefully you know who you are. One final thank you goes to Simon Smith of Morgan Sindall, Paul's workplace, for how he allowed Paul time off to come and be with his family and for sending the chocolates despite never having met them. He still asks after Conner now, which shows how sincere he was.

When I think of Conner's story, and of those of my grandad, Danny McCormack and many other tough Geordies I feel thankful for the genes I have. Seems they may come in useful one day.

YOU MIGHT GET HIT BY A BUS

"Seeing my son lying there dead told me that I should practice what I preach."

Mark and Emma consider themselves extremely fortunate that Conner survived. Some parents have been through similar situations but with a tragic outcome that is hard to ever truly come to terms with. Less than a year after his hospitalisation, Conner's friend Tyler was killed in a motorbike accident. Just a few months ago a popular lad from Taunton died from a drug overdose. Another parent who lost his son was Pete from Denmark, who is responsible for the quote that began this chapter. He went through something no parent should ever have to, and it could have been the final straw, but instead he was in time inspired to live by the qualities he most admired in the son he lost.

"I had a very sub-optimal childhood and have been dealing with that for a good part of my adult life," he explains, "In the late eighties I had been keeping the demons in check with various substances and living life in the fast lane but when I applied for a different job in my unit and my boss replied with the question 'Give me three reasons for letting you stay' I had a moment of clarity."

Pete acknowledged that his way of life, although it may have been helping him to stay afloat in the short term, was going to hold him back and perhaps even destroy his future. He made a deal with his boss; he had a year to change direction and get his life back on track, and if he succeeded then the new job would be his. Sometimes the inspiration for change can come from someone else showing they care and that they believe in you. Remember the police officer who helped Rico to get support for his drug addiction rather than throwing him in a cell and telling him he was scum?

If someone is already feeling bad it's unlikely that they will be inspired to feel better by their negative self-image being reinforced. In the same way that closing soup kitchens is unlikely to increase the ambition of rough sleepers, castigating someone who is already punishing themselves is less likely to inspire change than showing understanding, whilst recognising that there is a problem. At this point Pete ramped up his dedication to fitness, which made him feel stronger both physically and mentally, and ultimately allowed him to get the new job. Around this time he also became a father. When his son was born, Pete would run along pushing him in a pram, then pulling him along on a trailer whilst cycling. A second son would soon follow, and the trailer got bigger, but his training didn't slow down. It gave him a new degree of confidence, but not a huge amount, because after completing some shorter triathlons he decided against trying any longer ones because someone had told him he couldn't do it.

Pete had made real progress in his life; getting his addictions under control, getting fit and healthy and being a good father, but there were monumental challenges ahead that would have been a huge test for anyone.

"As things went I got divorced," he says, "I think I knew for a long time the marriage wouldn't work, but I had it in my head that my children would not have the same start in life as me, and so I really tried to keep it going. My demons from the past started showing their ugly head."

Far worse was still to come. In 2012 Pete was devastated when his son drowned whilst diving near Stavanger, Norway. It had been his dream to become a professional diver, and Pete was inspired by his dedication in pursuing it. If anything good was to come of this horrific loss it would be that Pete would become a better person and live in a way that honoured his son.

"When I was standing next to my son, who was lying dead on a table, I vowed that I would follow my dreams. Some would take time, but they would get the appropriate attention."

Pete reflected on the way his son had been following a dream by moving to Norway and doing the job he'd always wanted to. It had cost him his life, and it brought home to Pete how short and precious life is, once the initial devastation he obviously felt had become a dull ache of grief that would fluctuate in intensity. A friend who lost his wife a few years ago said that time doesn't heal but you learn to manage the pain. Grief, I think, is something that effects people always. Every time we lose someone the world becomes a slightly different place, and when it's someone so close it doesn't stop impacting upon us no matter how much time goes by.

"Nineteen years ago I had a second moment of clarity when I bumped into an old girlfriend who'd dumped me because of my way of life," recalls Pete, "This time I listened to her. We went on a trek together to Northern Sweden, where my son's death was allowed to, in the lack of better words, sink in. She is my wife now, and I realised that my son had lived the way I wanted him to be able to; following his dream, and now it was time to practice what I'd preached to him and follow mine."

To get a picture of Pete's childhood, and what shaped his view of himself and the world, he speaks of how in Denmark there are some unofficial 'rules' known as the law of Jante that provide a subtle undercurrent to the way people live.

They are: -

1. You're not to think *you* are anything special
2. You're not to think *you* are as special as *we* are
3. You're not to think *you* are smarter than *we* are
4. You're not to imagine *yourself* better than *we* are
5. You're not to think *you* know more than *we* do
6. You're not to think *you* are more important than *we* are
7. You're not to think *you* are good at anything
8. You're not to laugh at *us*
9. You're not to think anyone cares about *you*
10. You're not to think *you* can teach *us* anything

I guess what you take from the law of Jante could depend on your personal outlook to a degree. Looking at it as an outsider, I'd say at best these 'rules' could be taken as a reminder to always be humble, not to brag and to consider the feelings of others. At worst though they could fill you with self-doubt, or even self-loathing. Looking at the placement of the italics, I'd say the law of Jante was intended to prioritise the importance of the collective rather than the individual. It's the same thinking behind communities. That's for most of the points anyway. Point 1-6 can be taken that way for sure, even though without the italics a couple of them seem fairly brutal. Point 1, when put alongside point 2, is basically saying the same thing. Points 7-10 I struggle with. You are not to think *you* are good at anything? Surely key to the collective success and well-being is that everyone does have their individual strengths, and each of these are equally important to the whole? Also, point 9 – You're not to think anyone cares about *you?* Surely there's only one way that can be taken? Pete thinks his childhood would have been very different if the law of Jante hadn't been there. He grew up with an inferiority complex that persisted into adulthood, and when people showed belief in him he responded, but then something would happen to set him back.

When his son died, and after taking some time out to try to come to terms with his horrific loss and figure out how he could carry on, he started to be inspired by the way his son had pursued his dreams. He began to figure out that by telling his son to do this he'd also been telling himself, without realising.

"There may or may not be more to this world than we can see," ponders Pete, "But I just feel that doing the best I can do is the best source of hope. Knowing that I have done things, helped people and trained/raced as well as I can is the best formula for doing greater things."

He has completed a number of Ironman Triathlons and ultramarathons, which he was told he couldn't, and through his work he has been deployed to seven different war zones around the world. He has learnt a lot from both.

"When I stood in the Sahara Desert with my tiny backpack at the start of the Marathon Des Sables in 2015 I was humbled," he recalls, "I had all I needed to live a whole week in that backpack and I'd never felt more free. I think that we modern humans fill our lives with too much junk, which can be both physical and mental. We set too many parameters for success and doing so gets in the way of being happy with what we have achieved."

A number of the stories in this book would back up what Pete is saying. Often simplicity leads to the greatest fulfilment. We spend so much time focusing on the wrong things. This is something that really hit home to Pete when he spent time in war zones.

"I have also learned that it's possible to pursue my dreams whilst encouraging others to follow theirs," he reflects, "I'm not saying I never get sad nowadays, but when I do I allow myself to be sad and at the same time I try to look for any good in the situation."

Of course Pete will always be devastated to have lost his son. This doesn't go away. He has managed to carry on though by "Facing my fears and tackling them, dreaming big and living life to the max." Living life to the max doesn't have to mean running through the desert for days. It's about focusing on what's most important and not being half-hearted in pursuing it. If it's being there for those close to you that's most important to you then that's living life to the max. The point Pete is making is that you can do both. Of course when somebody else relies on you then your own dreams have to take a back seat to a degree. That's true for everyone, and is the way it should be. In the fullness of life though there's no reason why there shouldn't be room for both. To me another drawback of social media is that we are bombarded with images of what others have done and think it's somehow better or more important than what we do, so we can lose sight of what is important to us in trying to keep up with everyone else, or despairing that we can't. I don't remember this being so intense before the internet. Perhaps then we just looked around us and thought the same but it seemed far less full-on. I realise I'm repeating myself in making this point.

What Pete is also saying is to make the most of every day, because you could be hit by a bus. Well that's exactly what happened to Leon Gray, aka 'Hit by Bus Guy.'

Leon wasn't a young man when he was hit by the bus, but he was a very active 64-year-old. He was president of both a trail running group and a road running group, had run several 50ks and had been training for a 50 mile race. I will let him continue.

"I was cross training on my bike when I was hit by the handicap bus," he states, "The handicap bus made me handicapped. Well at least it wasn't a hearse."

Leon got to ride to the hospital in a helicopter, but because there's no NHS in America it ended up costing him $19,500, or at least it would have done had his health insurer not finally agreed to pay it. They weren't too pleased about the outlay. A sobering thought. He had a shattered pelvis, a broken leg and several fractures, and was in a coma for two months, then had to stay in hospital for another two weeks before spending two further months in a nursing home and then another two months with a live-in nurse during the week. Around seven months after the accident he developed a hernia, then a month after having an operation to get it removed he developed a hematoma, which got infected with MRSA. It was back to the hospital for all of January of the year following his accident. Feeling dizzy?

A friend of mine named Dan was hit by a bus around five years ago but never woke from his coma. Leon did, but his difficulties were far from over. Like he said though, he had survived. It was clear that his running skills would have been somewhat hampered by his injuries, but he didn't want what had happened to stop him from enjoying his hobby. There were numerous peaks and troughs when he tried to get his fitness back.

"2014-2015 were good years, with twenty races from a 5k to a 24-hour race, in which I clocked 62 miles. Some were on road, some on a trail," he recalls, "2016 sucked with plantar fasciitis, knee and hamstring injuries. In 2017 I did a lot of walking, then I did a technical 12k in January 2018, which took 3:31. I used to do it in about 1:30. I have a 30k trail race in November and a 50 miler, and will probably bump up to 100k in February 2019."

How has he recovered from his injuries? Do they still trouble him?

"I do suffer from Peripheral Neuropathy in both feet but they don't really hurt that much, just more of a bother. I'm quite fortunate because it can be very painful, but now it's just numb and heavy with hypersensitive skin on top of the feet. I just deal with it and go on. I'm now blind in one eye, my balance is super wonky, my right leg doesn't lift all that well so doing technical trails is a real challenge. There I've got the speed of a three-legged, slightly inebriated tortoise."

I like Leon already. Similarly to Conner, he has a way about him that must be infectious to those around him, and has not focused on what he can't do but what he can do.

"I can't do what I used to do but I still get out all the time and DO what I can. I put on about a third more of my existing weight during the several months I was in hospital, and I started to get a pot belly. I said to myself 'I am NOT going to be a potbelly stickman, and now I'm happy."

When I asked him what the main things were that he'd learned from all he'd been through he was similarly to the point.

"I'm often told I'm a miracle and an inspiration to others," he states honestly, rather than with braggadocio, "The miracle part I agree with but I just feel like almost anybody who's had a traumatic experience should try to get better. Just don't say 'woe is me' and expect everyone to do everything for you."

There have been a bunch of stories in this book of people who've recovered from things they easily couldn't have on paper. What they have in common is the fact that they all found hope and they all fought. Leon reasoned that although it sucked getting hit by the bus, and all the complications that followed, he was still alive and he could still use his legs. The former was ridiculous in itself. The latter was pretty mind-blowing considering how badly he was hurt. Like the Karl

Meltzers and the ageing marathon record holders from the previous chapter, Leon has shown that age doesn't have to be a barrier to activity. Around 70 years old now, he just wants to keep doing what he loves to do. It seems the only thing that will stop him will be if he is hit by a hearse another time. Like Justin Gloden, a lifetime of running seems to be his goal. His three-legged inebriated tortoise pace may prevent him from chasing Masters gold medals, but it's far more important for him to be out there in the first place. Despite being such an easy going guy, there are things about the modern day that rile him, one being similar to most people if those in this book are anything to go by.

"I don't like seeing several people who are supposedly out together and all have their faces buried in their phones. Put them away and TALK. Also, many younger people of today are flat out wimps and easily offended by everything."

I can almost hear this page being torn out of books by the thousand (wishful thinking about the size of my audience), but if so stop and think. Does Leon have a point? This may seem a little harsh, but being offended does seem to be the in trend nowadays. Couldn't all that time spent being offended be put to better use? Maybe I'm somewhat guilty myself. I had a message via my author page saying that my first book was one of the worst things ever written, and that I was one of these millennials who should stop feeling sorry for himself. I do retreat into self-pity sometimes I admit, but I'd like to think the review was a little harsh as I've heard from plenty more people who said they really got something out of reading it. Something good I mean.

Anyway, if we are to blend the messages behind Pete and Leon's stories we can say that awful things happen. Things that are unfair, and that can make it hard to find the strength to carry on sometimes. To be sad about these things is only natural, but in time the only option is to try to look for reasons to carry on. These reasons always exist, even though it may not always seem that way. You could get hit by a bus tomorrow, literally or metaphorically, so make the most of today. That doesn't mean you should live recklessly, just mindfully. Mindfully of the fact that every day matters, and that the people you care about will not always be here, so while they are, and while you are, live like it matters. Because it really does.

EPILOGUE

"With a deep sigh, Henry collapsed back into his chair as the computer whirred into life. This was the most beautiful sound on earth to him, and following the syringing it was now embellished with extra intricacies. Sounds he'd never heard before. A world of possibilities contained within that screen. A chance to dream. He reached up and pulled the window shut, cancelling out the cacophony of birdsong. He drew the curtains closed and gained shelter from the blinding light of the outside world, retreating into the comforting glow of the technological arena he called home. The final checks commenced. Half a bottle of cherryade and huge unopened bag of beef and onion crisps would see him through the next few hours until it was time to call up for his daily meal. Where would it come from today? Who cared? He was good for it. Vibezone kept tipping money into his account faster than he could ever spend it, even as reckless as he was with his finances. What he made in a good morning paid all the costs associated with this place for a month. It was never a bad morning. His people hung on his every word, and even though he got a tiny fraction of the money Vibezone made from him, a tiny fraction was still a small fortune. He didn't care about this either. Vibezone needed the money more than he did. They were the ones who kept the world spinning. They gave him a big enough slice of the pie that he never went hungry; literally, metaphorically, categorically. That was the thing. He just didn't care. At least not about anything except the one thing that had been his focus all this time.

He took a few extra deep breaths, holding for two seconds at a time before exhaling slowly. It was almost time. Today would be the day. 25 million kudoes. Up to number 7 in the rankings, and within another million of everyone up to 4th place. The top 3 weren't gonna be shifted any time soon, but they could wait. They'd go off the boil, and people would be sick of them by Christmas. Richard Crogworthy would be at number 1 for another year even if he got no further kudoes in all that time, but his days were numbered too. The rise to the top would never be in doubt, because Henry was wiser than all of them, and getting to number one was literally all he cared about....."

The Mexican man in the mariachi band bounces down the street with a trumpet in his hand. Not a care in the world, he's feeling good. He woke up this morning and knew he would. Across the seas there's an icy breeze, a man huddles in a doorway trying not to freeze. He's getting old, no fixed abode, life gave him lemons and they grew mould. With a hacking cough he counts the cost and cries about everything he has lost.

The opening paragraphs I wrote before I had read the book 'Ready Player One' this year. My friend Neil posted it to me because he thought I might enjoy it. He was right. It was also basically what I had been trying to write, but I felt it did a much better job than I was doing. I wasn't disappointed. Besides, for the second time in my life a work of fiction I invested a lot of time and energy into was swept aside, making way for a work of non-fiction that was probably the far better option for me to be writing in the first place. Most fiction is loosely based on reality anyway. I love a good novel, and luckily for me the world has plenty of good novelists. I think writing about real life is

EPILOGUE

my thing, but there's always a bit of room for some prose-style writing in there. The other paragraph was just something I wrote that explains how some people appear to need hope far more than others, but just because someone has it in abundance doesn't mean they don't need it too. The need for hope is something everybody has in common.

Besides, what I wrote, I discovered, was what more people than I realised were thinking. Nearly everyone I spoke to for this book thinks the world is too technology-driven and that we have retreated too far into a virtual reality. It wasn't a loaded question with any of them as far as I can recall. I simply asked them what they didn't like about the modern world, not what they thought of the increasingly technological nature of it. We spend too much time on technology. By 'we' I mean the vast majority of us, before anyone gets too offended, which many would also say is a very modern trait. I wasn't around in Tudor times and so I don't know if people were constantly offended then. It would go some way towards explaining the barbaric punishments dished out by Henry VIII on others who didn't see the world his way. It has to be said though, people seem far more offended now than I ever remember them being when I was growing up. I got called a 'misogynist and quite possibly a racist' last year for suggesting that Beyonce wasn't the best role model for young girls. My reasoning was that her message seemed to actually be anti-male, and I see a lot of that on Facebook. 'Men are scum, women rule' – not about making sure women are treated with respect but that all men are treated like dirt because some of them behave like peldrigudes. I might be wrong, but I just saw something I felt should be highlighted and so I did. Several people who would describe themselves as being ultra-liberal and in favour of free speech weren't very liberal towards my free speech. Never mind though.

What can be done about the all-encompassing power of the digital age? Another book I read on a similar subject, which shall remain nameless as I don't want to put people off reading it for themselves, suggested that there was probably nothing we can do. While I don't exactly disagree with the fact that there will never be a return to simpler ways unless it is forced upon us, I do think there is something we can all do as individuals. I can't speak for you, so I'll just say what I plan to do, which is the same as I've been planning to do for a long time. I plan to have at least one block of four hours or more in each day during which I won't look at my phone at all unless somebody calls me. I might even leave it behind when I go out, as much as this will invoke rage in anyone who does try to contact me during those hours. I will dedicate far more time to meaningful activities, or even just activities I enjoy that aren't technology based. I can research new skills online and get inspiration there but once I have learnt those things I will practice them frequently offline. Any time I do spend on the internet, apart from a short while I will allow myself some days, will have a purpose. Be it contacting an old friend, organising something, trying to sell something, researching a topic or a skill, whatever it may be, it won't just be mindless time. I will read more books. I will exercise every day in some way, and will get fitter than I have ever been. I will finally sort out my diet and maintain it. I will find new ways to earn money, including regular employment, and work harder. I will do favours for people without expecting anything in return. I will make lists and action every point on them. I will keep my car tidy. I will keep myself tidy. I will fight for causes I believe in. I will try to be far less of a twerp. I won't ever let myself lose hope again.

At this point I take a deep breath. I continue. I will get

a guitar and play it every day, even if it's just for five or ten minutes. I will play it because I enjoy it, but I will get better. I might even record some covers of songs I like, and practice singing so they don't sound terrible. I might even write a few of my own. I will try and become somebody those who haven't given up on me, even though I've given them all so many reasons not to, can be proud of. I will try and be a good influence and a good role model. I will try and get this book to as wide an audience as possible, because the people who have spoken to me for it deserve to have their stories heard. I will try to put my metaphorical, and perhaps literal money where my literal mouth is and try to do something about the issues I've highlighted in this book rather than just saying how terrible they are and then going on with my life as if they're not happening. I will look to get closer to God again, and have a serious look at myself and work out why there have been barriers. I will remember Billy Isherwood's story, among others, and realise that not every Christian has always been a shining example of one, and that people found it hard to follow God even in biblical times. I will not wave a bible in anyone's face unless they ask for one, but I will try to be a much better example. Not just for me but for everyone I come into contact with, even if I think they're a twerp. Takes one to know one. On December 15th 2018 it will be 1,000 days until I'm 40. On that day I will write a list (maybe 10, maybe 100, maybe anywhere in between) of goals to achieve over those 1,000 days. Most of them will be ambitious but all will be realistic. I won't let myself lose sight of hope ever again, no matter how desperate things might seem.

That's enough about me and my hopes. What about hope in general? Wojtek told me his piano teacher would always say "Hope springs eternal." When in the worst situations the way to keep moving forward is to believe that things may get better, and to act upon this belief. Some situations are so horrific that finding hope within them can be like searching for a needle in a haystack, but if you are to find that needle then the hope can become the haystack. A haystack of hope is more than enough to get you through the day. Whether you find your hope in God, in other people, in music, in nature, in a new flavour of Lucozade you are desperate to try…. Wherever you find your hope, you can't deny that you need it. To bring hope where there is despair is the most amazing gift you can give to somebody, and sometimes just being there is enough to give a glimmer of hope. Just getting in touch, or choosing to abandon your Game of Thrones marathon to spend a bit of time with someone close to you. Sometimes what might seem like a tiny gesture of kindness to you could actually be a major turning point for somebody. Sometimes just to know that somebody cares can have a huge impact.

It had a huge impact on me to know that everyone who spoke to me for this book cared enough to spare a bit of their time. If I can repay them all by getting their stories heard and it leading to some kind of opportunity that will help them to maintain hope, then I've helped in some way……

"Is it time?"

The question hung in the frosty air. The man with the icy stare kept his eyes fixed on the screen. It remained to be seen whether he'd heard. He didn't say a word, just kept on staring; his expression cold, blank and uncaring.

The man who'd asked the question took a step back towards the comforting darkness of the shadows. His breath created great plumes of steam in the space between the shadows and the screen. His heart was pounding at a raised tempo, with a slight echo. On the screen a man was speaking fast, his eyes

EPILOGUE

wide as his head moved from side to side....

"Thank you for joining me for another great day on Vibezone. The sun's shining out there, and it's a beautiful day. At least that's what they'll tell you, but you know what sunshine really means? That's right; sunburn. Sunburn, wasps, sweat.... the list goes on. You're much safer in Henry VIIII's court. I'm not like the last Henry – he was doing just fine until he had all those wives of his. They made him go beserk and act like a total berk. I'm not gonna make the same mistake. Now it's time to hear from a few of my subjects...."

The man on the screen smiled straight at his audience as he said this, but he received nothing back from either man in this room. They kept watching in silence. The man in the shadows thought about repeating his question, but fear held his tongue like it was encased in concrete. It was the total absence of emotion from the man sat in front of him that created the aura of terror. The way he could do the things he did without seeming to feel a thing. Perhaps that was just it. Perhaps he'd done so many terrible things that he couldn't feel a thing any more. Did he even consider what he did to be bad? He considered it to be necessary; that's all anyone could gather. Had he gone past the point where conscience could be any part of his person? Maybe he wasn't human? Whatever the reason for his emptiness, it forced respect upon anyone who stood in his presence. The man on the screen continued.....

"Ok, so Kenny Burns says 'Your majesty, I'm glad to 'hear' your ailment has been cured...'"

Henry guffawed and slapped his thigh with great intensity, trying not to wince from the pain.

"Oh Kenny, your humour is music to my 'ears.' Your message continues, but as you know I have hundreds to get through. My lunch won't eat itself, but my stomach will if it's not filled soon, and I'd like to get to the end of this column before that has a chance to happen. Thank you, Kenny."

The man in the shadows wondered how much more of this he'd have to watch, but at the same time he was strangely in awe of the man on the screen. They'd been aware of him for many years, and were fairly certain he posed no threat, but he'd climbed the 'Tree of Vibezone' over the past few years, now being only seven leaves from the very top. Without their help it might take him another three years to get into the top five, but he seemed to have an astuteness about him that could one day see him climbing all the way. He recognised that less is more. He was the only one of the top 10 who didn't have his camera on 24/7, and that made him an enigma to thousands. Henry VIIII appearing in Vibezone was an event, and when he left it was an event too. There were conversations from people all over the planet about where he might be, and what he might be doing. Nobody knew what he looked like off-screen, because of the outrageous costume he wore on it. Therefore as long as he didn't draw attention to himself he could probably go anywhere and not be recognised. Maybe some of them had met him a number of times and never even realised. There were many forums dedicated to just that topic. He was like Banksy but far more daring. These two men watching him on the screen in the cold room knew where he lived. They always had done. They could have made it public at any time.

"It's time," said the man sat at the screen, without turning round or even shifting his gaze at all, "Set up a meeting."

"Thought you'd never ask!" said the man in the shadows, stepping forward to the keyboard as the man who was seated moved to the side. He did have a flicker of guilt at what he was about to facilitate, just like he always did, but he knew it would pass, just like it always did too. It had always been difficult for

EPILOGUE

him to feel too much sympathy for these people. If they were stupid enough to walk into a trap, and blinded by their own egos, then surely they deserved everything they got. On the other hand, if their fame showed them the way to the truth then they could end up being powerful allies. Even better. Either way, any threat would be neutralised.

The man who had been sat down stood and left the other man to type his message. He ran two slender, callused fingers through a straight lock of his slightly receding fringe, a few hints of silver now beginning to show amid the jet black as he stood on the cusp of his fiftieth year. He strolled across to the alcove where the whiskey bottles were kept, instantly gravitating towards a forty-year-old Scottish malt and pouring a small measure into a tall glass, topping it up with ginger beer from a can that he had already opened an hour ago. He took a sip, carrying the glass back over to the screen and not offering his accomplice a drink

"Are we going to tell the others?"

"Not yet," he replied, taking another small sip, "Not until he's been properly assessed."

The man at the screen nodded, turning back to complete his message. Something about this one was different to any he'd set up before. He couldn't quite tell what it was, and of course he didn't share his feelings with the man next to him, even though he'd spent most of every day with him for the past ten years. He found himself wondering how he could spend so much time with someone and yet know so little about them. He didn't even know his name.

"If he can meet tomorrow we'll meet him tomorrow," said the mysterious man, "If he can't then make sure it's soon........"

That was another chapter of the novel I'd been writing. Again, it was very 'Ready Player One', even though I'd never read that book. There is nothing new under the sun. You know where that quote's from? Some postmodernist thinker, right? I thought so too, but it's actually from the book of Ecclesiastes in the bible. The writer of that book, believed by many to be Solomon, who had lived a life that was full and travelled each and every highway, metaphorically speaking, was saying there was nothing new under the sun in a time before memes, before the internet, before the industrial revolution. There was nothing new then? What he meant was that all of the things he thought were so important turned out to be meaningless. Can anyone relate to that?

In the chapter above the main character, an internet celebrity who called himself Henry VIIII (I was in the midst of a Tudor obsession at the time) was holding court to his 'subjects', basically his online followers. I look at the world nowadays and this is what I see. Also in the chapter was a shadowy figure and his henchman, who were seemingly plotting Henry's demise because he was threatening to become more powerful than them. Seeing as the novel will never be finished, let me tell you what was going to happen.

Ok, so to give a little background and context, Henry's parents had died in a car crash when he was quite small, making it difficult for him to get close to anyone. He had a girlfriend who he adored, and she adored him too but his reluctance to open up to her made her grow distant from him, as did his growing obsession with Vibezone, and with building his following on there. Eventually she left him without warning, and he hadn't seen her since. This paved the way for him to pursue his online fame as far as it would go. It was his sole focus, but unknown even to him was really just a mask for the despair he felt at losing the love of his life. At the time she was growing tired of him spending more time on there he thought

EPILOGUE

she was just getting tired of him in general and so retreated further into the virtual world to try and block out the pain. Also unknown to him, a few years later, was that his ex-girlfriend had left because she was pregnant and she wanted to find somebody other than Henry to be a father figure. She didn't want her child's father to be someone who would be too busy online to spend any proper time with them, and felt certain he wouldn't change his ways. As the story continues, the shadowy characters meet up with Henry. They basically run Vibezone, which is all of social media combined into one big virtual reality world, and they offer him a level of fame he could never reach on his own in return for him basically working for them. He has some kind of instinct that working for them will have terrifying implications from which he might not be able to walk away, but he also knows that he will achieve what he's been working so hard for in a fraction of the time, if he ever could on his own at all. He does the deal. At exactly the same time his ex-girlfriend is sending him a message asking if they can meet.

After much deliberation he meets with his ex-girlfriend, and of course is still hopelessly in love with her. What's more, she absolutely floors him by telling him he has a three-year-old son, and wants them to meet. At first he is furious that she kept this from him, and goes on a drinking binge, but when he wakes up with a hangover he spends the rest of the day thinking about his whole life, and realising that although what she did might not have been fair on him, his ex must have had her reasons, and when the resentment fades he contemplates the life changing news that he is a father. He has no idea how to be father, so instead of going back on Vibezone he tries to research the subject as much as he can, and agrees to meet his son. He knows his current way of life makes him a terrible role model, and so he vows that he will change. He tells the shadowy men that he wants out, and they explain to him in a chilling way what will happen if he walks away from the deal.

To cut a long story short, Henry doesn't meet his son and his ex thinks she was right all along and that he's a terrible man. He has colossal fame on Vibezone but behind the mask he is falling apart, and knows he has to do something. Just as he's at his lowest ebb he is approached by somebody who somehow knows who he is outside of Vibezone, and says he can move him into hiding so he can live out the rest of his days in peace. It would mean the world would think he had died, as had happened with a number of celebrities who may have exposed the true nature of the shadowy organisation who run Vibezone, and he could never see anyone he loved again, but he would be out of his current life and would always be safe. Henry agrees, and says he will meet this man at a specially arranged location, making sure he isn't followed.

He writes a letter to his son saying that he never met him because he knew he was dying, and didn't want his son to have to witness this at such a young age, and gives him some advice on how to live a completely different life to him so he doesn't make the same mistakes. The man he met promises he will deliver it. Henry goes to the secret location to meet him, and finds the shadowy leader of the organisation sat there with a cold expression. The novel ends with a single nod, indicating that Henry will be dealt with for what he was going to do.

The epilogue is the letter Henry wrote to his son. When it ends we realise that his son had been reading it out to someone, then we realise that it's actually Henry. His son has grown up and didn't believe what he read in the letter, so tried to find out the truth. When he recklessly went after the shadowy leader of the organisation, he was astonished to discover that all along he had been saving people from being killed by the

EPILOGUE

organisation rather than being responsible for their demise. The other man Henry met had been the only person in the world that man trusted, and they had been working together. Henry had been in hiding all of these years, and was living a simple life in a community made up of people who'd had to be rescued. Henry's son and his ex-girlfriend, who had never really been able to move on, had come to live there with him. The epilogue ends with us learning that Henry's parents are alive too, and have been all along, and that they were the first people who had to be saved from the shadowy organisation, when they were running whatever they were running before Vibezone was a thing. We all cry, and vow to always be nice to everyone we love from now on, and to spend far less time on the internet.

So yeah, I think I had a cracking idea for a novel there, but luckily someone had already written something that said similar things, and in fact had some startling similarities to the point that reviewers would have said I was ripping the other novel off. Besides, to stretch an idea to novel length is a skill I don't yet possess. Maybe one day, but not now. Anyway Henry, like Solomon, had been pursuing material things and they seemed so important that everything else faded away, but when he realised that he mattered to somebody else all of the things he'd thought were so important suddenly seemed meaningless. They were meaningless.

What is important to you? Now you've read all the stories in this book has it reminded you of the answer to this question? Has it changed your mind in any way? If so I'd love to hear about it. If not then I must try harder. I'm not very good at endings, and so I'll leave you with another coincidence. I love coincidences in case you hadn't realised. When I was writing the book about the national marathon record holders it had been inspired by an accidental discovery about a man named Karl. Here it is…..

"So, allow me to let you in on the reason for this book's existence. By that I mean the discovery I made that was most directly and tangibly responsible for planting the seed that led to this book being written. It was all because of a man named Karl from an island nation named Nauru, and a marathon that he ran in 1968. I have tried to get in touch with Karl, in a number of ways in fact, but none of them have proved successful, and so instead I must merely imagine what took place. To give a little background info, it was through an accidental view of the national marathon records, via an unrelated Google search, I discovered that had I been born a citizen of Nauru and yet achieved the exact same running feats as I have, then I would be the national record holder in the marathon. This led to me looking up many other national records and attempting to get in touch with a whole load of the men who ran them. All through this I was thinking to myself that the real icing on the cake would be to speak to the man who had inspired it all, but I just couldn't get any of my communications through, despite trying a number of different avenues. Instead I can merely try to guess what happened when Karl ran his 3:38 marathon back in 1968, and so here is my version of events (NB – this is, barring the most incredible coincidence the world has ever seen, a totally fictional account) ……

Karl was a lonely boy who never took to school. He didn't dislike the other children, he merely watched them go about their interactions with each other, and their games, and wondered why he never felt as confident as they appeared. Each day he couldn't wait until school was over so he could go back to his family home, where his mother and father would ask him about his day. He would always tell them it was a good

EPILOGUE

day, with a smile, for he didn't want them to know how lost he felt on the inside. They were the best parents a boy could hope for, and to tell them how sad he felt when he was away from home would feel like he was saying they hadn't done a good enough job.

So why did he feel so sad? Why did he lack confidence? Well, when he was eight he ran in front of others for the first time. It was a games lesson, and he and the other children in his class had lined up to sprint form one end of the yard to the other. It wasn't a race, they were told, but Karl wanted to do well. "On your marks....." said the teacher, "Get set.......GO!" The children all sprinted off. They were half way across the yard and Karl was near the front of the field. He was beginning to feel his lungs having to work a lot harder, but he knew he could maintain his pace to the finish. Momentarily he closed his eyes, but in that moment he had failed to notice a stone in front of his left foot. His foot landed half on the stone, his body jolted in surprise, he stumbled, he fell.

For a moment he just stayed still as his brain caught up with what had happened. His knee and elbow were a little sore where they'd hit the ground but he didn't cry. He was Ok. The rest of the children had got to the other side of the yard by now, but when they realised what had happened they'd come and make sure he was Ok. Maybe they'd get another chance to run in a minute. He'd look where he was going this time.

He heard the sound of laughter, and began to smile, but then looked up to see that all the children were pointing at him and guffawing, whilst taking mock tumbles. The teacher was doing the same. Well, it was pretty funny he supposed. He laughed too, and stood up to go and join them, but they started to call him names. Not in the joking, friendly way that he and the other children occasionally would, but in the way that he'd seen the mean older siblings call the main characters of the books his parents read to him when he went to bed. He hesitated.

"Don't fall over again," shouted one child, and all of the others guffawed again, one even picked up a small stone and threw it in his direction. He wasn't sure whether to go and join them or just stay where he was. He didn't want to be there anymore. He wanted to be back home where he felt safe. It was time to go back to class, and the others ran towards the school building, but Karl remained rooted to the spot. He felt something he'd never felt before. He couldn't describe the feeling, but up until that point in his young life he'd always felt happy and confident. Now he felt uncomfortable in being who he was. He thought that maybe he was different from all of the others, and wished he could just be the same. His lip quivered and he felt tears forming behind his eyes. He hadn't even noticed the girl who was standing in front of him. It hadn't really registered with him at the time, but she hadn't been laughing when the others had. In fact she'd been standing to one side with a look of empathy in her eyes. He hadn't really noticed her before because she was the quiet one, and no-one really spoke to her. She just gazed at him for what seemed like several minutes, before she softly spoke.

"Don't worry about what they think. I like you."

She smiled, but he couldn't smile back. He felt like bursting into tears at her kindness. She kept smiling.

"Are you coming back to class? It's lunch soon. You can sit with me if you want to."

He nodded.

"I'd like that," he murmured.

They headed back to class, and he was prepared for more teasing when he walked in but the other children had already

EPILOGUE

forgotten about his mishap. He hadn't. In fact from that day onwards Karl was never quite the same in school. Previously he'd always thought the other children liked him, but now he just didn't know. He did become good friends with the girl who had been kind to him. Her name was Eva. She would often call for him after school and they would walk down to the ocean and sit sometimes in silence just watching the waves break on the shore, sometimes they would talk about their families or about what lands lay beyond the seas.

This would continue for the best part of the next ten years. Neither of them were popular at school, but they had each other and they didn't really need anyone else apart from their families. Karl's undercurrent of melancholy morphed into full blown despair though when the local guys started to notice Eva in her late teens and began to pay her attention. He wouldn't have minded, but he'd been trying to drum up the courage for years to tell her how he really felt about her and now she was showing an interest in others. He felt it was pointless to tell her now, because these other guys were confident and had skills and abilities that he had never learnt because he was too shy to get anyone to teach him. One guy in particular, Paul, really seemed to impress Eva. Most nights she wouldn't call for Karl any more, and when she did she would only ask if he was Ok. He'd lie that he was, just as he still did to his parents, but under the surface he was in torrents of searing emotional agony.

The pain was unbearable, and he would have done anything to block it out. He even considered heading down to the bar and looking for comfort at the bottom of a bottle of the local beer that seemed to turn some of the folks around town crazy, but it just wasn't him. He couldn't sleep at night, so one night he decided to head out for a run. He'd avoided running at all costs since that terrible incident when he was eight, but he walked everywhere and so had a basic level of fitness. The thought of running still filled him with dread even now, but if he was out at night and stayed away from the town then surely he'd be alright.

On that first run he knew he'd have to start off slow. He was running so slow he almost felt like he wasn't moving at all, or may as well have been running into a ferocious headwind, but he wasn't getting out of breath and so he must be doing something right. He took great care to look where he was going at all times; even though there was no-one around he just knew that if he was to take a tumble it would be at the exact moment a large group of people were walking past on their way back from the bar. Even worse, it would be the exact moment Eva and Paul walked by arm in arm. This time she would probably laugh along.

Before long he came to the beach, and began to run on the sand. His legs and lungs both had to work a little harder, but by not forcing the pace he was still able to keep running. A breeze along the shoreline whipped sand up against his legs, stinging his skin a little, and the waves crashed against the beach. He was reminded, inevitably, of all the time Eva and he used to spend at the beach. Tears formed in his eyes at the simplest memories, and for just a moment he stopped in his tracks. Something made him continue. He reasoned that if he had been sat alone in his room he'd still have been thinking of her, and would probably be missing her even more intensely, as he would feel imprisoned by the four walls. Out here he had to face his sense of loss directly, but at least he could keep moving, and the images in his field of vision would change. Perhaps he could keep running forever. Maybe he could even outrun his torment at some stage.

That evening he probably covered around four miles, but it

EPILOGUE

had felt like he was running for hours, and when he got home he felt sad about Eva still, but this was more of a dull ache now than searing agony. The run had really taken the edge off things.

During the night he dreamt of Eva; of her having moved on from him and thinking it best that they went their separate ways in life. He woke up feeling more alone than he had ever felt. It was a Saturday, and all the remaining hours of the day were stretching out in front of him. Stretching out like the miles of a marathon. When taken as a whole they seemed just too imposing, and so he tried to break them down into smaller sections. There were twenty-four hours in a day, twenty-six miles in a marathon. He didn't know anyone who'd run a marathon himself, but had heard of them. It was a superhuman feat of endurance that only the very top athletes could complete. Or was it? Something struck Karl in that moment. It was only twenty-six miles. What if you broke that down; divided it by ten? Two point six miles. That's nothing. He had run further than that last night. Surely he could do that ten times if he ran slowly. If he ran slowly he could run all day. Maybe he wouldn't run it in the fastest time, but he would get there. He was going to run a marathon. He would train for a year, and then on this day next year he would do it. There was a ramshackle athletics track just outside the town. He would run it there. People would watch or they wouldn't, but he'd need someone there to verify that he'd done it. At least one person. Somebody everyone trusted.

He went out and ran again that day, and this time he ran into Paul but Eva was not with him. When I say ran into Paul I mean he looked up and Paul was standing right in front of him with his chest puffed out. Karl stopped in his tracks, the dirt that scuffed under his feet making a dust cloud that went right up into Paul's face. He didn't change that steely expression one bit.

"Karl."

Karl didn't know what to say. He thought maybe he shouldn't say anything and should just walk by, but Paul had other ideas.

"Karl, we need to have a chat," he said, "Not here. Come this way."

Paul lumbered around the corner and away from the street to a yard where there were a few busted old crates and a bit of seaside debris but nothing much else. Karl followed at a distance, wary of what was to come. Paul turned on his heel and glared, cracking his knuckles against his other hand.

"What do you want, Paul?" said Karl, suddenly feeling the injustice of this situation. Paul had won. Why did he have to rub salt in the wounds?

"You," Paul growled, "You're ruining everything for me, man."

"What do you mean?"

"You know what I mean" Paul shouted, taking a few steps forward and towering over Karl.

"No, I don't," Karl growled back, "I really don't."

Paul grimaced and cracked his knuckles again.

"You're all she ever talks about," he raged, "It's 'Karl' this, 'Karl' that. If I hear her talking about you once more I swear I'll...."

For a few moments there was silence. Karl felt braver than he'd ever felt before, and more angry. He didn't feel like himself, and what he did next absolutely shocked him to his core. He took three steps towards Paul and launched himself forward, pushing his adversary in the chest with all his weight. Paul staggered back, more out of amazement than anything else. He looked up at Karl with wide eyes.

"And how's that my fault?" Karl shouted through gritted teeth, "I don't know if you've noticed, but I don't control what comes out of her mouth."

EPILOGUE

At least that was what Karl envisaged in his mind, but in reality he had taken five steps back and was pleading with Paul not to come any closer.

"See? You're pathetic," Paul sneered, "And you're going to make sure Eva knows it."

"What do you mean?"

"You're going to tell her that you never liked her and that you were only her friend because you felt sorry for her. Then I'm going to come round the corner and see how much you're upsetting her and I'll beat you. Then she'll see how pathetic you are."

"No," said Karl.

"What did you say?"

"I said no," he replied, the words just coming out without him thinking, "If I knew Eva thought badly of me it would be more painful than any kind of beating you could give me. So you can do it anyway if you want."

Paul just glared at him in the hope that he'd back down, but in that moment Paul learnt what would ultimately be the undoing of him and Eva. He could easily intimidate Karl, but the one thing Karl was more afraid of than physical pain was the thought of losing any chance he had of Eva choosing him over Paul some day. One day Paul's jealousy would make that happen if he couldn't make her hate Karl in the meantime. He knew he couldn't just tell her anything about Karl though; she'd want to hear it from him as well before she believed it. He felt anger rising and wanted to take every ounce of it out on Karl there and then. He wanted to beat him until no-one would recognise his face any more.

"Anyway, are we finished here? Because if we are I'm going to finish my run" said Karl.

"You're not going anywhere" snarled Paul.

Karl looked him in the eye and saw pure hatred. If he did nothing this would probably end in a beating. If he stood up to him it would probably end in a beating anyway. Either way there was just a small chance that nothing would happen, but he didn't know what to do. He wasn't good at dealing with situations like this. He was such a peaceful man that he saw this kind of thing as being pointless, and so when it happened he just wasn't equipped to act.

"I said you're not going anywhere," Paul repeated, taking another step forward, but just one. Just then Karl saw something else in Paul's eyes. Trepidation. Maybe he'd never actually been in a fight in his life.

"Yes I am," said Karl, surprising himself, "I'm finishing my run."

He turned and began to jog away. He didn't sprint off in fear, but just ran off comfortably as if he'd stopped for a chat.

"You'd better run," he heard Paul shout after a little while, "And you'd better hope I don't bump into you again."

When Paul had seen that he couldn't be intimidated there was no longer any danger. He didn't want to push the matter and try to intimidate Paul, because if it ended in a fight he still didn't fancy his chances of winning, but somehow he just never thought there was any threat after that day. Paul was just a bully; he only asserted himself because he knew Karl wouldn't stand up for himself. As soon as he was proved wrong it changed everything.

Karl continued to run most days, and before long he felt like he would be able to run for hours without stopping. The marathon was in the bag. But how fast would he be able to run one? He'd read in the newspaper about a man named Derek Clayton from Australia, who'd just run a marathon in 2 hours and 9 minutes or so, and it was a world record. Obviously he wouldn't be able to run that fast. What would be double that time? He quickly worked out that it would be 4 hours and 18 minutes. That would be his target.

So far his training hadn't really had any focus; he just ran. How would he find out how he could train better? Nauru didn't really have many running coaches, and there were no professional athletes. He didn't even know if anyone from Nauru had run a marathon before, although there was the running track he knew of on the edge of town. It had been built as part of a government initiative to try and get more young people interested in sports, but he'd never been there because it was near where Paul lived. This didn't worry him anymore, but running into Paul and Eva did; seeing them together might send him into a deep despair, but surely it couldn't be much worse than what he imagined in his head on a daily basis. In his mind, nobody had ever loved anyone as much as Eva had loved Paul. When he was with her he wasn't the scowling, aggressive guy Karl knew him as. He was sensitive, kind, knowledgeable, witty and basically all of the things Eva would want him to be, plus as far as she knew he was tough and could protect her. Of course Karl knew differently about everything, but maybe Paul was a great guy really. How would it feel for Karl if he and Eva were together and she never stopped talking about Paul? Surely it would get pretty tiresome. Maybe Paul was only the way he was because he imagined that the time Karl and Eva used to spend together was the most wonderful time any two people could ever spend together, and it was something he could never live up to.

He actually began to feel bad for Paul, and wondered if he should stay away from the running track, but then he couldn't spend the rest of his life trying to avoid them (as tempting as it was), so on a Wednesday evening he jogged the couple of miles down to the track. When he arrived it was deserted, as it always was, and that suited him just fine. He decided to run round the track a little faster than he would normally run elsewhere, just to see how long he could keep up the pace for. The first couple of laps felt pretty comfortable. He was breathing a little harder than usual but his legs felt great. Then half way through the third lap he started to gasp for air and his legs began to feel like jelly. He dug in, hoping that it would pass, but then nausea hit his stomach with great force and he ground to a halt, retching by the side of the track.

He managed to avoid vomiting, but as he took a few deep breaths he heard laughter from off to the side.

"What's wrong, Karl? Not tough enough?" sneered Paul.

"Don't say that," said Eva, gently, "He's trying his best."

Those four words stung far more than anything Paul could ever say. 'Trying his best' basically meant he was no good. He knew it.

"He's always out running. He should be better at it by now" said Paul.

"I'm not used to running that fast," said Karl, taking his hands off his knees and drawing up to his full height, "Could you do better?"

"Of course I could" he laughed.

"Come on boys, stop it!" said Eva, "You know I wish you two would just get along."

Paul and Karl looked at each other and then at Eva.

"I'm sorry," said Karl, "Anyway, I think I might do a few more laps."

"Shall we race?" said Paul.

Karl looked at Eva, expecting her to lead Paul away, but she was looking at him and waiting for his response.

"Ok," said Karl, "Well I'm training to run a marathon. Why don't you train too and we'll race that? I could do with some company on the track."

"You?" cackled Paul, "You, running a marathon?"

"Yeah. What's wrong, Paul? Not up to it?"

Paul glared at Karl and clenched his fists, but relaxed as soon as Eva looked at him.

"Well, Paul? What do you think? I'd be so proud of you if you ran a marathon."

'What about me?' thought Karl, but of course he didn't say anything.

"Yeah, I'll do it," said Paul, "When?"

"How about six months' time?"

Paul didn't run at all at the moment, at least not any kind of distance, and he wasn't sure if six months would be long enough, but he had to do it now.

"Ok, that's settled then. I hope you're ready to lose."

"May the best man win," said Karl, and he wasn't just talking about the marathon. He had a notion in his head that maybe if he could run with enough heart and determination he might impress Eva enough to win her heart in the long term.

As the months went by he trained and trained. This was 1968, so there was no strava, facebook, garmins, fancy running shoes or any of the things so many take for granted in the modern day. People just went out and ran. Imagine that. He had very few resources available to tell him the best way to train for a marathon, but he persisted with his faster track running sessions and was surprised to find that they got easier with time. In fact within a few months he could run round the track quite a few times at a fairly decent pace. It hurt a little, but he was able to use his experience to know that he could manage the pain for a certain amount of time. He knew he wouldn't be able to manage that level of pain for 26.2 miles, and once again thought of Derek Clayton – how was it possible for someone to run at such a blistering pace for so long without collapsing by the side of the track? He wondered if Australians were superhuman.

As well as the track sessions he ran most days at an easier pace along the coast, sometimes walking back and sometimes running. He estimated the longest run he did in training to be almost twenty miles, which had taken him a little under four hours, but he still felt like he could run further at the end and had to exercise a lot of restraint not to. The pain of Eva not being around dulled when he ran, sometimes he even felt joyful, but it never went away completely. Sometimes somebody can leave such a mark on you that no matter how hard you try, and how many reasons you can think of why it could be for the best that they're not with you, it just feels like something's missing when they're not around. He began to think beyond the marathon. This marathon had given him a focus; something to give every day a purpose, and something to distract him for a while from the pain he continued to feel. If Eva had been happy with Paul, and it had obviously been the case, he felt he would have just had to find a way to let go, but at the back of his mind was the nagging feeling that maybe she'd be happier with him. This is why he remained in limbo.

He'd been looking forward to the marathon for so long, but now it was getting closer he hoped that day would never come round. If he finished this one then perhaps he could start training for another as soon as he'd recovered, but he wasn't sure if it would be the same. He was dreading the moment he crossed the finish line. What would he do with himself once it was over? Maybe he should look for a job and save some money, head overseas and try and start a new life elsewhere. Despite his doubts about Eva and Paul, the fact was that she had chosen Paul over him. There must have been a reason

EPILOGUE

for that. If she wasn't with Paul she probably wouldn't be with him either, because they'd been so close before that surely if they were meant to be together than they would have been. Maybe Karl just wasn't meant to be a husband or a father. Maybe he was meant to be alone. The thought of this made him excruciatingly unhappy, but then he'd always felt more comfortable on his own in a strange kind of way. He'd be calmer on his own, but would he be happier? He very much doubted it.

The next day he went down to the track and ran harder than he ever had before. He could feel his lungs were working too hard, but he wanted to sustain the pace for as long as he could. He needed to. He wanted to feel like Derek Clayton, if only for a short while. His calf muscles were on fire as he charged round the back stretch, but he kept on running. By the end of the third lap enough was enough and he collapsed to the ground on purpose, absolutely gasping for air.

'Derek Clayton is not human' he thought to himself.

"Hey Karl, get up. It's my turn to use the track now."

Karl didn't look up. He knew that voice anywhere. He just shuffled over so he was a few metres from the track.

"It's all yours" he mumbled.

"What did you say?"

"I said it's all yours," he said a bit louder, looking up to see Paul swaggering towards him, Eva following a few paces behind, "I'm finished."

"Yes, I'd say you are by the look of you."

Karl forced a weak smile and hauled himself to his feet, beginning to walk away.

"Hey Karl, wait" said Eva.

He didn't want to stick around, but he remember how she had picked him up the first time he fell, and despite the agony he felt every time he saw her and Paul together now, he also felt a degree of comfort at the memory. Paul hit the track and started to run round at a fairly impressive pace. Karl was beginning to think he might be humiliated when it came to the race, but would it really matter if he didn't win? He'd set out to run a marathon, and that's what he was going to do no matter what happened.

"Karl, you don't have to do this," said Eva.

"Yes I do," he replied, "Pretty much all I have right now is this."

"I'm sure that's not true."

Karl realised how it must have sounded. He knew that men who doubted themselves and had no direction weren't impressive to women, but then neither were men who lied. He really did have nothing apart from his running. Apart from Eva it was pretty much all he thought about from the time he woke up until the time he went to sleep. Surely this wasn't right, but what else was there right now? He knew he'd have to get a job at the end of the summer because he wasn't going off to study anywhere and the money his parents had given him, which they'd been saving since he was born, wouldn't last forever.

"Ok, well maybe it's not all I have," said Karl, "But I need to do this."

"That'll do," said Paul between breaths as he caught up to them, "I only need to do one lap; haven't got much competition, have I?"

"Don't, Paul" said Eva, and he scowled at Karl.

"It's Ok," said Karl, "I'm not in it to win anyway. I just want to be able to say I've done it."

"Yeah, you'd have to say that," smirked Paul, "Otherwise it'd be embarrassing."

"Anyway, have a good day" said Karl, starting to walk away.

"No," said Eva, "Why don't you come with us? It would mean

EPILOGUE

a lot to me if you two could get on, you know."

Although they'd never discuss it, there was one thing here that Paul and Karl could agree on. Eva just didn't understand men.

"I would, but I've got to see someone about a job," lied Karl, "Maybe another time?"

"Yeah, maybe another time" said Paul. Eva could tell that both of them were hoping that other time would never come, but she decided to let it go for now.

They didn't bump into each other again before the big day. Karl had been unable to sleep the night before, not for more than an hour or so anyway, and on the morning of the race he was too nervous to eat much, but he didn't think it would matter. Today his efforts would transcend any kind of physical limitations that might hold him back. He would run with his heart, and the power of his will to succeed would carry him across the finish line even if his body was screaming at him to stop miles before he got there. He made his way down to the start line a couple of hours before the race was due to begin, and when he got there he was shocked to see that a timing clock had been installed next to the finish line, with 'Start' carved on a huge piece of driftwood some way back. Eva's Uncle Tony was pacing around next to the start. Karl had met him several times when he was younger but hadn't seen him to speak to in a number of years.

"Karl, are you ready?" he beamed, flashing that same unmistakable smile he had when they'd first shaken hands.

"I've been waiting for this for a long time," Karl replied, "I'm going to finish."

"You gonna win?"

"It doesn't matter," Karl said truthfully, "I don't mind if Paul finishes an hour before me as long as I go the distance."

Tony looked at him with a touch of sadness.

"Eva really misses you. You do know that, don't you?"

Karl had to take a deep breath.

"I miss her too," he replied, "But if she really is happy then who am I to stand in her way?"

"That's just it," said Tony, "She's not happy with Paul. I know she may say she is but he's not a good guy. The way he treats her.....well I don't like it. She deserves better, but she thinks she has to stay with Paul because she doesn't realise how special she is."

Karl looked at his feet.

"Tony, I don't mean anything by this but shouldn't you be telling her that?"

"Oh, I've tried. Believe me," he sighed, "But she won't hear a word against him. She always makes excuses for him, because when she was younger she never thought any guy would want to be with her. She thinks now she has him she has to keep him because there won't be anyone else."

"Why are you telling me this though, Tony? What can I do?"

"Karl, you have to win this race."

Karl looked up to meet Tony's gaze. He seemed genuine, but what if this was something Tony had cooked up with Paul so he'd start off too fast and run out of energy? Surely not. Tony had always seemed honest. He tried to put it out of his head.

"Where did the clock come from anyway?" he asked.

"Ah, the government got hold of that," said Tony, "There's gonna be quite a few people coming to watch the race you know?"

"What?"

"Yeah of course, don't you read the papers? Don't your family?"

For a while he'd felt like his parents were trying to keep

EPILOGUE

something from him. Not something bad either. He hadn't read the news in years, because he was tired of reading about people who were making a better job of life than he was. What had happened?

"This is quite the contest you and Paul have got going on," laughed Tony, "Got a lot of interest. Hasn't anyone spoken to you?"

For a long time he'd only been out running at night, and during the day he'd kept himself to himself. No one really could have told him.

"Yeah, here come a few now."

Karl looked round and saw a group of people he recognised a little from the town walking towards the track. They nodded to him as they went past and positioned themselves a little back from the track edge. As the minutes ticked by more and more people came along until there was quite a crowd gathered around. What's more, the atmosphere was electric. This was the most exciting event Nauru had seen in some time. The clash of two brave warriors, giving their all to do what seemed impossible to many of the people who came to watch it take place.

Paul strolled nonchalantly towards the track with minutes to spare, just as Karl was finishing his warm-up. Eva was by his side as always and she smiled at Karl. He smiled back, but didn't want to hold eye contact for long because he had to focus on the task in hand. Before he started though there was one more thing he had to know. He jogged over to where Tony was standing.

"Tony," he said, "Why do I have to win this race?"

"Do I really have to answer that?"

A few moments of silence passed.

"Yes."

"Come on, Karl. If you win this race then Eva's yours. Surely it's obvious."

"I wouldn't be too sure about that."

Tony tutted.

"Man, you don't make it easy for yourself do you?"

"What do you mean?"

"Women like confidence. Surely you know that."

He knew it only too well, which is why he knew he couldn't go on faking that he had an ounce of it for too long, so it was pointless trying.

"I know what you're thinking," said Tony, "But man, do you think I'm confident? Really? Under the surface?"

"Probably."

"Well let me tell you something, Karl. I aint. All you have to do is make a good job of pretending."

Karl sighed.

"But I can't, Tony. Eva already knows everything about me. She knows that I'm not confident; she only talked to me in the first place because she felt sorry for me."

"Ah, Karl," smiled Tony, "There's one thing she doesn't know about you yet."

"What's that?"

"She doesn't know that you can win this race. Once she knows that she'll see you in a whole different light. Then it's up to you what you do with that, but let's just say if she didn't believe in you before she will after you've won."

Karl didn't quite know what to say.

"Anyway, get on that start line."

He walked over to the start, where Paul was already waiting.

"You're lucky," snarled Paul quietly, so only Karl could hear.

"What do you mean?"

"If all these people hadn't been here I'd have put you out of

EPILOGUE

the race."

"Eva would have been here."

"Yeah well," he seethed, "I would have had to make sure her back was turned, wouldn't I?"

Karl said nothing more. He tried his very hardest to remain noble and to rise above it, but from that moment he knew that he wanted nothing more on earth than to win this race. He wanted Paul to know how it felt to be on the losing side. The seconds ticked down and Tony shouted "Go," his booming voice seeming to echo round the arena.

Karl settled into a comfortable pace straight away, and Paul headed off a little quicker to begin with, but soon looked over his shoulder and allowed himself to be caught up, then matching Karl stride for stride.

"Don't think you stand a chance, Karl."

"We'll see."

These were the last words they spoke to each other for the next five miles. Karl was pleased with his pacing strategy, feeling stronger as the laps went by, and he couldn't quite believe it but Paul seemed to be struggling. He was breathing fairly heavily by now, and once or twice he almost fell off Karl's pace. Karl actually felt bad, and momentarily wondered if he should slow down, but he had a feeling it wouldn't matter. Paul wasn't going to finish.

"I thought you'd be done for by now," Paul muttered, "Are you even tired?"

"Paul, have you actually done much training for this?" said Karl, ignoring the question.

"Didn't think I'd need to."

Karl couldn't believe it. Surely Paul would have known how many people were coming down to watch. Why didn't he prepare?

"Karl, you have to drop out. Please."

"What?"

"Karl, I'm not gonna be able to run much further. This'll be so embarrassing for me. Drop out and then I'll pretend I couldn't carry on because I felt bad for you."

"Why should I do that, Paul?"

"Come on, please."

Something began to nag at Karl round the next lap. He knew all too well what it was like to be humiliated. In the moment before the race he'd wanted Paul to feel like that, but now the moment had arrived when he was about to it just didn't feel right. No-one deserved to feel humiliated. He thought about going along with Paul's wishes, but how could he? He'd spent so long preparing for this day, and there wouldn't be another chance. No-one would believe him if he claimed to run a marathon after that. No-one would come and watch him try. Every bit of work he'd put in over the year would go to waste. This was his one chance to feel like he'd proved himself. If he didn't he'd always be that boy who stumbled and fell in the playground, who everyone had laughed at. If he did then Paul would always be the guy who couldn't finish a quarter of the marathon.

"Paul, why didn't you do the training?"

"I told you, I didn't think I'd need to."

"But why didn't you train so you could finish the marathon?"

"I was just planning to do what I said, and then Eva's family would change their mind about me."

"But what about the next time?"

"What do you mean?"

"Do you think you could keep deceiving them forever?"

Paul sighed. Or at least tried to between breaths.

"Man, do you know what it's like to be me?"

EPILOGUE

"What do you mean?"

"Do you know what it's like to know that it's only a matter of time before your woman finds out who you really are and then goes off with this guy she hasn't stopped talking about the whole time you've been together?"

This hadn't been part of the plan. Karl was beginning to think he would just have to do the right thing, but was it really the right thing?

"Paul, none of these things are my fault."

"Well if you'd had the guts to ask her out in the first place then I wouldn't even be in this position, would I? She would never have been with me, she'd have been with you. I'd have met someone else."

"So why can't you still? Do you love Eva?"

"Not really. But that's not the point."

Karl looked over and shrugged.

"Well it's not, is it? If I lose Eva to you then no other girl's gonna be interested in me are they? I'll be a joke."

With that comment went every ounce of sympathy Karl had built up for Paul. He kept on running at the same pace, not wanting to make his break too early.

"Look, Paul," he said, "Just grit your teeth and try and finish. That's what I'll be doing too."

"You're not gonna help me?"

"Why should I help you?" said Karl, "What have you ever done to help me?"

As he said this he began to have doubts once again. It shouldn't matter that Paul had never helped him. If he didn't help Paul anyway was he not a good person? In the end the decision was out of his hands.

Just a few steps later Paul took a huge swing at Karl. Karl ducked out of the way and kept running while Paul tumbled to the ground. A huge collective gasp rang out around the crowd of spectators as Tony ran forward and dragged Paul off to the side of the track.

"Disqualified," he said sternly, "Now get out of here."

Eva glared at Paul as he started to leave.

"You coming with me?"

Eva shook her head.

"Fine."

That was the last anyone saw of Paul, although word got back to the island that he'd moved to Australia and got a job as a mechanic. Karl didn't let the incident put him off his stride at all. A mile or so after it had happened he did feel a little queasy in the pit of his stomach, thinking how close he'd come to being clattered to the ground in front of all of these people. That was the moment his mind had really wavered, and the unthinkable happened.

Karl's wandering mind had meant he stopped focussing on putting his feet one in front of the other, or at least where they were landing, and he tripped and came crashing down, just as he had all those years ago. He prepared himself for the inevitable cacophony of laughter, but only for a split second. A new understanding came over him; if they were laughing now they wouldn't be when he finished the marathon. It would be forgotten if he could do what he set out to do. He sprung to his feet and carried on running. No-one laughed, in fact a collective round of applause rang out all around him. Karl was attempting something that everyone who was watching would be too afraid to, and so he had their respect.

The fall gave him a burst of adrenalin that actually made him run a little too fast for a lap or two, but he soon settled back into his comfortable pace and managed to sustain this for many more laps without feeling too tired.

EPILOGUE

"About six miles to go" said Tony after what hadn't seemed like all that long. He'd been so focused on keeping moving forward that he'd passed the twenty mile point. This whole time Eva had been watching, and she'd shouted encouragement each time he went past. When Tony had said there were six miles to go she'd even seemed to have a tear in her eye. She hadn't gone after Paul, she'd stayed to watch him the whole time. How could this be? Was everything going to change from now on? If it wasn't then he wasn't sure he wanted this marathon to end. Nothing could hurt him out here; he was doing what he loved to do and all of the things that bothered him each day couldn't get to him. He thought about slowing his pace for a moment, even though he still felt strong, because then he could just keep on running for longer and delay the inevitable.

That was just it though. No matter how slowly he kept moving forward, the passage of time would eventually mean the end of the race. Could he keep going beyond marathon distance? No, surely no-one could do that. Once this marathon was over it would be time to stop running. Well he might as well put that speed training to use and do it in style.

There was a chorus of gasps when Karl put his foot down, just as there had been when Paul had taken a swing at him. He'd already run twenty miles, how could he have the energy to run faster? Was it simply because he knew the end was in sight? Would he collapse over the finish line when he got there? He hadn't increased his pace massively, but it was definitely noticeable. The laps seemed to go by quicker than he could count them, but it felt manageable. How fast would he have been able to finish if he'd started quicker? It was pointless wondering; if he'd started quicker he may be crawling by now.

Tony would shout out each time another mile went by.

It was only when there were two miles left that the efforts of the past 24 miles really began to catch up with him. Karl was beginning to fade, but he knew he just had to dig in and the finish line would come. Just two more miles. That wasn't much. If he could keep up this pace he guessed it would take about fifteen minutes to get there. Just fifteen more minutes. How would he get there? He began to ponder many things; the stories his mum had told him when he was a child about the polar explorers she'd heard tales of, and of a ship named the Titanic. Why would anyone want to go to the South Pole? It sounded horrible there. He wondered why everyone doesn't just get along, and why some people are allowed to be so much richer than others when not everyone has enough money for food and shelter. These things were making him think so much that he'd barely even registered when Tony had told him there was a mile to go. When it sunk in he finally allowed himself to acknowledge the fact that his parents were there. All he'd even wanted, apart from to win Eva's heart, was to be able to make them proud. Now he had a real chance to. And Eva. A huge crowd had gathered, but it was only those three people, and Tony, who he really wanted to impress. The people who'd been kind to him when no-one else was.

Eventually Tony told him that there was only one lap to go, and he decided to give it everything he had. He somehow found the last reserves of energy he had left, and gradually accelerated. The noise of the spectators was building to a huge crescendo, and everything seemed to go in slow motion for him as he ran round the final bend towards the finish line. It had all been worth it. He was about to complete a marathon. When he crossed the line the crowd went wild and Eva, his parents and Tony ran towards him and gathered him into their arms......

EPILOGUE

Of course I'd love to tell you that this was the point when Karl's life changed forever and nothing would ever be difficult again but I can't, because that's not what life is. Less than an hour had passed since his triumph when Eva went looking for Paul to try and figure things out. His legs ached for days afterwards and he wasn't really able to run for a week or two. He was very proud of what he'd achieved, but when a week had passed things began to get almost back to normal and he started to feel that he needed a new challenge. What was left to achieve though? He'd run a marathon in three hours, forty-eight minutes and six seconds. To this day nobody from Nauru has run one faster. A number of people who were there that day to witness Karl's heroics were inspired to run, and some of them completed marathons, but none of them really challenged Karl's record.

This wasn't the moment when Eva and Karl could finally be together, but they did see more of each other, and would even sometimes go and talk for hours on the beach just as they had when they were growing up. He even told her how he felt. He had the day after his marathon. She'd told him that Paul had only just left and it would be far too soon for her to think about loving anyone else. He was sad, but she hadn't said that there would never be a chance, and so he had hope to hold onto. Besides, he'd survived for this long without her and so even though it would be painful every day he knew he'd continue to. That doesn't mean he wasn't heartbroken when she moved overseas just two years later to be a nurse in New Zealand. On some of Karl's worst days he wondered if she was lying and she'd actually had a letter from Paul, and had moved to Australia to be with him.

While Eva was away, Karl had been approached by the government of Nauru and had accepted a job as national sports minister. He would train runners and in later years would select Nauru's team for overseas competitions, but nobody would run a marathon faster than he did. That's until one day in 2014, when Karl was in his sixties, and had received an e-mail telling him there was something he must look at. It seemed to be an article from a runner who claimed to be the marathon champion of Nauru. Had his record been broken? He felt almost relieved, because he wanted to see his record broken. He wanted more talented athletes to emerge from his nation. It turned out it was from a runner in England who had run a marathon faster than Karl did, and so if he was to apply for citizenship he would be Nauru's marathon record holder. Karl was even more amazed when he was forwarded an e-mail from this very runner asking if he would be willing to answer some questions as research for a book about national marathon record holders. For a moment he was thinking he'd be honoured to talk, but then it wasn't long before he realised that he didn't want to be famous. Clearly a story like his would be made into a film; a huge blockbuster movie that would make pots of money. That runner from England would probably get rich from it, but it wouldn't be Karl's story. Surely it would have to be embellished, and the role of Karl would be played by one of those American actors with a chiselled physique and perfect white teeth. It wouldn't be real. Karl closed the e-mail down and smiled to himself. He didn't need to say no, because surely that runner would believe that e-mails wouldn't reach Nauru; that whoever did the website he found the address on would be pretending Nauru had the internet when actually they only had carrier pigeons. He would think it was impossible to get hold of Karl, and so instead might just guess what his great marathon run may have been like. Nothing more needed to be done.

EPILOGUE

He switched off the computer and went into his living room, where Eva was sitting with his grown up sons, who had come to visit. His eldest son had just told her that he wanted to run a marathon, and would break Karl's record.

"I'm sure you will, son" said Karl, with a smile.

Eva had returned from New Zealand after just six months, saying that she'd simply missed Karl too much, and had missed Nauru too much. She didn't want to be away any longer.

Their life together wasn't a fairy tale. Sometimes it was a real struggle; at one point they wound each other up so much that they split up for a few months, but they were drawn back to each other, and over a number of years they managed to figure everything out. Eva's uncle Tony was killed in a motoring accident just as they were really beginning to feel that things were moving in the right direction, and for some time she wasn't herself. She became very distant from Karl, but he was strong enough by this point to realise that it would just take time and so he allowed her space but let her know that he was there if she needed him.

There were a number of other setbacks, but they got through it all. Karl never ran another marathon; he didn't need to. That day in 1968 he'd proven what he needed to, and after that he was just able to run for enjoyment. One day he learnt that people did run further than marathon distance, but he had no real interest in giving it a go. A marathon was far enough. Last Thursday he was walking down the street in Nauru's main town and one of a group of youths who were congregating by a restaurant could be heard saying to his friends

"That's Karl. He's a legend; the best athlete Nauru has ever seen."

"I'm not a legend," he laughed, "I'm just a man named Karl."

.....

So... the coincidence, which I'm sure you'd forgotten about by now, was that some time after this a man named Karl gave me the biggest opportunity of my writing career to date. What? Not much of a coincidence? Sweet story though, hey? That's it. Try not to give up hope.